TRANSITION ECONOMICS

Maturity Models

Transition Economics Maturity Model™
CSQ RESEARCH

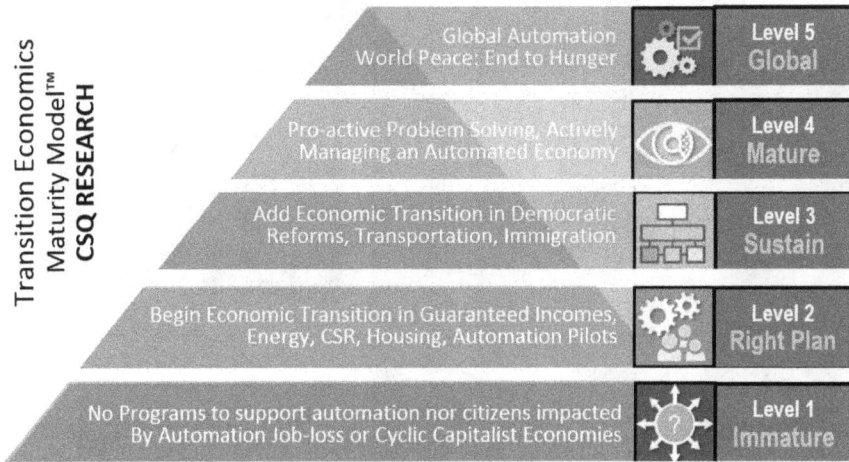

	Level
Global Automation World Peace: End to Hunger	**Level 5** Global
Pro-active Problem Solving, Actively Managing an Automated Economy	**Level 4** Mature
Add Economic Transition in Democratic Reforms, Transportation, Immigration	**Level 3** Sustain
Begin Economic Transition in Guaranteed Incomes, Energy, CSR, Housing, Automation Pilots	**Level 2** Right Plan
No Programs to support automation nor citizens impacted By Automation Job-loss or Cyclic Capitalist Economies	**Level 1** Immature

A Teaching and Learning Framework designed to make Economics relevant again. From the Author who wrote the book on Common Sense 101, Transition Economics, Teaching Doers, SUSTAIN Project Management, Modern Love and World Peace - The Transition.

EDWARD TILLEY

"End of War" is Edward Tilley's latest release in this Sustainable Societies Series. End of War – Managing Mature Capitalisms is a project that applies lessons in Transition Economics and SUSTAIN Project Method

Get a **FREE AUDIOBOOK** when you pre-order the three-book Sustainable Societies Collection hardcopy set - and save...

Go to CSQ1.org/order

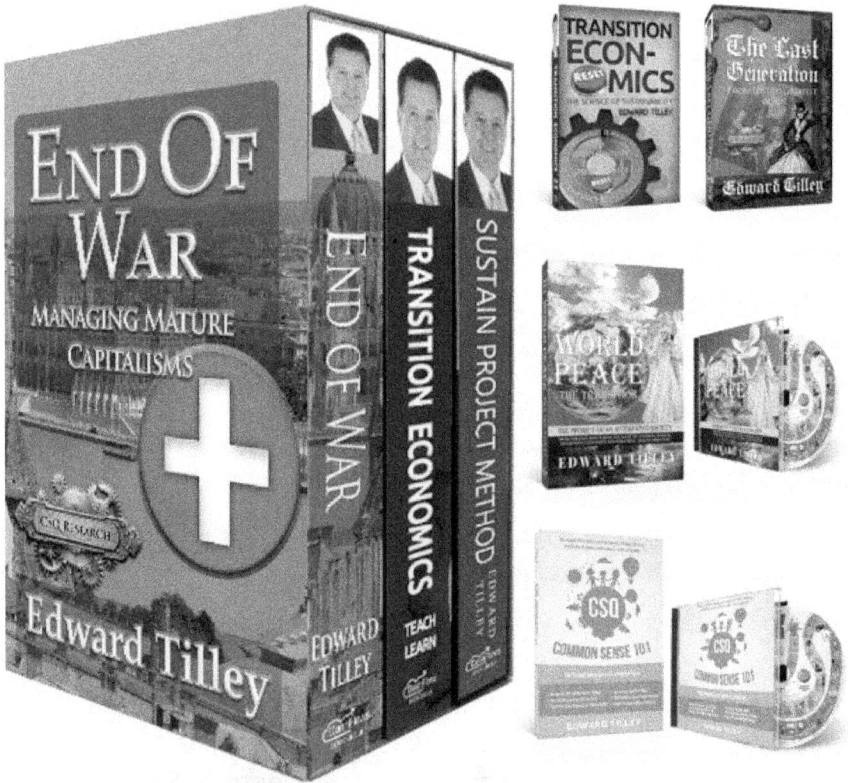

Ask your favorite bookseller for Edward Tilley's books in hardcover, paperback, and audiobook formats. Positive reviews online helps build Good Lives and Sustainable Societies too, so consider adding yours to these books at Amazon, GoodReads, Apple and other major media outlets

To Samuel & Meghan

CONTENTS

ACKNOWLEDGMENTS

Writing prodigious books about worthwhile subjects, for me, culminates in Transition Economics and its Maturity Modelling subset of the much larger Reference Guide. TE is a framework of policies & method proven scientifically to steer economies reliably toward a sustainable Good Life, American Dream, and away from Collapse.

We had a Good Life in North America and many G20 countries; and now 72% of our developed nations have lost it.

Sustainable societies support freedoms and new human rights too, and so it is from society's point of view that Transition Economics are explained in this book. A Transition Economics for Business and Banking book could follow easily.

Cycle Economists like Nickolae Kondratieff, Harold Schumpeter, and Hammurabi, King of Babylon contributed as did global automation efforts ongoing in technology and industrial centers worldwide.

Failing to support families in economic change causes collapse; and as collapse is the underpinning of revolutions and world wars in a mature nuclear era; collapse is not an option today. We must reset with new incomes and spending-power and thinking as we build sustainable renewable automation – that's Transition Economics.

Finding a way through complex problems in society can be frustrating, but there can be no more worthwhile goal either.

Chapter 1

-

Transition Economics Maturity Models

Our Manual Economies are automating. Shortly, the construction of 250 well thought-out Connected Smart Factories will lift mankind's 10,000-year manual civilizations into a new era of sustainable Automated Economies.

Transition Economics (TE) is a new Social and Engineering Science that explains how to direct our transition to Automation with the same social and economic policies needed to reset our normal Economic Cycles too.

TE Maturity Modelling is an important subset of Transition Economics that explains how closely aligned are a Country's Policies with TE Mature Policy proven to reset Economies by ensuring Incomes and renewing Spending-Power. Simply follow the chart of policies laid out here to assess your country's TE-Maturity and then set a course to improve quickly.

Cycle Economists realize that over Capitalistic Society's 4000-year history, economic controls have been enforced successfully to manage recurring sixty-year cycles of peaks and then troughs that have occurred routinely in one-after-another succession.

Transition Economics provides an important teaching and learning framework that restores Economics as an important tool in the correction of a world in which fully 72% of global economies are in a Collapse Trending today.

"Truth is ever to be found in simplicity, and not in the multiplicity and confusion of things."

Isaac Newton, Physics & Co-Founder of Calculus

Aristotle's systems of thought leadership are perhaps the most famous in all history. He is the founding father of both Scientific Method and also our University Curriculums; and therefore, all of our subordinate school curriculums as well.

According to Aristotle's "Scientific Method", any approach that does not take into consideration real world observation cannot be considered true. Without this constraint, he realized that academically peer-reviewed theory was at risk of becoming theoretical fiction.

Jeffery Sachs of Columbia University included a discussion of Cycle Economics in his recent book; William Thompson at Indiana University has published influential papers and books documenting eighteen K-Waves dating back to 930 AD in China's Song Province as well; and I will wrap up this aside with Michael Snyder who wrote "It should be noted that economic cycle theories have enabled some analysts to correctly predict the timing of recessions, stock market peaks and stock market crashes over the past couple of decades." (Snyder, 2014)

Thought Leadership

Building Thought-Leadership requires both strong individual contribution, and a strong process that consistently harvests ideas and best practices from new engineers, thinkers, and even random great ideas - on a regular basis. Too often, Administrators view their role as Chief Idea Creators when rather - a good administrator must instead nurture ideas from all of his or her resources – whether from within an organization or even an entire country. With good ideas in hand, he or she must next understand how to build an Expert Panel of SMEs and Engineers that can recommend the projects needed to realize those best-and-brightest ideas reliably.

It takes some character to not let one's ego confuse what is a leader's role in Thought Leadership.

Individual Contributors

"Sometimes it's the people that no one imagines anything of, who do the things that no one can imagine."

The Imitation Game 2014 - Andrew Hodges

We can never under-estimate people nor pre-judge another person's abilities. So often it is those who you might never expect to change the world that do - and the surest way to disincent someone from making important change is to not support nor permit their work, nor to acknowledge their contribution.

This is true for the very great majority of us, whose contributions and passions lead us to raise families and build tremendous communities too. Recognition is certainly as important for people among us who are different in that they do incredible, groundbreaking work with their fantastic contributions in science, technology, mathematics, medicine, and all other fields of study.

Gifted people and savants often struggle when interacting with the rest of us. "Gifts", are double-edged swords because even when a savant takes an active interest in communicating to the outside world, you can imagine that they might find that there are very few others who understand their interests with the same dexterity.

A man or woman who can play any song ever heard in any key or style on a piano, is not going to find very many interesting others in even a concert hall filled with other pianists. A man who can read a theatric play and hear the music just once before performing it perfectly - like my Anglican Minister and friend Ross Norton, will spend a lifetime waiting patiently for even the Mensa club members at his table to catch up. This can be frustrating - so when gifted people also feel bullied or ignored by less capable others, it can be a great challenge for them to take time for relatively unimportant social propriety.

As an aside, the ability to memorize a page and its contents on sight is an invaluable memory skill that I discuss can be developed by most of us in CSQ Common Sense 101. Like remembering names and developing good study habits, improving memory takes effort, a process, and a lot of practice for the rest of us - who are not gifted like Ross.

The surest way to disincent someone who does ground-breaking, thought-leadership work with fantastic performance, is to not acknowledge, recognize their value, nor permit their contribution.

Alan Turing, founder of Computer Science - and one day perhaps founder of World Peace too, was reclusive and permitted by his government to be chemically castrated by local authorities with the result that he committed suicide at the age of forty-one. Over the four years from 1940 to 1943, Mr. Turing built and made work from concept, an electro-mechanical computer capable of deciphering Enigma - the most sophisticated mechanical encrypting computer ever built – used to protect messages between German forces throughout World War II. By 1945, he had redesigned his Turing Machine with wholly digital components similar to the binary computers that we all use today.

Mr. Turing's genius and contribution are estimated to have saved the lives of twelve million people and reduced World War II by two years – as documented in the 2014 movie "The Imitation Game".

Albert Einstein (founder of the Theory of Relativity and Atomic Energy) was relegated to a patent clerk and ignored by academia for two decades; in 1989, Stanley Pons and Martin Fleischmann discovered Cold Fusion but academic peers condemned them to disgrace when they could not recreate their findings. It took twenty-five years to discover failings in the in the peer-review formulations of nickel and palladium nano-powders and then they did indeed create cold fusion reactions.

Years lost; reputations slighted; contributions ignored and a future of clean energy delayed.

And those are just three of a dozen examples that come to my mind.

For Business, Government and Academia

Thought leadership is squandered routinely today in business, in government, and in academia. The importance of a well-thought out process to recognize, protect and encourage great ideas from all sources cannot be over-emphasized. A Chief Thought-Leadership Officer position is a very important addition to every organization and is an essential component of Strategic Planning certainly.

Resetting Collapse Trending Economies is Critical

This topic is important to discuss and resolve as carefully and well as we possibly can. Our past 20-year period of increasingly competitive workplaces, have spawned management teams that led 72% of all nations' globally to report a collapse trending today. The Socio-economic impacts of Collapse include Recessions, Depressions, Populism, Racism, Social Problems, Religious Intolerance, high incarceration rates, military spending, terrorism, increasing cost of living, lower standard of living and human rights - on and on. Young people cannot start lives in family-friendly communities without stable homes suitable for young children.

Turning-around economies requires that decision makers of policy are not be bureaucrats nor politicians – but SMEs (Subject Matter Experts). SMEs are twenty-year experienced thought-leaders, engineers, authors, experts, and major project builders with experiece from many countries and corporate settings – and not career admins nor generalists.

Expert Panels: Experts and Executive Advisory Boards can fill this need in many cases. However, when expert organizations are denied grants and supporting incomes, or when SMEs become unhirable in a competitive job market - as they are today; societies will probably continue the status-quo collapse trending that have led to revolution in 20% of Winter Economic Cycles; and unnecessary social problems in the other 80% of troughs historically.

Look to Expert Panels and Executive Board Advisors with wide consulting and building experiences to safeguard thought leadership impartially and objectively.

We really cannot afford to not look at policies that reset economies actively now.

Countries that correct these problems and successfully reset their economies, keep their heads above water - even in difficult economic times. Statistics confirm that they position themselves for prosperity sustainably.

The countries that are good examples of sustainable policy making today include The Netherlands, Japan, China, Germany (except in Energy), Russia, Italy, Norway, and twenty others discussed in the Transition Economics Maturity Modeling discussions that follow.

As a society, we cannot want dumbed-down business and government workplaces. We want instead, to encourage thought-leadership and lessons-learned in solutions that have turned around economies reliably.

Transition Economics implements Engineering Safety-Nets and Advisory Committees within Projects that ensure that we never have our best, brightest, and most experienced, sitting idle without productive output.

Thought-leadership is a complex but very solvable training challenge.

Learning from Smaller Economies

The consequences of socially irresponsible management and policy are not easily correlated in a large economy and population like the United States and China. America's GDP is the largest in the world and the population is twenty times that of many others at 340 million people; China and India populations are almost four-times higher than the U.S. again.

Rather than listing Economics studies alphabetically as does Harvard, Transition Economics suggests a cyclic teaching start. Sometimes a policy works well and sometimes the same policy does not work at all; policies that work well short-term do not always work well long-term either.

Transition Economics explains when a policy is appropriate; when is it most likely to move a society forward; and when will it move an economy toward collapse.

In much smaller countries, like the Nordic States – populations are between five and twenty million people – so the impacts of offshoring engineering and creating trade deficits (importing more than exporting), were felt severely within a short few years after policy implementation. Because these populations were small, they could also vote for socialistic policies that were more sustainable more easily too; democratic voters could react to bad policy almost as soon as the impacts were felt – and in this way corrections were made quickly that turned around the problems.

In the U.S., the Federal Reserve's 2010 Budget confirmed that 160 million Americans (40% of the population) had nothing (their wealth totaled just 0.3%) – and these individuals had no vote to effect change because the U.S. has a two-party system where the majority 60% are living well enough to feel they must protect what they have. American's can be legitimately worried to lose their jobs and health benefits after seeing the reality of life for the lowest 40% of income earners, for the unemployed, and for those without health benefits.

Who benefits from Inequality? No-one - is the correct answer.

Winning Battles and Losing Wars via Policy

Inequity is the natural result of Capitalism; and inequity is also capitalism's highest Opportunity Cost. Opportunity Costs are the potential incomes lost from other alternatives; and often these loses are recoverable by enacting a few smart policy changes too.

Cherry-picking of statistics, and logic-gaps in the conclusions that facts within GDP statistics reveal, are frequent in media and in the economics articles printed in our major news publications. One always hopes that each country's management team and economic performance are well protected once highly paid PhDs coach economic best-practice to their body politic. And yet, we do arrive poorer for it. Collapse Trending is a verifiably valid observation; so Science demands we rethink current best-practices.

In this Transition Economics Maturity Modelling, I cite statistics for 180 countries. The G7 countries include France, America, Germany, Canada, Italy, Japan, and the United Kingdom. The G8 adds Russia. The G20 adds Turkey, Saudi Arabia, Mexico, China, Indonesia, India, Brazil, Australia, Argentina, South Africa and South Korea (there are just nineteen countries in the G20 at present). The Nordic States include the three Scandinavian Kingdoms of Denmark, Norway, and Sweden plus Finland, Greenland, Aland Islands, and the Faroe Islands.

Consider that the costs of inequity are at least two-fold initially. First, in the United States there is a constant revolution where welfare, military and incarceration spending is roughly five-times more per capita than the next-highest G7 nation (the U.K. is second in incarceration rates). Second, the Opportunity Cost of having 160 million people who are unable to contribute to the productivity of the country's Gross Domestic Product (GDP) is tremendous. The U.S. has an Export-per-Capita of just $5,000 where TE-Mature nations like the Netherlands are six times higher at $33,000.

Canada, the U.K., and Australia each bypass $600 billion in exports annually by protecting inequality; by not providing support systems for their citizens like Guaranteed Incomes, Engineering Safety Nets, Day Care and Higher Education.

Complaints that Canadians raise too few children are used to permit the diluting of its own world-famous culture through the highest immigration rate in the G7 - with little or no governance protecting quality of life impacts here.

Germany, and recently France and Switzerland, have been shoring up their socialistic policy quite a bit; Germany enjoys the strongest per capital GDP of the G7 in large part due to socially responsible reforms.

Pre-Perestroika - before the U.S.S.R changed to a Capitalist model in 1986, Moscow citizens were the last of the G8 to lose the American Dream. By "American Dream", I mean to say that all Muscovites had an exemplary definition of freedom; modest apartments were provided to young people when they wanted to move out after age sixteen; at nineteen they could marry and started a family in a larger assigned home; and all families were assigned a family cottage (Dacha) outside the city if requested. 21-year-old women were often the oldest among their friends if their first child had not arrived already, and both parents could continue university degrees and post-graduate studies while raising their children at home. If their marks were high, the couple's student salaries were increased as well - so that they could afford a car for the family.

Little money was a constant complaint, quality and variety of goods could have been better too, and yet basic needs were provided. Homelessness was illegal in the U.S.S.R. states and many are uncomfortable with the new situation today where 3.5% of the population are homelessness in Russia. There are between 30,000 and 50,000 homeless people in St Petersburg alone. They are called Bomzhi - having no fixed abode - the official status of those who lack the Propiska; a stamp in the internal passport verifying an official place of residence. Without a residence permit, the homeless are deprived of employment, medical services and social welfare, and can be sent to prison for up to two years for "vagrancy, begging or leading a parasitic life." ("Homeless in Russia: A visit with Valery Sokolov, by Jan Spence, Share International Archives," 1997)

Unlike China, Russia failed to monetize their productions while operating as a communist government; this means that they failed to sell their watches, machinery, jets, and automobiles to other countries in sufficient quantity. These freedoms came to an end when Mikhail Gorbachev changed to the Capitalistic Policies suggested by U.S. President Reagan and other major trading partners at the time.

Most would agree that China is an economic powerhouse and even a force-of-nature, but how did they get there? In the west, students are taught that Communism (communistic or socialistic policies) are policies that result in a terrible financial failure – the U.S.S.R.'s challenges in monetizing their Communist economy is usually brought forward as an example. But what of Communist China's undeniable success?

The Chinese not only own 10% of U.S. Debt, and also own much of the most prestigious real estate in the United States, Canada and the United Kingdom too. Why invade another country if you can just buy the bits that are worth having – and leave the headache of managing lower-class indigenous people to local governments?

This is what brilliant planning and responsible management looks like; North Americans and European leaders might actually like to play a move or two of this strong planning chess game in their own defense once in a while.

The Netherlands managed better economically as a direct result of its adopting Socialistic Policies 25-years ago. At #5 on The CMI, the Netherlands guarantees living wages and incomes, maintains a trade surplus, has universal daycare, retirements; they implement graduated tax, offshoring protections, and housing controls that ensure that young families can get started. Dutch citizens earn three-times export per capita (new wealth) than a Canadian. Why? Because they can; their citizens are not forced to sit idly without the means to begin commercial businesses that make them productive.

Socialistic Policies are not the only solution for all phases of Economic Cycles, nor for all population-level countries, but you will come to understand why TE-Mature Socialistic Policy are the only choice in Autumn and Winter phases. Socialistic Policies are probably the only option that works in all economic phases for countries with populations of less than twenty million as well.

Like the Roosevelts and Bushes, I am the descendant of the 400-year Puritan family that originally helped to build Harvard University; my name is on the Mayflower Compact, and so it does not surprise that my own values prefer sustainable equality very much. I like them for both their business performance and obvious humanism.

The Netherlands, Norway, etc. make use of the productivity of 100% of their population through social supports - in keeping with their national values just the same.

Liking or nor liking something does not enter into research and observation, a socialistic policy may make a better business case – or it may not. Often I research a conclusion that I might like to prove correct only to find no support or that the opposite is even true.

To the question "Does Socialism make people lazy?" The answer is verifiable in GDP Export statistics as Absolutely Not. Inequity's Special Interest lobbyists jump quickly to cite negative examples in sub-communities – Canadian Indians are perhaps one example.

Based on GDP stats, and easily noticeable in CSQ Research's CMI Country Management Index, giving citizens the tools and means to be productive, is proven to make countries advance economically.

Transition Economics – Cycle Policy

Different phases in Cyclic Economies call for different Policy. Capitalist Economies are cyclic economies; play a game of Monopoly to see this cycle play out from start-to-end within sixty minutes or so.

Incomes and Renewed Spending Power are needed when Economic Controls are ignored in Autumn Economies and Inequity prevents the poor from contributing to economic production any longer.

Pure Capitalism is unsustainable by itself; a Monopoly Game must Reset every time and so too must Capitalist Economies. *Socialistic Policy*, and specifically the TE-Mature policies developed in

13

Transition Economics, are proven to increase production outputs similar to per-capita results seen in Nordic States, The Netherlands, Germany, Switzerland and others.

These countries are not in Collapse Trending today; their Economies are Advancing with positive Trade Balances and many of these nations boast Good Lives and live the American Dream still.

TE-Mature policies create a Sustainable Capitalism or Socialism that maintains citizen spending-power in housing, energy, healthcare and other needs through pragmatic Economic Controls.

Firing on all Cylinders

Think of a strong economy as one might think of a combustion engine. The strength of the engine relies on the production, or force, in each of its cylinders as each pushes to move a car forward. There are primary, secondary and tertiary economies that provide incomes to a labor force - but this labor force often comprises less than half of the citizens of any country.

Unemployment is often double the advertised rate and so is commonly 9% to 18%; the retired of most countries are 20%, and the rest of citizenry are children, students and disabled persons.

If you were to rely on the labor force alone, this promises an engine running at 41% to 55% efficiency at best.

Cash rich and strategically minded nations, profit by purchasing government debt from other nations or take ownership stakes in local companies, and this serves as another injector of wealth into the country.

The reason that programs like Guaranteed Living Incomes have such strong business cases is that they ensure that the unemployed, retired, and all others in an economy can contribute through their spending as well.

Finally, Renewable automation can begin to contribute to productivity and to a country's GDP as well. By targeting high-profit exports and expensive imports for automation first, we invest once and generate revenue many times – even while we sleep.

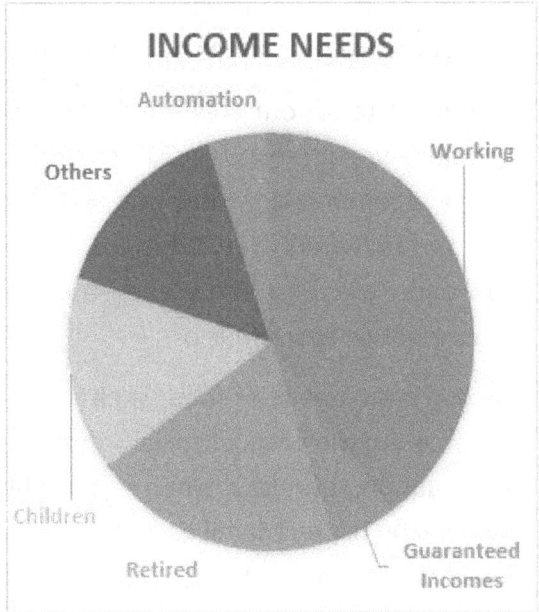

INCOME NEEDS

Automation

Others

Working

Children

Retired

Guaranteed Incomes

In our present economy, where automation is transitioning, and economies are transitioning too, an Engineering Safety-Net program permits skilled engineers to continue to develop very specific Renewable Automations.

With TE-Mature policies, now our economy is firing on all cylinders; now, we are focused on taking economic productivity from much more that just 40% of our working population.

With Transition Economics policies, our wealth distribution policies become wealth creation strategies. As evidence, I present the Netherlands' citizens who generate almost three-times the export wealth of a Canadian and six-times that of an American by running TE-Mature Policies.

Once incomes are in the hands of all citizens wishing to be productive; and once we restore spending power as well, we reset our economy for a new sixty-year cycle of prosperity in capitalism. This goals are the targets of a maturing Transition Economy.

We didn't teach our children Cycle Economics in high-school as we should have, nor did we teach them about other systems of housing policy, economic controls, etc. We taught our kids only about the systems that were status-quo today - and so now as adults, we have to wonder are these "new" cycle-appropriate Policies something that we should be suspicious of.

As our basic needs of food, shelter, transportation, and energy are automated, the costs of social safety-nets are reduced considerably. Automation, therefore, when responsibly planned and implemented, can clearly protect families from interruptions to their incomes and livelihoods – and that is the reason for having a government too.

Transition Economics Automation

"When you change the way you look at things, the things you look at change."

Max Planck, Quantum Mechanics in Physics

Automation is an important building block for civilization and humanity. Aristotle famously observed 2500 years ago that there will ever-be need of slaves until the assembly of the things we need in life are built by themselves. In 1960, George Jetson's futuristic science-fiction lifestyle featured 2-day, 3-hour work-weeks of brutal button-pushing between packing the kids and robot-maid onto journeys in their anti-gravity car. The Hanna-Barbera TV show "The Jetsons" was set in 1998 - and here in 2016 we still have barely begun.

Driverless cars, as with every other technology, was science fiction until an engineer – in this case an engineer with limitless resources -

made it work first in 2013 at Google; of course the engineer that I am referring to is Larry Page, Google's CEO.

In 2015, the World Peace Transition Projects - #WPProjects, explained the 250 Connected Smart Factories needed to automate every economy's basic needs of life – and then it assigned the workload to many hands by assigning one sustainable automation project to every country in an effort to create a profitable new international trade marketplace as well.

Without this sort of planning, automation is simply eliminating jobs at dizzying rates. Automation Job losses are projected by some experts to reach 50% of all jobs by the year 2035. We will talk about these next coming thirty-years of 972 jobs lost monthly, per million population – along with other TE Throttle Rate discussions.

Transition Economics uses TE-Throttles, to explain the responsible rate of change that permits the most effective automation of society - so that we can all see the benefits without unnecessary hardships.

Transition Economics Problem Solving

At each phase of an economic cycle, policies must solve problems unique-to and routine-within that phase.

Increases Interest Rates in Winter Phase:

Economies defend their currency valuation and national debt load by increasing interest rates. The upside of a lift is that this problem is now solved; however, there is a real downside in that as interest rates rise, mortgage payments also rise; first for variable mortgages and then for fixed mortgages. Housing Bubbles have forced many mortgage holders and real estate speculators to take on enormous mortgages that are many multiples of their salaries. As interest rates rise and owners cannot pay their mortgages, owners dip into retirement savings and then, if they cannot sell their homes, they lose their homes to the mortgage provider.

Evicted families turn next to an overstressed rental market and will often hold an overpriced rental without hope of returning to a home ownership position.

If homeowners lose their income as well, or cannot find income due to automation job-loss, high divorce rates, or high-unemployment, a large percentage of evicted home-owners will become homeless and 5% of homeless will commit suicide.

Regrettably, the status-quo answer in most capitalist countries today is to "do nothing" about this problem.

Now, Transition Economics are needed to save lives. See the Housing Policy in Chapter 7 below to see that many anti-eviction options, real estate bubble controls, and other proven, researched policies are available to balance the Interest Rate Increase.

What are other Problem Solving examples?

Automation: tests poorly with voters due to concerns for job-loss – and yet Automation is a direct economic production booster at the same time that it mitigates concerns of collapse entirely.

Consider also that no-one starves once food is automatically grown and delivered autonomously to everyone's door; and no-one goes without shelter once robots build serviced homes where and when needed too.

Guaranteed Incomes, Retraining, Engineering Safety Nets and perhaps even Corporate Automation Taxes, solve the job-loss problems at the same time they are proven to increase exports per capita (economic wealth creation) dramatically.

The needs of society to sustain families who no longer send someone to commute to office cubicles in order to sustain an income is now addressed. People can retrain, or begin worthwhile careers in fields that they love as opposed to repetitive labors.

For business, the savings from automation are substantial – consider that an automated shop floor has no need of night shift workers; can run 7/24 using equipment engineered to run for years at a time; and there is no need for even overhead factory lights in many cases.

For just two examples where Transition Economics save lives while building sustainable societies.

We discuss policy problem solving in much more detail in the Chapters ahead.

Chapter 2

-

Cycles and Phases in Capitalism

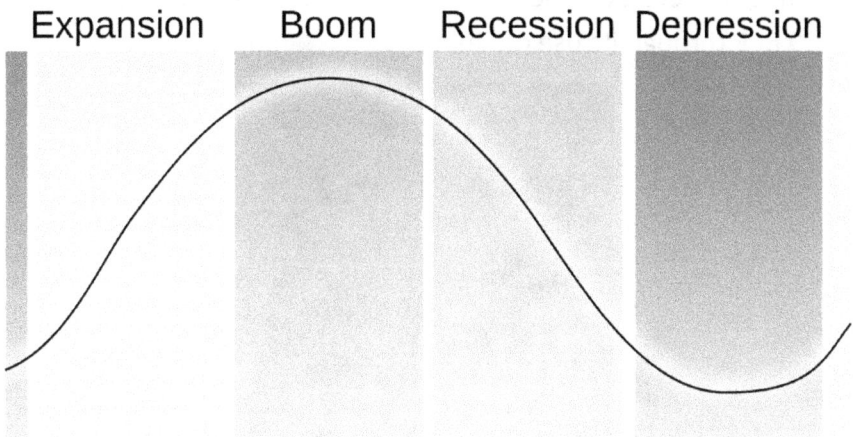

| Expansion | Boom | Recession Depression |

The sixty-minute game of Monopoly is a close approximation of Capitalism's sixty-year cycles. Would you be surprised to hear that there has been a Great Depression in capitalist economies consistently, give or take ten years or so, on record for 4000 years as well? The phases and cycle looks somewhat similar to the line and rectangles on this chart above.

Nicholae Kondratieff was the brilliant Soviet Economics Historian and Researcher who's book "The Long Wave Cycle" first documented the phenomenon first in 1925. He divided each cycle into four phases of Spring, Summer, Autumn and Winter - similar to the chart at the start of this chapter labelled Expansion, Boom, Recession, Depression.

I try to provide enough citations so that readers can validate presented facts for themselves. In this case, I encourage you to Google "K-Wave Economics" to confirm this point and encourage you to read more from the many citations referenced throughout this book.

K-Waves, or Kondratieff Waves or Longwaves, are proven in thesis back to 930 AD China (Snyder, 2014)("William Thompson | Department of Political Science | Indiana University Bloomington," 2016), and were documented on the Code of Hammurabi stone in 1760 BCE through its use of "Jubilees".

Code of Hammurabi - from the Louvre in Paris. (Bartz, 2005)

According to historical cycle records kept traced back to 930 AD, we are in a nineteenth Great Depression today. A Great Depression is simply a deep and pervasive recession and we will emerge from this time once our policies permit new incomes and spending-power.

Jeffery Sachs of Columbia University included a discussion of Cycle

Economics in his recent book; William Thompson at Indiana University has published influential papers and books documenting eighteen K-Waves dating back to 930 AD in China's Song Province as well; and I will wrap up this aside with Michael Snyder who wrote "It should be noted that economic cycle theories have enabled some analysts to correctly predict the timing of recessions, stock market peaks and stock market crashes over the past couple of decades." (Snyder, 2014)

And so the cycle has repeated, back through history. Longwave K-Waves are observable, well-documented and repeat regularly in Capitalistic societies. As enough evidence confirms the existence of these phenomena and as this is my third book in Economics that researches them too, I feel comfortable referring to Cycle Economics as not just a theory but a Science. Transition Economics endeavors to be scientific as well and so we will look at Automation and at methods to empirically pinpoint supporting TE-Mature Policy scientifically too.

What happens at the end of a game of monopoly? Does status quo get everyone back on track in the final hotel round? No - unfortunately not. All wealth must be thrown back into the game's bank; the game must be Reset, and money and properties redistributed an available to everyone again - so that a new game/cycle can restart.

When a Monarch ran the country, back in 1763 BCE Babylon (Egypt), King Hammurabi reset his economy every fifty years proactively - in anticipation of these sixty-year depressions. Universal Debt Forgiveness was called "Jubilee".

Today we are a Democracy – and regrettably, we are a democracy that is untrained in Cycle Economics. I say regrettably, because when we did not get these basic sustainability lessons in our high-school

Civics classes, we can now be easily misinformed and misled by special interests that might not like to have their status quo upset.

In the 1930s, Keynesian Economic Theorists distracted governments from wealth-distribution for long enough to create an opportunity for Adolf Hitler to come to power during Germany's 1930 revolution-vote – we call these elections "Populism" today. Brexit and Donald Trump are examples and there are many others in Spain, France and elsewhere following stride.

The democratic vote of Germans too long oppressed by slave-wages and Versailles Treaty oppressions – alongside a flaw in the then German constitution, permitted the forming of a Dictatorship that led to a World War which killed 60-million people.

War, therefore, is an observable result of Keynesian Economics' attempt to extend unsustainable capitalistic monetary policy indefinitely at the end of a K-Wave Economic cycle.

Keynes (pronounced "Canes"), dismissed the consequences of his progressively unsustainable practices by stating very ironically, "And then we are all dead". Let's hope he doesn't get to be right twice.

Financial industries and the rich flocked to Keynes' Theories as these systems protected their wealth by building layer upon layer of evasive and socially irresponsible protection tactics; each one more outlandish than the next - from Borrowing Fiscal Policy to Currency-Devaluing and Inflation-Driving Monetary Policy, to Distributive Justice (borrowing without paying it back), to Debt+Inflation=Prosperity mathematical logic gaps.

In the end, typical Keynesian tactics included government spending designed to stimulate very short-term demand, low tax, and under-investment in government sponsored projects (like automation) and business governance. In layman's terms, Keynes' theories were a study in short-sightedness almost from start-to-end.

Revolution and War are required in just about 20% of K-Wave Cycle restarts historically, and the more pervasive the Wealth Distribution, the longer and more prosperous is the new Cycle that follows it.

Let's look at K-Wave Cycles chronologically to see how wealth distributions have played out in the past:

- 1772's Credit Crisis was ended by the American Revolution's forced debt forgiveness – remember the Boston Tea Party? King George and the British Treasury got stuck with that bill for almost $1 million in 1776 dollars. France's $1.3 billion investment in the American Revolution went on to fuel the French Revolution.
- 1835's Great Depression was ended by the California Gold Rush which multiplied America's Gold Reserves ten-times
- 1883's Panic in the US was ended by new Immigrant Wealth
- 1929's Great Depression distributed wealth through WWII; and of course
- Academic Thesis have tracked K-Waves back to 930 AD in China's Song Province Capitalist Economy

"Jubilee" distributed wealth every 50 years for 1000+ years as carved on the Code of Hammurabi Stone – now located in the Louvre – ensuring that the misery of routine capitalist troughs did not turn into a revolution again the Kings of Babylon and Egypt.

Our last Spring Economy began around 1950. Wealth was well distributed and everyone had incomes that they needed - to buy homes and to afford a good life. Opportunities to get live and even become successful were readily available to all.

Summer was approximately 1969 to 1982. All was still very good and the boom of the American Dream began to afford a rich upper class now.

Fall, or Autumn, was much more difficult to explain and Winter was more difficult again – and so I will devote a chapter to discuss each individually.

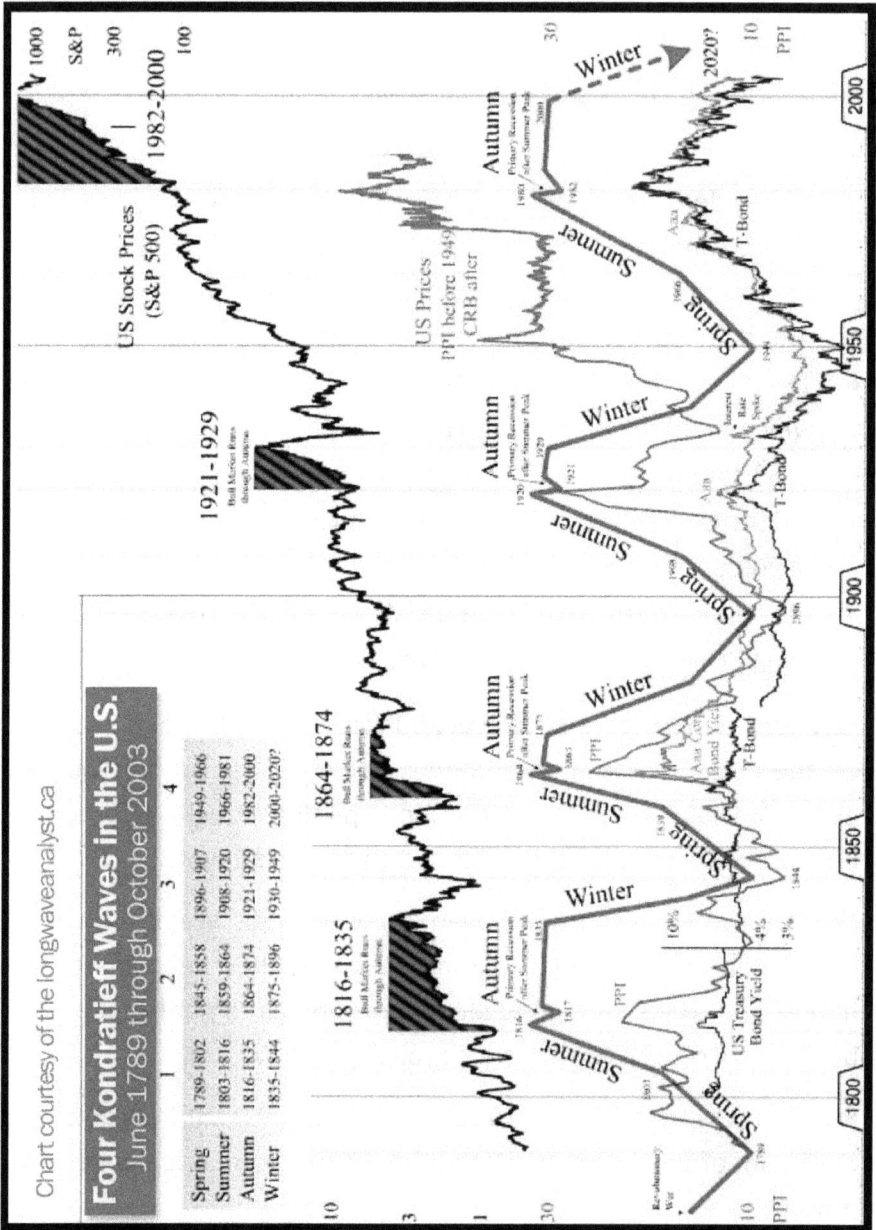

Chart courtesy of the longwaveanalyst.ca

Four Kondratieff Waves in the U.S.
June 1789 through October 2003

	1	2	3	4
Spring	1789-1802	1845-1858	1896-1907	1949-1966
Summer	1803-1816	1859-1864	1908-1920	1966-1981
Autumn	1816-1835	1864-1874	1921-1929	1982-2000
Winter	1835-1844	1875-1896	1930-1949	2000-2020?

Our most recent cycle is summarized in the following slides. You can follow along and view this slide deck in high-resolution online at: http://ow.ly/OKmj305xto1 (Edward Tilley, 2015).

Many topics in following chapters will make use of this deck as well.

Spring and Summer

Autumn

The next and last phase of the cycle is the **Winter** phase – our Great Depressions; the deep and sustained Recessions.

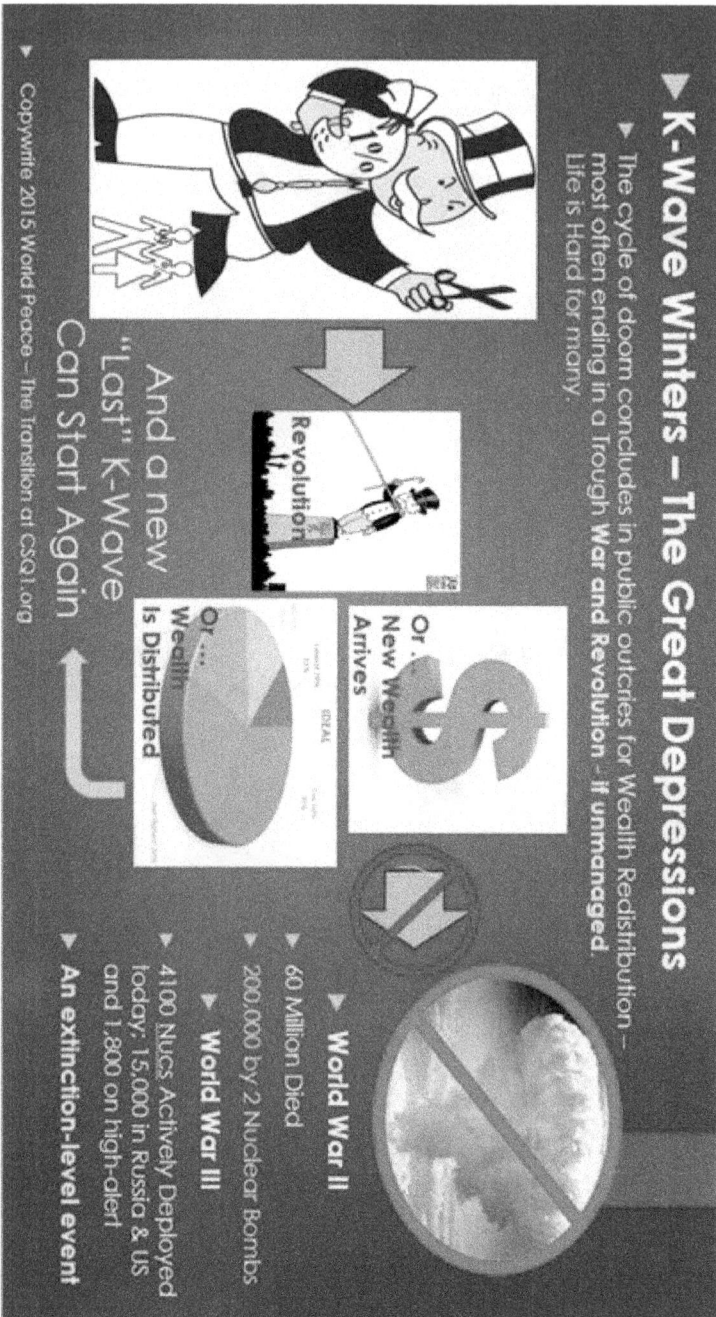

28

Boiled Frogs

Life feels very competitive in Winter Economies. With quality jobs scarce and affordable housing difficult to find in major cities, many couples are living paycheck to paycheck and cannot be ready to begin a family until well into their 30s and even 40s.

But it wasn't always this way...

A Good Life in the G8

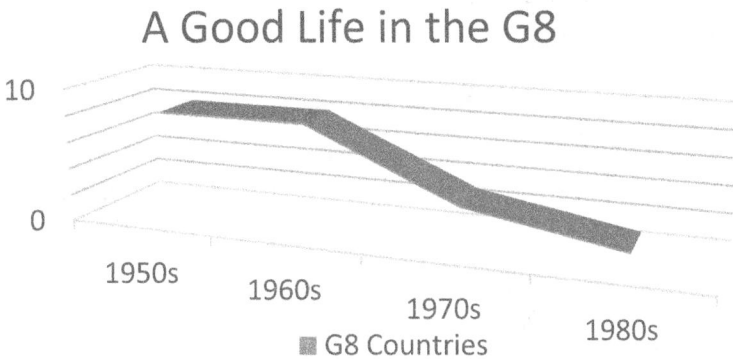

In all of the G8 countries, like the American Dream and Good Life in the USA of the 1950s up until the 1970s, a high-school education was sufficient to find lifelong employment with a full pension, healthcare, benefits, and to buy a home that would be paid free-and-clear its mortgage almost 100% of the time. A young family could begin life at the age of twenty without amassing the lifelong debt that we see today.

So too could Russian families, start a family and home easily until 1986's Perestroika changed their land-grants system to a North-American style open real-estate market.

All of our systems of pensions, benefits, insurance, childcare, education, etc. were built based on this one-job-for-a-lifetime model of benevolent capitalism. Back then there were plenty of jobs that paid retirements, drug and dental benefits, and just one income

29

afforded a comfortable living for most families with educations for family members as needed. Here in Canada, a plumber or steel worker could easily afford a nice cottage with a beach-front as well.

As pensioned, high-paying jobs disappear and gaps in wealth between the rich and the poor become more and more unequal, two-income families emerge as the new norm. Housing bubbles and billionaire-ranks grow alongside many more poor until the bottom 40% of Americas income earners came to own just 0.3% of America's wealth and income in 2010.

Remember that Rich people are making $3 to $5 million per day seven days a week for 30 years and longer now. That much inequity is not going to be overcome by asking workers to take two or three jobs.

Rate of Job Automation

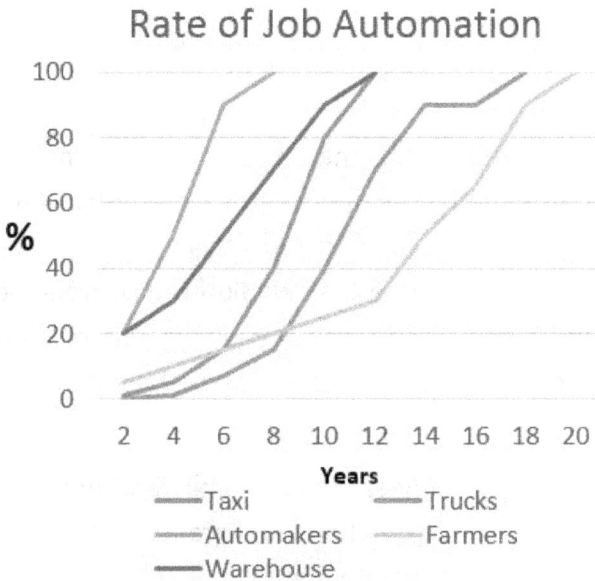

With Automations reducing repetitive jobs by up to 50% over the next twenty years, families will be fortunate to find a single high-paying conventional job.

In a large country like the United States, this represents 160 million people who own nothing and have no vote either. No vote, because 60% routinely vote to continue their status-quo – as per their basic in-class training and political instruction. The result is a modern-day American Revolution manifest in dramatic social problem statistics which include incarceration rates five-times higher than the next G7 country acts of onshore terror in 400 mass-shootings annually.

By applying the much higher GDP Export-per-Capita of socialistic country citizens from the Netherlands and Norway, it is possible to estimate the opportunity cost of keeping 160 million Americans unable to contribute to the economy. This opportunity cost is a staggering – an optimistic $8 trillion dollars annually; and in Canada, Great Britain and Australia where GDP Export per Capita is one-third and one-sixth, the costs of denying socialistic policies an average of $630 billion annually.

This serves as the basis of an estimate for what is the annual cost of protecting inequality in the G7 countries in a K-Wave Winter. I will expand on this discussion further in the book.

Country	GDP Export per Capita	Multiplier to Dutch Export/Cap	Export 2015 (in billions)	Opportunity Cost New Export (in billions)	Collapse or Advance Trending?
Netherlands	$33,652	100%	$477	$0	Advance
Norway	$28,807	117%	$103	$17	Advance
United States	$5,057	665%	$1,510	$8,538	Collapse
Sweden	$18,688	180%	$151	$121	Advance
Germany	$18,316	184%	$1,309	$1,096	Advance
Canada	$13,286	253%	$411	$630	Collapse
United Kingdom	$7,378	456%	$436	$1,553	Collapse
Australia	$10,446	322%	$188	$418	Collapse

Chapter 3

-

Transition Economics Maturity Model

Maturity Models are standardized measuring charts that help direct the services offered by any team within a specialization. These Models are commonly seen in Construction, Technology, and Transformation Project Management Offices and serve us well here in Economics too.

Maturity Models often discuss five or six major steps, which are usually just a series of building block projects that must be implemented to take a group from Immaturity – as a reactive fire-fighting organization; to Maturity – a pro-active, professional and transparent problem solver. The high-level maturity groups transcend their cost-center beginnings by offering products and

solutions that make them a profit generator and a strategic differentiator; a business-enabling force for their company – or for their country.

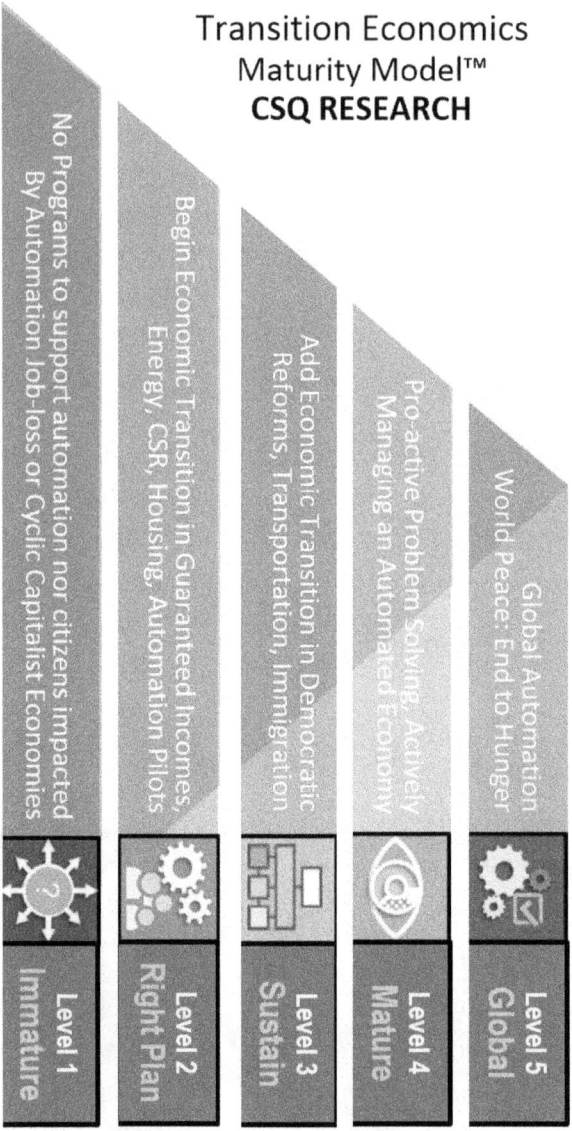

Transition Economics
Maturity Model™
CSQ RESEARCH

No Programs to support automation nor citizens impacted By Automation Job-loss or Cyclic Capitalist Economies

Begin Economic Transition in Guaranteed Incomes, Energy, CSR, Housing, Automation Pilots

Add Economic Transition in Democratic Reforms, Transportation, Immigration

Pro-active Problem Solving, Actively Managing an Automated Economy

Global Automation World Peace: End to Hunger

Level 1 Immature

Level 2 Right Plan

Level 3 Sustain

Level 4 Mature

Level 5 Global

Mature vs Immature

What would a mature Transition Economy look like? Surely it would be running the strongest policies that their business cases and ongoing monitoring confirm that they are sustaining a healthy, advancing economy. GDP reports would confirm that citizens have incomes and renewed spending power; and more than this, the most mature countries will have the time and best practices to help other countries achieve maturity the same.

A TE-Immature Country will be using policy inappropriate for this phase of our current economic cycle.

TE-Maturity and Calculus

Isaac Newton and Gottfried Leibniz solved the timeless problem of how to determine Instantaneous Velocity by inventing limits (called infinitesimals back then) and derivatives in Calculus. Leibniz went on to develop differential and integral Calculus as well, and both men could be easily regarded as giant contributors to science who made enormous advances in not only modern mathematics, but physics, science, philosophy, and economics.

Calculus is also an advanced mathematics, which is based on a very, very simple solution that allows us to calculate rise-over-run slope at point so small that there is no delta; at an instant.

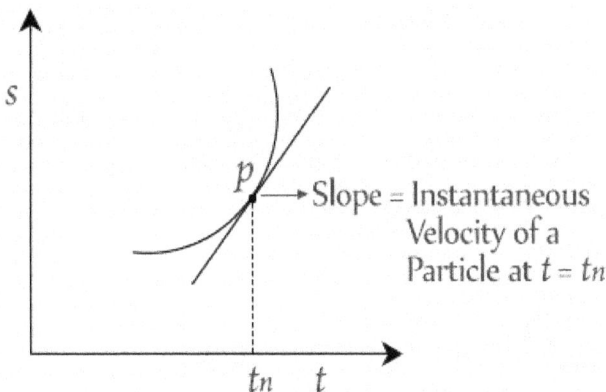

Slope = Instantaneous Velocity of a Particle at $t = t_n$

Similarly, the measure of Aggregate Performance for the many policies deployed within one country's economy, is suggested to be determined by TE-Maturity. We accomplish this measure by normalizing an arbitrary definition for Trending and then establish a baseline called "Collapse Trending".

Consider that Transition Economics policies are driven and monitored by a business case empirically, measurably; this means that the many and varied ways of implementing any single policy are defined and can be controlled so that differences between one *housing* policy and another, for example, can be easily compared. If the policy aligns with TE Maturity policy, we can assign a statistical value reliably like 1 or 0, "Yes" or "No", Like or Not Like, etc.

Draft Version .9 / Country	Collapse (C) / Advancing (A)	TE Maturity Model Estimate	GDP Export Per Capita	Wealth Distribution	Minimum Wage Targets	Graduated Tax (High Tax on Rich)	Guaranteed Incomes	Housing & Usury Law	End Tax Evation	Social Programs - DayCare	Social - Free Higher Education	Social - Universal Healthcare	Onshore Engineering	Wealth Creation	Quality Exports	Reduce Imports	Manufacture Locally	Local Profit	Transition Economics Maturity	Automation Project Safety Nets	Increase Spending Power	Renewable Automation #WPProjects
Afghanistan	C	1	$ 122	N	N	N	N	N	N	N	N	N			N	N	Y	Y		N	N	N

Non-Binary weightings and percentages can also be used, especially in artificial intelligence and analytic "deep-dives", but initially we want to prove that our method has value in simplest terms.

Each Country has sixteen policies as discussed here in this book initially. Countries with more TE Maturity-aligned policies, earn the assignment of a value greater than "1" – Immature Maturity. A more readable list of these policies is also in the Level 3 Maturity chart a few pages below.

The very detail-oriented among us will want to automate the assignment of maturity values as needed to build decision-support tools from models; and this will surely happen with TE Maturity Model adoption. Much can be learned about housing, and all other policies, from comparing collapsing and advancing groupings.

TE Maturity is not Calculus yet, but it is at the start of a wave of development as was when Newton and Leibniz began.

At this time there are just two countries that are deemed to be at a Level 3 and other maturing nations are Level 2. Maturity levels are defined in the next few pages.

Economic Trending

Collapsing

Collapsing (C) – In K-Wave Winter (which is where we are today), when policies are not proven to create incomes AND are not targeting renewed spending power policies AND a trade deficit exists, countries can be said to be trending in a Collapsing direction.

If that country is also in Fiscal Deficit that exceeds a year of GDP Exports (Incomes), one can say something about the rate of collapse as well, but for now we will simply state that the economy is in a Collapsing Trend.

Advancing

Advancing (A) – A country's economy is said to be advancing if its Trade Balance is in Surplus (GDP Exports minus GDP Imports GT 0) and is greater than 5% of GDP Exports. Get online at Wikipedia to find lists of GDP Imports and Exports listed for every country annually.

Growth of GDP alone is not considered an indicator of an advancing economy. Although the number is easily track-able, GDP cannot be easily correlated back to our ultimate goal of creating a sustainable Good Life. An increasing-GDP country with high levels of inequity could as easily be said to be headed for high social-problem spending and could be unsustainable or even unstable and moving toward revolution. Not to say that this is happening; rather simply GDP in itself tells us little.

GDP Export per Capita, alternatively, often shows a correlation with the GINI wealth distribution Index and with the United Nations HDI – Human Development Index, which are qualitative measures of the lives of citizens as well.

TE Maturity Math

By summarizing a list of 180 countries in this way (see the Charts below), we can make a number of important conclusions.

First, we can determine what percentage of countries have Collapsing or Advancing trends.

Changing the definition of Collapse Trending will change the resulting value but by drawing a best-effort line in the sand, we build a basis to start with. Recall that our goal here is find which combination of policies lead to reliably Advancing Economies.

All Countries				
	Trade Deficit	Trade Surplus	**Collapsing**	Advancing
	132	54	114	45
	71%	29%	72%	28%
G20				
	11	8	9	10
	58%	42%	47%	53%
G8				
	4	4	4	4
	50%	50%	50%	50%

Second, now that we know that some number (72%) of all nations measured are in Collapse Trending, with this control group - and baseline number, we can determine was our assumption about higher-TE-Maturity nations correct.

If our TE-Maturity Policy assumptions are correct, we should expect to see that a smaller percentage of TE Maturing countries are in a Collapse Trending; and if we are incorrect, we should see that our TE Maturing countries have a similar or worse Collapse Trending.

On reviewing our simple initial list, just one or perhaps two of the twenty TE-Maturing nations (nations with a TE-Maturity of 2, 3, 4 or 5), exhibit Collapse Trending initially. By this comparison, TE-Maturing countries show collapse rates from 5% to 10% compared-to much higher rates for G8 (50%), G20 (47%), and 72% Collapse Trending for all countries.

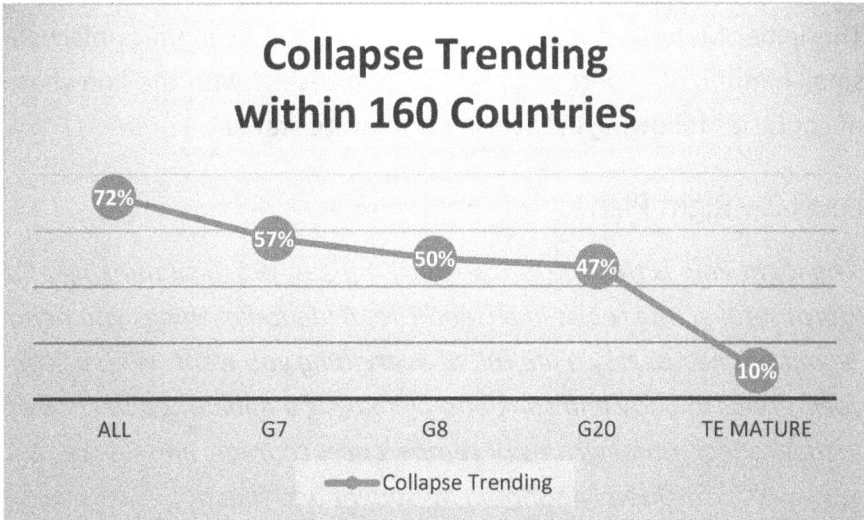

Collapse Trending within 160 Countries

Many adjustments can be made in policies and data collection accuracy is important too. Fine-tuning and optimizing country policies until the best economic and social results are measured is the point and value of this exercise. At the end of the day, TE Maturity permits all countries to make policy decisions that arrive at a predictable, measurably sustainable, and economically advancing society.

Which countries are trending towards Collapse? In the G8 - Canada, France, United Kingdom and United States; G20 nations also include Australia, India, Mexico, South Africa, and Turkey.

Let's consider TE-Maturity Level definitions next.

Level 1 – Immature

Immature – Indicates that a country has insufficient Transition Economic Policies & Programs to support incomes, a return of spending power, nor support of automation and automation-driven job-losses. A look at the Trending chart below shows what you might expect within our Current Global Depression; correcting these trends takes policies with GDP-proven results.

The initial Maturity Model table for Transition Economics places a small handful of countries at Level 3 and Level 2 with the lion share of countries following in Level 1 – Immature status.

Level 2 – Right Plan

The Right Plan is the one whose ends, means, practical thinking and purposeful action result in a Good Life. A life full of things you need – and not necessarily a life full of everything you want. With a little luck, goods in body and soul, and by making a habit of good choices that reflect moral virtues of temperance, courage, and justice, a Good Life should be sought and found.

Abridged from Politics 322 BCE (Messerly, 2013)

A **Right Plan** for transitioning our world and country, is a plan of well-researched, worthwhile Goals, Proven & Transparent Process, the Right People, Great Vision and business-case-driven projects.

WHAT DOES IT TAKE?
TO BUILD A RIGHT PLAN

- Worthwhile Goals
- Simple Steps
- Proven Process
- Right People
- Clear Directions
- Great Vision

A Country Right Plan:

- Ensures Incomes:

	Transition Economics Mature Policy 5% to 10% in Collapse	Collapse Policy 72% of All Countries are in Collapse
Working Families & Individuals	Graduated Tax, Big-Business Tax Avoidance Crackdown, Inequity targets, Local Business Ownership, Local Govmt Business Ownership	Low Tax, Trickle-down, Middle-Class Focus, Diversity, Cheap Imports, Immigration, Small Business w/o support
Unemployed	Guaranteed Cost of Living Incomes, Business Automation Revenue Sharing	No benefits for underemployed nor all unemployed
Retirement	Employee & Pension Fund Protections, Cost of Living minimums, CSR & Business Accountability	Offshoring, Misuse of female diversity rules, ignoring pensions
Children	Free Mastery-based Education & Transition Economics Voter Education	Failure to support 20-year-olds starting families, High Divorce Rates
Others	Cost of Living Benefits for Disabled	Insufficient Support, High Debt Servicing Costs
Automation	Engineering Safety Nets, #WPProjects & Renewable Automation Support, Multi-Party Long Term Strategic Planning	Innovation programs that fail to support Renewable Automations and Trade & Selling Needs

The table's top-left cell contains a pie chart labeled "INCOMES DISTRIBUTE" with segments: Automation, Others, Working, Children, Guaranteed Incomes, Retired.

- Returns spending power to citizens

SPENDING POWER RETURNS	Transition Economics Mature Policy 5% to 10% in Collapse	Collapse Policy 72% of All Countries are in Collapse
Healthcare & Benefits	Universal Healthcare, Employee Benefit Plans to Revenue Neutral Business Case targets	Private Plans, Patents that externalize Government R&D
Childcare	Universal Daycare & Free Education incl. University	Unaffordable Childcare
Housing	Public Housing (30%) Controlled to Inflation, Land Grants, Anti-Eviction, and Foreign Ownership Taxes	Energy Poverty, Housing Bubbles created by lax controls
Food & Goods	License Renewable Automation, Local Harvesting, Driverless Transport & Distribution, Local Self-Sufficiency & Abundance	Insufficient Farm Compensations, Failure to develop automation, Dollar & 99p Stores, Cheap Imports, Austerity Measures
Energy	Abundant Geo-Thermal, Hydro, Cold-Fusion, Thorium Nuclear, Zero-Pollution Fuels	Part-time Wind & Solar, Fossil Fuel Oil Pipelines, Energy Poverty
Transport	Driverless-cars & Automated Goods Delivery, Auto Road & Rail Construction	Infrastructure w/o Automation & Trickle-down Protection, Transit

- Affords Engineering Safety Nets and the re-shoring of Engineering
- Balance tax & revenue-neutral solutions that add living wage income supports
- CSR – Corporate Social Responsibility training programs

- Support and Planning for Pilot Automations in Energy, Housing, Food, Clean Water & Transportation

I have stressed that Economic Controls alone are sufficient to sustain a Good Life and economy for any country. In order to take advantage of the benefits of automation too, #WPProjects is an example Global Right Plan of Connected Smart Factories and supporting social Policy, that was introduced in my last book World Peace – The Transition.

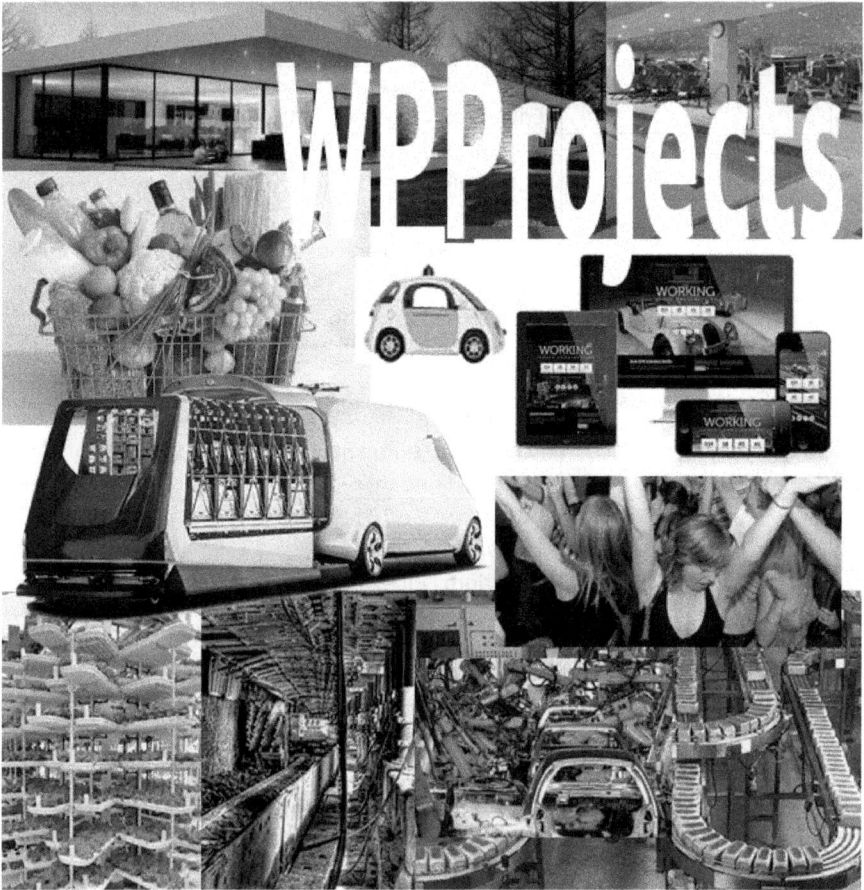

That #WPProjects Right Plan assigned 250 initial social and automation projects to 200 countries as needed to provide for the basic needs of food, water, top pharmaceuticals, furnishings, shelter, roads, automatic delivery and transportation, and so on.

The Right Plan needed for your country requires just a subset of these projects.

For most countries, just one automation project is typically required to build a new international trade network in hi-tech robotics and to spread the workload and expense of the automation project work. And what better way to leverage international expertise, experience, and also to include everyone as well?

The 250 WPProjects Connected Smart Factories can be found in the books Transition Economics – The Science of Sustainability, World Peace –The Transition, and you can visit the #WPProjects planning page online at http://csq1.org/world-peace-transition-projects-faq/

Level 3 – Sustain

The Projects needed to achieve this next level of maturity include wide Transition Economics training and adoption, Reversal of Housing Bubbles, Engineering On-Shored and Safety-Nets provided, Immigration Policy, and advances in Renewable Automation Programs.

This example Voting Chart is a summary list of policies proven to create profitable Social Program Business Cases with positive economic results. This book will spend time in explanation of every policy and point in the Chapters to come.

To create a chart like this for your country, simply replace Political Parties along the top of the chart and fill it in per the policies of each group running election-by-election. Elections for Housing are typically regional or municipal; Energy is often a State or Provincial Election issue; Tax Avoidance, Exports & Immigration are Federal.

The Chart below is an aid to help democratic voters and politicians stay focused on sustainable policies that improve your Country's Transition Economics Maturity and economies ongoing.

#	A+ Priority Social Policy	Canada			
		Cons	Lib	NDP	Grn
1	Long Term Right Planning	No	No	No	Yes
2	Bench Strength of MPs for Project Execution	Maybe	No	No	No
Wealth Distribution					
3	Pension Controls				
4	Minimum Wage Targets	No	Maybe	Yes	Yes
5	Graduated Tax	No	No	No	Yes
6	Guaranteed Incomes	No	No	Yes	Yes
7	Housing & Usury Controls	No	No	No	No
8	End Tax Avoidance	No	No	No	No
9	Daycare, Healthcare, Higher Education	No	Maybe	Yes	No
10	Onshore Engineering	No	No	Yes	No
Wealth Creation					
11	Increase & Automate Quality Exports	No	No	No	No
12	Reduce Imports	No	Yes	Yes	Yes
13	Sellers Automate Manufacture Locally	No	No	Yes	Maybe
14	Local Profit becomes Investment & Tax Revs	No	No	Yes	Maybe
Transition Economics Maturity					
15	Engineering Project Safety Nets	No	No	No	Yes
16	Increase Spending Power & Opportunity	No	No	No	No
17	Renewable Automation #WPProjects	No	No	No	No
18	TE Maturity Model	No	No	No	No
	If Yes=2, Maybe=1, No=0	3%	13%	47%	53%
	Leaning	Right	Left	Left	Left

46

Level 4 – Mature

Countries with a Mature Transition Economics plans are now actively monitoring and Release-Controlling improvements to their automated infrastructure. If the United Nations and member countries adopted projects similar to #WPProjects tomorrow, they could all be living sustainably within as little as five years.

The positive impact on equality and human rights should be tremendous for the first countries to reach Levels 4 and 5. Rewards will also be higher for early adopters - as would risk in development investment. This risk is addressed by revision control, automated upgrades and life cycle management supports in each project.

Transition Economics sets reasonable goals that exceed U.N. Global Goals with timings perhaps eight years sooner than Global Goals' 2030 targets. The reason for the productivity improvement can be found in the planning and in the SUSTAIN Project Planning Processes introduced later in the book.

Level 5 – Global Transition

These are the Strategic Differentiators and Game Changing Countries that build their local needs and then carry on to assist Global teams with consulting, thought leadership and best practice.

With a Good Life well on its way to being rolled out locally, Level 5 countries can now contribute to ensuring that these solutions are rolled out and running well with partners and global communities as needed. Our sustainable automations were designed to scale to this level quickly, and by now we are at release 2.0 and release 3.0 levels of technology maturity so that systems are reliable, renewable, and even elegant.

TE Maturity List by Country

All aforementioned Maturity measures are scored on the chart for every country based on the sixteen policy areas listed above; Healthcare, Guaranteed Incomes, and the other policy measures as discussed in the chapters that follow. At present, maturity levels are evaluated one country at a time and each country can request an assessment of how close or distant are they to their next maturity milestone.

As mentioned above, Right Plans are suggested to detail the projects needed to advance one's policies and country through these five levels of maturity. The transparency of this process will improve so that anyone has the ability to grade their own country more fairly than we have graded them here in isolated research.

The v1.0 initial list follows; see CSQ1.org online for the latest updates to the Transition Economics Maturity Model charts countries are welcome to update their data on this list by sending an email to info@csq1.org.

Country	Collapsing - C / Advancing - A	TE Maturity Model Estimate	GDP Export Per Capita	Wealth Distribution	Minimum Wage Targets	Graduated Tax (High Tax on Rich)	Guaranteed Incomes	Housing & Usury Law	End Tax Evation	Social Programs - DayCare	Social - Free Higher Education	Social - Universal Healthcare	Onshore Engineering	Wealth Creation	Quality Exports	Reduce Imports	Manufacture Locally	Local Profit	Transition Economics Maturity	Automation Project Safety Nets	Increase Spending Power	Renewable Automation #WPProjects
Afghanistan	C	1	$ 122	N	N	N	N	N	N	N	N	N	N		N	N	Y	Y		N	N	N
Albania	C	1	$ 3,481	N	N	N	N	N	N	N	N	N	N		N	N	Y	Y		N	N	N
Algeria	C	1	$ 4,414	N	Y	N	N	N	N	N	N	N	N		N	N	Y	Y		N	N	N
Angola	A	1	$ 4,315	N	Y	N	N	N	N	N	N	N	N		N	N	Y	Y		N	N	N
Antigua and Barbuda	C	1	$ 9,269	Y	Y	Y	Y	N	N	N	Y	Y	Y		Y	Y	Y	Y		N	Y	N
Argentina	A	1	$ 1,969	N	N	N	N	N	N	N	N	N	N		N	N	Y	Y		N	N	N
Armenia	C	1	$ 2,099	N	N	N	N	N	N	N	N	N	N		N	N	Y	Y		N	N	N
Australia	C	1	$ 8,728	Y	Y	Y	Y	N	N	N	Y	Y	Y		Y	Y	Y	Y		N	Y	N
Austria	C	1	$ 26,517	Y	Y	Y	Y	Y	N	Y	Y	Y	Y		Y	Y	Y	Y		N	Y	N
Azerbaijan	A	1	$ 8,352	Y	Y	Y	Y	N	N	N	Y	Y	Y		Y	Y	Y	Y		Y	Y	N
Bahrain	A	1	$ 9,216	Y	Y	Y	Y	N	N	N	Y	Y	Y		Y	Y	Y	Y		N	Y	N
Bangladesh	C	1	$ 576	N	N	N	N	N	N	N	N	N	N		N	N	Y	Y		N	N	N
Barbados	C	1	$ 6,616	Y	Y	Y	Y	N	N	N	Y	Y	Y		Y	Y	Y	Y		N	Y	N
Belarus	C	1	$ 10,780	Y	Y	Y	Y	N	N	Y	Y	Y	Y		Y	Y	Y	Y		N	Y	N
Belgium	A	2	$ 35,359	Y	Y	Y	N	N	N	Y	Y	Y	Y		Y	Y	Y	Y		N	Y	N
Belize	C	1	$ 5,164	Y	Y	Y	Y	N	N	Y	Y	Y	Y		Y	Y	Y	Y		N	Y	N
Benin	C	1	$ 327	N	N	N	N	N	N	N	N	N	N		N	N	Y	Y		N	N	N
Bhutan	C	1	$ 3,025	N	N	N	N	N	N	N	N	N	N		N	N	Y	Y		N	N	N
Bolivia	C	1	$ 2,709	N	N	N	N	N	N	N	N	N	N		N	N	Y	Y		N	N	N
Bosnia & Herzegovina		1	$ 3,048	N	N	N	N	N	N	N	N	N	N		N	N	Y	Y		N	N	N
Botswana	A	1	$ 8,683	Y	Y	Y	Y	N	N	N	Y	Y	Y		Y	Y	Y	Y		N	Y	N
Brazil	A	1	$ 1,887	N	N	N	N	N	N	N	N	N	N		N	N	Y	Y		N	N	N
Brunei	A	2	$ 57,652	Y	Y	Y	Y	N	N	Y	Y	Y	Y		Y	Y	Y	Y		N	Y	N
Bulgaria	C	1	$ 10,759	Y	Y	Y	Y	N	N	Y	Y	Y	Y		Y	Y	Y	Y		N	Y	N
Burkina Faso	C	1	$ 463	N	N	N	N	N	N	N	N	N	N		N	N	Y	Y		N	N	N
Burundi	C	1	$ 57	N	N	N	N	N	N	N	N	N	N		N	N	Y	Y		N	N	N
Cambodia	C	1	$ 1,999	N	N	N	N	N	N	N	N	N	N		N	N	Y	Y		N	N	N
Cameroon	C	1	$ 585	N	N	N	N	N	N	N	N	N	N		N	N	Y	Y		N	N	N
Canada	C	1	$ 13,262	N	N	N	N	N	N	N	N	Y	N		N	N	N	N		N	N	N
Cape Verde	C	1	$ 2,240	N	N	N	N	N	N	N	N	N	N		N	N	Y	Y		N	N	N
Central African Rep.		1	$ 70	N	N	N	N	N	N	N	N	N	N		N	N	Y	Y		N	N	N
Chad	A	1	$ 672	N	N	N	N	N	N	N	N	N	N		N	N	Y	Y		N	N	N
Chile	A	1	$ 7,144	Y	Y	Y	Y	N	N	N	N	Y	Y		Y	Y	Y	Y		N	Y	N
China	A	2	$ 3,489	Y	N	N	N	Y	N	Y	Y	Y	Y		Y	Y	Y	Y		N	Y	N
Colombia	C	1	$ 2,215	N	N	N	N	N	N	N	N	N	N		N	N	Y	Y		N	N	N
Comoros	C	1	$ 237	N	N	N	N	N	N	N	N	N	N		N	N	Y	Y		N	N	N
Costa Rica	C	1	$ 4,876	N	Y	N	N	N	N	N	N	N	N		N	N	Y	Y		N	N	N
Croatia	C	1	$ 9,168	Y	Y	Y	Y	N	N	N	N	Y	Y		Y	Y	Y	Y		N	Y	N
Cuba	C	1	$ 3,752	N	N	N	N	N	N	N	N	N	N		N	N	Y	Y		N	N	N
Cyprus	C	1	$ 11,321	Y	Y	Y	Y	N	D	Y	Y	Y	Y		Y	Y	Y	Y		N	Y	N
Czech Republic	A	1	$ 22,402	Y	Y	Y	Y	N	N	Y	Y	Y	Y		Y	Y	Y	Y		N	Y	N
Denmark	A	2	$ 24,347	Y	Y	Y	Y	N	N	Y	Y	Y	Y		Y	Y	Y	Y		N	Y	N
Djibouti	C	1	$ 1,712	N	N	N	N	N	N	N	N	N	N		N	N	Y	Y		N	N	N
Dominica		1	$ 3,396	N	N	N	N	N	N	N	N	N	N		N	N	Y	Y		N	N	N
Dominican Republic	C	1	$ 3,110	N	N	N	N	N	N	N	N	N	N		N	N	Y	Y		N	N	N

Country																		
Ecuador	C	1	$ 3,178	N	N	N	N	N	N	N	N	N	N	N	Y	Y	N	N	N
Egypt	C	1	$ 1,954	N	N	N	N	N	N	N	N	N	N	N	Y	Y	N	N	N
El Salvador	C	1	$ 2,049	N	N	N	N	N	N	N	N	N	N	N	Y	Y	N	N	N
Equatorial Guinea	A	1	$ 28,543	Y	Y	Y	Y	N	N	N	Y	Y	Y	Y	Y	Y	N	Y	N
Eritrea	C	1	$ 234	N	N	N	N	N	N	N	N	N	N	N	Y	N	N	N	N
Estonia	C	1	$ 22,228	Y	Y	Y	Y	N	Y	Y	Y	Y	Y	Y	Y	Y	N	Y	N
Ethiopia	C	1	$ 172	N	N	N	N	N	N	N	N	N	N	N	Y	Y	N	N	N
Fiji	C	1	$ 4,556	N	Y	N	N	N	N	N	N	N	N	N	Y	Y	N	N	N
Finland	C	1	$ 15,178	Y	Y	N	Y	Y	Y	Y	Y	Y	Y	Y	Y	Y	N	Y	N
France	C	1	$ 10,987	Y	Y	Y	Y	N	N	Y	Y	Y	Y	Y	Y	Y	N	Y	N
Gabon	A	1	$ 11,312	Y	Y	Y	Y	N	N	Y	Y	Y	Y	Y	Y	Y	N	Y	N
Georgia	C	1	$ 3,200	N	N	N	N	N	N	N	N	N	N	N	Y	Y	N	N	N
Germany	A	3	$ 23,113	Y	Y	Y	Y	Y	Y	Y	Y	Y	Y	Y	Y	Y	Y	Y	Y
Ghana	C	1	$ 1,683	N	N	N	N	N	N	N	N	N	N	N	Y	N	N	N	N
Greece	C	1	$ 7,759	Y	Y	Y	Y	N	N	Y	Y	Y	Y	Y	Y	Y	N	Y	N
Grenada		1	$ 2,923	N	N	N	N	N	N	N	N	N	N	N	Y	Y	N	N	N
Guatemala	C	1	$ 1,726	N	N	N	N	N	N	N	N	N	N	N	Y	Y	N	N	N
Guinea	C	1	$ 357	N	N	N	N	N	N	N	N	N	N	N	Y	Y	N	N	N
Guinea-Bissau		1	$ 244	N	N	N	N	N	N	N	N	N	N	N	Y	Y	N	N	N
Guyana	C	1	$ 5,539	Y	Y	Y	Y	N	N	N	N	Y	Y	Y	Y	Y	N	Y	N
Haiti	C	1	$ 311	N	N	N	N	N	N	N	N	N	N	N	Y	Y	N	N	N
Honduras	C	1	$ 2,201	N	N	N	N	N	N	N	N	N	N	N	Y	Y	N	N	N
Hong Kong		2	$ 126,467	Y	Y	Y	Y	N	N	N	Y	Y	Y	Y	Y	Y	N	Y	N
Hungary	A	1	$ 20,711	Y	Y	Y	Y	N	N	N	Y	Y	Y	Y	Y	Y	Y	Y	N
Iceland		2	$ 24,183	Y	Y	Y	Y	N	Y	Y	Y	Y	Y	Y	Y	Y	N	Y	N
India	C	1	$ 1,345	N	N	N	N	N	N	N	N	N	N	N	Y	Y	N	N	N
Indonesia	A	1	$ 2,270	N	N	N	N	N	N	N	N	N	N	N	Y	Y	N	N	N
Iran	A	1	$ 5,017	Y	Y	Y	Y	N	N	Y	Y	Y	Y	Y	Y	Y	N	Y	N
Iraq	A	1	$ 2,892	N	N	N	N	N	N	N	N	N	N	N	Y	Y	N	N	N
Ireland	A	3	$ 50,338	Y	Y	Y	Y	N	Y	Y	Y	Y	Y	Y	Y	Y	N	Y	N
Israel	C	1	$ 10,887	Y	Y	Y	Y	N	N	Y	Y	Y	Y	Y	Y	Y	N	Y	N
Italy	A	1	$ 9,927	Y	Y	Y	Y	N	N	Y	Y	Y	Y	Y	Y	Y	N	Y	N
Jamaica	C	1	$ 2,706	N	N	N	N	N	N	N	N	N	N	N	Y	Y	N	N	N
Japan	A	3	$ 5,366	Y	Y	Y	Y	Y	Y	Y	Y	Y	Y	Y	Y	Y	N	Y	Y
Jordan	C	1	$ 5,004	Y	Y	Y	Y	N	N	Y	Y	Y	Y	Y	Y	Y	N	Y	N
Kazakhstan	A	1	$ 8,879	Y	Y	Y	Y	N	N	Y	Y	Y	Y	Y	Y	Y	N	Y	N
Kenya	C	1	$ 496	N	N	N	N	N	N	N	N	N	N	N	Y	Y	N	N	N
Kiribati		1	$ 195	N	N	N	N	N	N	N	N	N	N	N	Y	Y	N	N	N
Kosovo	C	1	$ 1,547	N	N	N	N	N	N	N	N	N	N	N	Y	Y	N	N	N
Kuwait	A	2	$ 58,696	Y	Y	Y	Y	N	N	Y	Y	Y	Y	Y	Y	Y	N	Y	N
Kyrgyzstan	C	1	$ 1,516	N	N	N	N	N	N	N	N	N	N	N	Y	Y	N	N	N
Laos	C	1	$ 1,795	N	N	N	N	N	N	N	N	N	N	N	Y	Y	N	N	N
Latvia	C	1	$ 13,280	Y	Y	Y	Y	N	N	N	Y	Y	Y	Y	Y	Y	N	Y	N
Lebanon	C	1	$ 10,742	Y	Y	Y	Y	N	N	Y	Y	Y	Y	Y	Y	Y	N	Y	N
Lesotho	C	1	$ 1,159	N	N	N	N	N	N	N	N	N	N	N	Y	Y	N	N	N
Liberia	C	1	$ 284	N	N	N	N	N	N	N	N	N	N	N	Y	Y	N	N	N
Libya	C	1	$ 14,181	Y	Y	Y	Y	N	N	N	Y	Y	Y	Y	Y	Y	Y	Y	N
Lithuania	C	1	$ 19,633	Y	Y	Y	Y	N	N	Y	Y	Y	Y	Y	Y	Y	N	Y	N
Luxembourg	C	2	$ 185,119	Y	Y	Y	Y	N	N	Y	Y	Y	Y	Y	Y	Y	N	Y	N
Macedonia	C	1	$ 6,258	Y	Y	Y	Y	N	N	N	Y	Y	Y	Y	Y	Y	N	Y	N
Madagascar	C	1	$ 425	N	N	N	N	N	N	N	N	N	N	N	Y	Y	N	N	N
Malawi	C	1	$ 361	N	N	N	N	N	N	N	N	N	N	N	Y	Y	N	N	N
Malaysia	A	1	$ 19,062	Y	Y	Y	Y	N	N	Y	Y	Y	Y	Y	Y	Y	N	Y	N
Maldives	C	1	$ 12,977	Y	Y	Y	Y	N	N	N	Y	Y	Y	Y	Y	Y	N	Y	N
Mali	C	1	$ 513	N	N	N	N	N	N	N	N	N	N	N	Y	Y	N	N	N
Malta	C	1	$ 27,266	Y	Y	Y	Y	N	N	N	Y	Y	Y	Y	Y	Y	Y	Y	N
Mauritania	C	1	$ 2,030	N	N	N	N	N	N	N	N	N	N	N	Y	Y	N	N	N

Country			$																
Mauritius	C	1	$ 9,620	Y	Y	Y	Y	N	N	Y	Y	Y	Y	Y	Y	Y	N	Y	N
Mexico	C	1	$ 5,197	Y	Y	Y	Y	N	N	N	Y	Y	Y	Y	Y	Y	N	Y	N
Moldova	C	1	$ 2,061	N	N	N	N	N	N	N	N	N	N	Y	Y	N	N	N
Monaco	C	1	$ 23,204	Y	Y	Y	Y	N	Y	Y	Y	Y	Y	Y	Y	Y	N	Y	N
Mongolia	A	1	$ 4,259	N	Y	N	N	N	N	N	N	N	N	Y	Y	N	N	N
Montenegro	C	1	$ 5,904	Y	Y	Y	Y	N	N	N	N	Y	Y	Y	Y	Y	N	Y	N
Morocco	C	1	$ 2,422	N	N	N	N	N	N	N	N	N	N	Y	Y	N	N	N
Mozambique	C	1	$ 333	N	N	N	N	N	N	N	N	N	N	Y	Y	N	N	N
Namibia	C	1	$ 4,122	N	Y	N	N	N	N	N	N	N	N	Y	Y	N	N	N
Netherlands	A	3	$ 39,090	Y	Y	Y	Y	Y	Y	Y	Y	Y	Y	Y	Y	Y	Y	Y	N
New Zealand	C	1	$ 10,442	Y	Y	Y	Y	N	N	N	Y	Y	Y	Y	Y	Y	N	Y	N
Nicaragua	C	1	$ 1,881	N	N	N	N	N	N	N	N	N	N	Y	Y	N	N	N
Niger	C	1	$ 214	N	N	N	N	N	N	N	N	N	N	Y	Y	N	N	N
Nigeria	C	1	$ 1,011	N	N	N	N	N	N	N	N	N	N	Y	Y	N	N	N
Norway	A	2	$ 25,230	Y	Y	Y	Y	Y	Y	Y	Y	Y	Y	Y	Y	Y	N	Y	N
Oman	C	1	$ 27,035	Y	Y	Y	Y	N	N	N	Y	Y	Y	Y	Y	Y	N	Y	N
Pakistan	C	1	$ 608	N	N	N	N	N	N	N	N	N	N	Y	Y	N	N	N
Panama	C	1	$ 13,787	Y	Y	Y	Y	N	N	N	Y	Y	Y	Y	Y	Y	Y	Y	N
Papua New Guinea	A	1	$ 1,348	N	N	N	N	N	N	N	N	N	N	Y	Y	N	N	N
Paraguay	C	1	$ 3,996	N	N	N	N	N	N	N	N	N	N	Y	Y	N	N	N
Peru	A	1	$ 2,795	N	N	N	N	N	N	N	N	N	N	Y	Y	N	N	N
Philippines	C	1	$ 1,824	N	N	N	N	N	N	N	N	N	N	Y	Y	N	N	N
Poland	C	1	$ 11,324	Y	Y	Y	Y	N	N	Y	Y	Y	Y	Y	Y	Y	N	Y	N
Portugal	C	1	$ 10,916	Y	Y	Y	Y	N	N	Y	Y	Y	Y	Y	Y	Y	N	Y	N
Qatar	A	2	$ 105,868	Y	Y	Y	Y	N	N	Y	Y	Y	Y	Y	Y	Y	N	Y	N
Romania	C	1	$ 7,965	Y	Y	Y	Y	N	N	N	Y	Y	Y	Y	Y	Y	N	Y	N
Russia	A	2	$ 7,163	Y	Y	Y	Y	Y	N	Y	Y	Y	Y	Y	Y	Y	N	Y	N
Rwanda	C	1	$ 212	N	N	N	N	N	N	N	N	N	N	Y	Y	N	N	N
Saint Kitts and Nevis		1	$ 7,328	Y	Y	Y	Y	N	N	Y	Y	Y	Y	Y	Y	Y	N	Y	N
Saint Lucia		1	$ 4,823	N	Y	N	N	N	N	N	N	N	N	Y	Y	N	N	N
Saint Vincent and the Grenadines		1	$ 2,869	N	N	N	N	N	N	N	N	N	N	Y	Y	N	N	N
Samoa		1	$ 1,768	N	N	N	N	N	N	N	N	N	N	Y	Y	N	N	N
Saudi Arabia	A	1	$ 28,280	Y	Y	Y	Y	N	N	N	Y	Y	Y	Y	Y	Y	N	Y	N
Senegal	C	1	$ 587	N	N	N	N	N	N	N	N	N	N	Y	Y	N	N	N
Serbia	C	1	$ 5,306	Y	Y	Y	Y	N	N	N	Y	Y	Y	Y	Y	Y	N	Y	N
Seychelles	C	1	$ 18,766	Y	Y	Y	Y	N	Y	Y	Y	Y	Y	Y	Y	Y	N	Y	N
Sierra Leone	C	1	$ 820	N	N	N	N	N	N	N	N	N	N	Y	Y	N	N	N
Singapore	A	3	$ 157,680	Y	Y	Y	Y	N	N	Y	Y	Y	Y	Y	Y	Y	Y	Y	N
Slovenia	C	1	$ 21,555	Y	Y	Y	Y	N	N	N	Y	Y	Y	Y	Y	Y	N	Y	N
Solomon Islands		1	$ 1,128	N	N	N	N	N	N	N	N	N	N	Y	Y	N	N	N
South Africa	C	1	$ 4,007	N	N	N	N	N	N	N	N	N	N	Y	Y	N	N	N
South Korea	A	1	$ 18,525	Y	Y	Y	Y	N	N	N	Y	Y	Y	Y	Y	Y	Y	Y	N
South Sudan	C	1	$ 369	N	N	N	N	N	N	N	N	N	N	Y	Y	N	N	N
Spain	C	1	$ 10,656	Y	Y	Y	Y	N	N	N	Y	Y	Y	Y	Y	Y	N	Y	N
Sri Lanka	C	1	$ 2,188	N	N	N	N	N	N	N	N	N	N	Y	Y	N	N	N
Sudan	C	1	$ 323	N	N	N	N	N	N	N	N	N	N	Y	Y	N	N	N
Suriname	A	1	$ 9,427	Y	Y	Y	Y	N	Y	Y	Y	Y	Y	Y	Y	Y	N	Y	N
Swaziland	A	1	$ 3,697	N	N	N	N	N	N	N	N	N	N	Y	Y	N	N	N
Sweden	A	2	$ 19,768	Y	Y	Y	Y	N	N	N	Y	Y	Y	Y	Y	Y	N	Y	N
Switzerland	A	2	$ 41,527	Y	Y	Y	Y	N	Y	Y	Y	Y	Y	Y	Y	Y	N	Y	N
Tajikistan	C	1	$ 482	N	N	N	N	N	N	N	N	N	N	Y	Y	N	N	N
Tanzania	C	1	$ 604	N	N	N	N	N	N	N	N	N	N	Y	Y	N	N	N
Thailand	A	1	$ 10,590	Y	Y	Y	Y	N	N	N	Y	Y	Y	Y	Y	Y	Y	Y	N
Togo	C	1	$ 548	N	N	N	N	N	N	N	N	N	N	Y	Y	N	N	N
Tonga		1	$ 945	N	N	N	N	N	N	N	N	N	N	Y	Y	N	N	N

Country																		
Trinidad and Tobago	A	1	$ 19,227	Y	Y	Y	Y	N	N	Y	Y	Y	Y	Y	Y	Y	N	Y	N
Tunisia	C	1	$ 5,228	Y	Y	Y	Y	N	N	N	Y	Y	Y	Y	Y	Y	Y	Y	N
Turkey	C	1	$ 4,818	N	Y	N	N	N	N	N	N	N	N	N	Y	Y	N	N	N
Turkmenistan	A	1	$ 10,259	Y	Y	Y	Y	N	N	Y	Y	Y	Y	Y	Y	Y	N	Y	N
Uganda	C	1	$ 397	N	N	N	N	N	N	N	N	N	N	N	Y	Y	N	N	N
Ukraine	C	1	$ 4,120	N	Y	N	N	N	N	N	Y	N	N	N	Y	Y	N	N	N
United Arab Emirates	A	2	$ 60,417	Y	Y	Y	Y	N	N	Y	Y	Y	Y	Y	Y	Y	N	Y	N
United Kingdom	C	1	$ 15,432	N	Y	N	N	Y	N	N	N	Y	Y	Y	Y	Y	N	Y	N
United States	C	1	$ 25,670	Y	Y	Y	Y	N	N	Y	Y	Y	Y	Y	Y	Y	N	Y	N
Uruguay	C	1	$ 4,703	N	Y	N	N	N	N	N	N	N	N	N	Y	Y	N	N	N
Uzbekistan	A	1	$ 1,429	N	N	N	N	N	N	N	N	N	N	N	Y	Y	N	N	N
Vanuatu		1	$ 1,430	N	N	N	N	N	N	N	N	N	N	N	Y	Y	N	N	N
Venezuela	C	1	$ 4,762	N	Y	N	N	N	N	N	N	N	N	N	Y	Y	N	N	N
Vietnam	C	1	$ 4,441	N	Y	N	N	N	N	N	N	N	N	N	Y	Y	N	N	N
Yemen	C	1	$ 1,207	N	N	N	N	N	N	N	N	N	N	N	Y	Y	N	N	N
Zambia	C	1	$ 1,644	N	N	N	N	N	N	N	N	N	N	N	Y	Y	N	N	N
Zimbabwe	C	1	$ 540	N	N	N	N	N	N	N	N	N	N	N	Y	Y	N	N	N

Data Quality

Note that TE-Maturing nations (Nations greater-than GT > 1) appear at a much lower 5% to 10% collapse trending rate initially.

Although statistically significant, we recognize that much is dependent on quality of research data and we continue to improve data collection. We will keep an update of this list on the Transition Economics Maturity Model page at csq1.org.

Chapter 4

-

Automation as a Renewable Resource

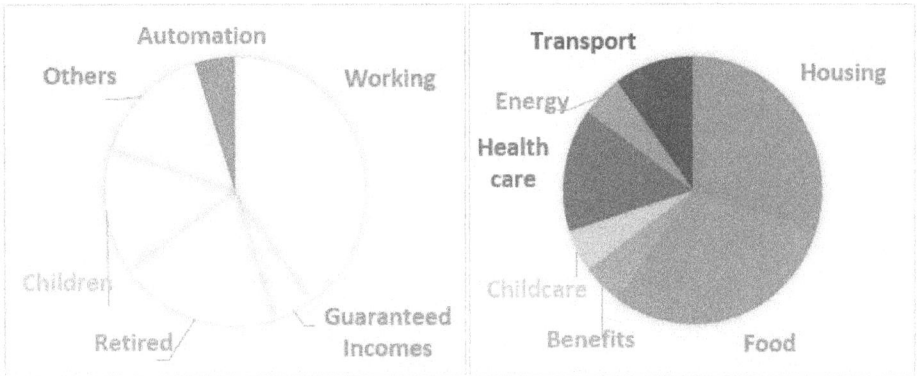

Automation is mankind's most important evolution since manual economies and civilization began 10,000 years ago. Well-planned projects in Automation have the power to create a renewable, sustainable infrastructure that provides for the basic needs of a Good Life reliably, scalably, and flexibly.

Progress has been slow in creating this Renewable Automation due to an absence of central planning, and still Automation is widely acknowledged to be proceeding well on its way toward outmoding as many as 50% of today's jobs within the next twenty to thirty years.

Politicians and Government staff alike will admit openly that Automation does not "test well" in populations worried about unemployment. How do we fix this?

Jobs that can be better accomplished by Automation are important to automate, but the incomes lost to these changes must be maintained too. Losing jobs in a Winter Economic Phase is a normal event historically; and both unemployment and automation both force governments to shift focus to Income distribution policies, and not simply focus on trickle-downs to middle class via unsustainable Job creation; middle class usually have incomes already as well.

Rate of Job Automation

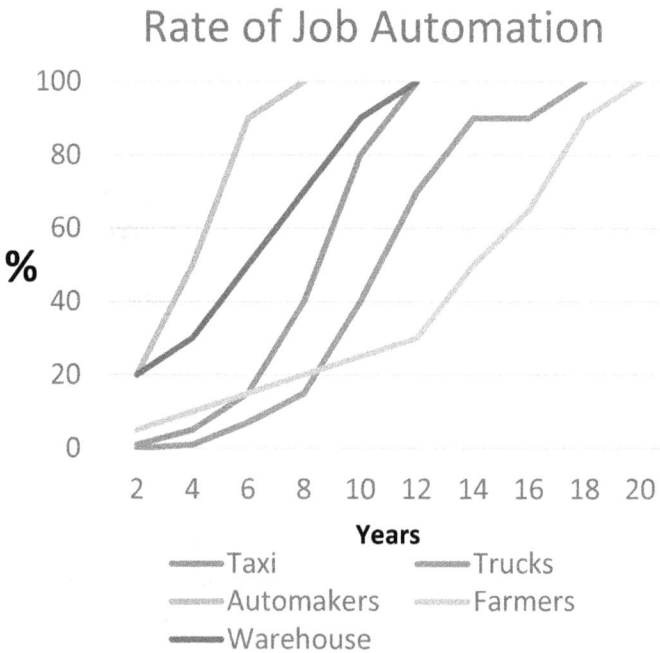

Guaranteed Living Wages and Incomes are the surest method of directly distributing wealth as needed to permit beneficial Job Automation and to begin a new Economic Cycle. Engineering Safety Nets on top of these minimum incomes, support Renewable Automations and give governments who coordinate both of these activities, benefits many times.

Renewable Automation is a new industry and now is the time that Governments will want to establish rules to either have, share, or control communal ownership of their food supply, public housing, transportation and energy.

The last thing that should be permitted is a repeat of what happened with Cancer Research. Billions were given to Cancer Research over 30-years – by Governments and by Charities. In this time, Cancer:

- Has reached epidemic proportion – society is suffering; people are dying.
- Has a handful of companies that profit exorbitantly from their pharmaceutical treatments - which were discovered leveraging the research R&D and Scientific Education spending mentioned
- Has very few approved treatments; fewer cures; and ...
- Healthcare and Insurance systems are fighting an unsustainable battle to afford the pharmaceuticals developed by all of this thirty-years of R&D investment.
- Those with no medical coverages are ignored and left to die – despite Charity and Government investment for a generation.

How did rich pharma companies run away with all the profits while externalizing all of this R&D cost? The answer is in very poor government sustainability planning and controls.

Governments want to encourage renewable automation, which means assisting or paying for R&D; and heavily supporting rapid development. Society should take the time now to ready laws and patent rules that ensure this automation will be used to eradicate homelessness, hunger, energy poverty, alongside improving the human rights of all - in healthcare, education and support for the young and elderly - sustainably.

This time, governments want to license the financial rewards of Renewable Automation - to Business; ensuring that services are available for all, and ensuring that we can recover our investments in R&D and guaranteed incomes and Engineering Safety Nets. Perhaps governments should look to own or part-own all renewable automation smart factory patents in law too.

Consider in all of these discussions that anything less works against a sustainable society, leaves us with the unworkable Cancer industry model above, and therefore has to be considered poor planning that is in no-one's best interest.

In 2015, #WPProjects - the World Peace Transition Projects, explained step-by-step what are the 250 initial Connected Smart Factory projects needed to automate our economy's basic needs of life – and then this planning assigned the enormous workload needed to many hands as well. The work-packages in these automation projects are large by themselves, and so assigning one sustainable #WPProjects automation project to every country on the planet creates inclusiveness, a profitable new global trade market, and important social needs like automated food delivery, energy, shelter, transport and more.

As our economies become ever more unsustainable here in the Winter Phase, the automation of our essential needs reduce our reliance on money too.

Does anyone believe they will starve once food delivery to their door is automated - as ordered and as needed? No, of course not. Will anyone go without a home for his or her family once life-cycle-managed shelter is automated? Will elderly or school-children be unable to get to their doctor's appointments and schools once transportation is automated? And finally, will we freeze or go without clean water once clean abundant energy is available for everyone automatically? No.

Can we really automate everything?

A driverless car, as with every other technology, was science fiction until an engineer – in this case the engineer was someone with unlimited resources - made it work for the first time in 2013. That engineer was none other than Larry Page, Google's CEO.

Singapore was the first city to launch driverless taxi services in September 2016. Now ask yourself honestly; if you had not seen a driverless car working in real life five years ago, would you ever believe such a sophisticated automation would ever be possible?

Many of us might think it was impossible in our lifetime; most people would think that this technology was just too advanced.

The reality is very different: the Driverless Car took just two years of development to get to Alpha - and then Beta tests. The car's testing was so successful that Ford has committed to mass-producing autonomous passenger automobiles within five years. Driverless trucks are driving on our roads in automated testing today as well - and have been for most of the past year.

This explanation is as true for Leonardo da Vinci's Helicopter – which was a 4-Year Project that was realized in 1939 by Ukrainian-American Igor Sikorsky. His Armored Tank was a 2-year project realized in 1916 by the British Army. It was the same for Jules Verne's Nautilus submarine; Nautilus was two 3-year Projects of the U.S. Government; the first launched a diesel submarine in 1930 and then a nuclear submarine followed in 1954. Mr. Verne's Trip to the Moon was a seven-year Project accomplished by the U.S. Government & NASA.

These example technologies were all a fanciful science fiction for hundreds of years, but today we look back at these machines that are obviously viable and proven. Often we even forget that they were once science fiction.

Science Fiction is just a HiTech Project

Leonardo Da Vinci 1452-1519

Helicopter realized 1947

Tanks, Robots, Planes Bicycles, and more.

Jules Verne 1828 - 1905

Nautilus realized 1940

Earth to the Moon 1969

Hanna & Barbera 1910-2001 1911-2006

Video Watches realized 2016

Robot Maids realized 2025

Gene Roddenbury 1921 - 1991

Communicators realized 2013
Universal Translator realized 2015
TriCorder XPrize 2016
HypoSpray 1960 perfected 2015
Replicators Today & 2032

Spread Limited of Kyoto, Japan, looks as though it may become the first company to build a completely automated farm once it begins delivery of 30,000 heads of lettuce daily in operations scheduled to start late in 2016. Automated Lettuce - is not sexy — but it is an important first and now automated farms are no-longer science fiction.

Are the automated Mushrooms (assigned to El Salvador), Cabbage (Angola), Bananas (Ecuador), and 100 other top-100 grocery store sales items on the #WPProjects' list any different? These projects are the same. And there is no science fiction in these automation projects either because everything needed is already working today. These projects simply have not been integrated together because no central plan has recognized the importance yet.

In any recession, infrastructure spending - like road construction - is often recommended - and all that this plan is changing is that now we are building automated road builders - instead of simply roads.

What do Sustainability Robots look like?

Many of us think of robots as mimics of humanoid workers; we can watch robots perform as a human might in his or her factory work – in a YouTube video easily. A Star Trek "Replicator" - if you never saw the show - was a machine that converted energy to matter and produced a wide variety of goods based on a user's voice command. WP Projects emulates this - by taking your request - for food, a car, a TV, an appliance, etc. - on a phone app or a Call Center Operator. Each order starts a sub-routine that automatically assembles, distributes and ships the ordered product to your door - automatically.

Very shortly, Audi Automotive will be building some of the finest driverless automobiles in the world, on assembly lines that are completely automated and require almost no human workers on the shop floor at all. In this example, it is the Assembly Line that is the sustainability robot; and the autonomous cars are their automated, robotic products.

Each self-driving automatically-built car is a sophisticated robot unto itself, but again - it is the sustainability robot that we are more interested in creating; again and again, in order to ensure repeatable scalability and abundance worldwide.

In the example of Spread's automated lettuce farm, the assembly line that pieces together its hydroponic components, complete with robotic farm-attendants, is the sustainable robot that we want to build.

Self-driving taxis, delivery vans, fuel trucks, GPS-driven tractors, trains, drone cargo planes, mining equipment, fishing trawlers, even emergency vehicles - will soon be entirely automated in this way.

Once designed and tested, these completed Sustainability Robot/ Assembly Lines for each product will be rolled out to produce many farms throughout many countries, and many regions, in sizes and configurations as needed by the local communities.

Robotic assembly lines add limitless and easy scalability that creates abundance - as opposed to our current scarcity-based financially limited systems today.

These services will eventually install and life-cycle-manage your appliances, homes, etc.; and most of the things we need can be delivered in just 250 projects. Each of these projects could deliver a v1.0 product within just one or two years as well. These projects can all start at once, so the entire program of products could complete within just two years too.

These are big automation projects, but 90% or more are entirely pilot-able within just a year. In some more complex examples, pilots might have to happen within two or three years at maximum.

House-building Sustainability Robots build robots that travel to building sites and assemble homes; and not just the same home, but multiple models and floor-plans for apartments, townhomes, semi-detached, and single family dwellings whose designs are enhanced year over year. If a third or fourth child surprises you, a granny suite and bedroom can be added to some of these home automatically upon request and need. One can only be limited by a failing of imagination really.

Having variety in home layouts, finishing, rooflines, furnishings, etc. adds needed practical utility and also adds charm and visual appeal to our neighborhoods. Renovations or upgrades can be planned in; appliances can be installable in an automated and as needed way as well.

Energy Robots build the automated robots that create Power Plants, and then repeat that construction again and again, until power is abundant and reliable. Road building robots, train and train-track building robots, mining and metal processing, ships and shipbuilding robots – are all a part of the plan.

As I said, difficult – but far from impossible, and this complexity is the reason that automation projects must be distributed to many countries with a consistent and sophisticated SUSTAIN Project Management Method.

The Necessity of Planning

Without planning, automation will have the simpler effect of eliminating jobs at dizzying rates and few governments appear to have a clear direction on how to prepare their citizens for this kind of change.

It is socially irresponsible for governments to not prepare for automation, and clearly today there can be no excuse to say they did not realize this was coming either.

The safe and responsible transition to an automated economy and prosperous new economic cycle lies entirely in good planning. I discuss Guaranteed Incomes in the next Chapter. This next slide is #20 of The Transition Slide Deck.

Algorithms in Automation Transition

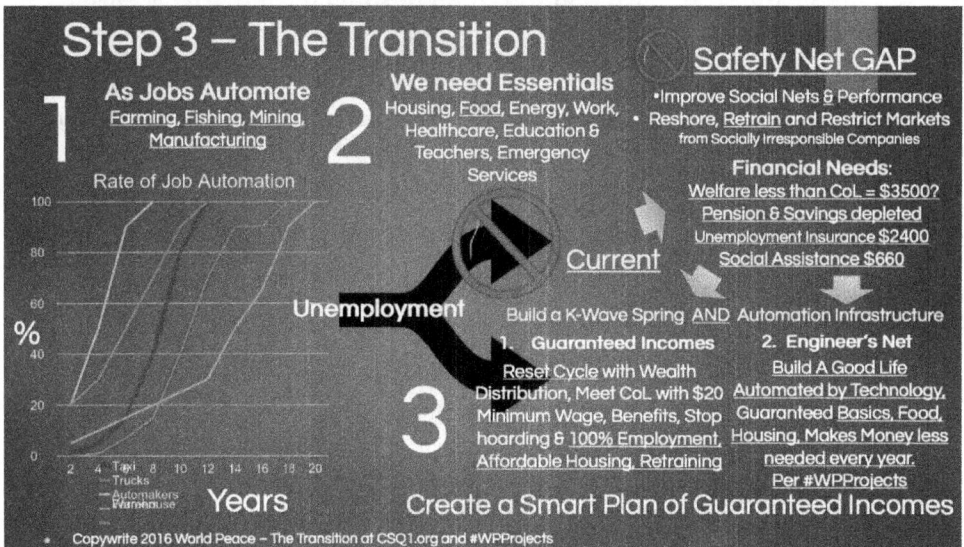

The Engineering Safety Net

#WPProjects' 250 automation projects plug together in a plan that creates a direct economic benefit – a Renewable Automated assembly line of monetizable products and sustainable products that are needed by society every day. These projects are professionally managed and tracked, so that the funding of Engineers who might wish to participate in Automation Construction Programs, can share learning and progress. These supports should well afford their salaries as needed to pay the bills for a home and family life.

Engineering Safety Net workers are much more than productive tinkerers. The work is worthwhile and profitable and warrants funding at the rate of an "IT Architect", Engineer, or "Senior Project Manager". Engineers need to afford the computers and internet access required at a minimum, and then any further funding and space must be made available within automation labs as needed to support their work both remotely and in group facilities – perhaps even within educational institutions. Easy access to free education, project knowledge-bases, benefits programs for healthcare, dental, and medications are also needed to be productive and are essential.

Engineering Leadership

The "Tail can never Wag the Dog" in Transition Economics projects. This means that concerns for insurance, legal, patent, and accounting must take distant second importance to the primary goal of progress in society. Progress and building to a Right Plan is our primary goal, so concerns presented by "the tail" cannot be a weak-link in the chain and so these professionals are tasked with correcting the problems and overcoming any obstacles – just as are engineers.

The sentences "We cannot" or "the law will not permit" are the words of the wrong resource for the job. Everything needs considered and everything needs resolved as best can so that people can eat and have the basics of shelter that they must be afforded.

Progress as a society means that legal obstacles, software and other broad patents, special interest lobby groups, licenses or material price gouging; anything - that forces obstacles in the way of completing automation work with minimal frustration, needs to be understood as a second priority by all levels of government and our legal systems as well. The way must be made clear of these obvious frustrations and obstacles and they cannot become show-stoppers.

Our current slow rate of automation is surely evidence that these obstacles have already dramatically deterred advances over these past forty-five years.

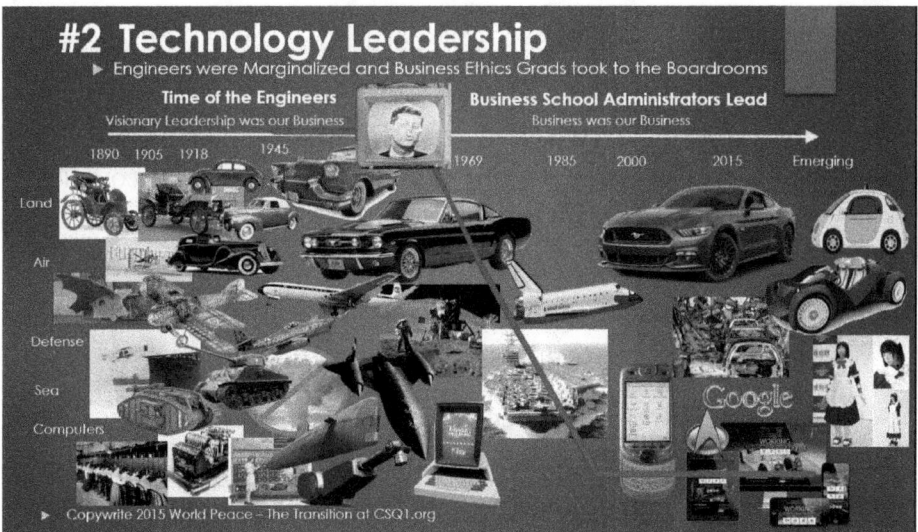

Other spending for automation include educational programs that contribute to #WPProjects. This is a very good optimization of Education Spending because this spending is not only educational, but it is also productive and it engages the next generation of beneficiaries directly too.

Return-on-Investment Business Case calculations for the *Engineering*

Safety Net should include patent and other financial proceeds accumulated during this work. Obviously each engineer's work generates tangible value and also products that promise to return a financial reward. These revenues should be take full advantage of.

Intellectual Property and Patent Ownership

When Engineers enter into Engineering Safety Net programs with a lot of their own propriety information to begin with, ownership of that proprietary knowledge should remain with the engineer as owner and patent holder. In this case, perhaps the government can assist patent development with provisos that profits and employment for these patents stay within the country - or similar simple but fair and effective ownership strategies can be discussed.

When Engineers enter into Safety Net programs with only their own time and "sweat equity" contribution; with very little or no proprietary work in advance, they are remunerated with a salary and worthwhile project work. In this case, ownership for discoveries might stay with the project team and with the country that paid for the work. To promote performance and acknowledgement of contribution, perhaps a profit sharing and awards/rewards formula can be arrived with engineers as well.

Personal incomes from Engineer Safety Net supported projects, from all sources, should be capped (perhaps at a $4 million per year maximum for example) and the rest taxed and poured back into automation project development.

Balancing contribution and investment, acknowledges the promise that society had to make in advance to support everyone's success. This is true for most businesses and these programs can easily be considered Conservative Investments. This message of Balance should be reinforced in Business Accountability rework discussions and Business Ethics courses immediately too.

Rate of Automation

Projects can begin more easily once Automation initiatives are afforded by Income Safety Nets in society. These programs should not be seen as a dependency however; Automation can also happen at a rate that our other GDP incomes can absorb responsibly and many countries will begin without these safety nets in place at the start. Planning is always best and Guaranteed Incomes are a smart planning building-block.

Business Plan for Renewable Automation (ROI-RA)

Consider that the country that plans a business & revenue return on its investment (ROI) in renewable automation infrastructure, probably has a bright future ahead. Even slippery-slope (impossibly worst-case) discussions regarding automation investment, can hold little merit in a country that will shortly receive groceries and other basic needs door-to-door automatically. No-one need starve nor suffer even if money were to be removed completely from the equation; and money would never need to be removed as long as there is benefit in keeping it - in reality.

A famous American slippery slope argument from the 1930s was the introduction of the speed limit on its highways. Detractors made slippery-slope arguments to say that once these freedoms were limited, that eventually we would all be driving five miles per hour.

Once an economy has been automated, the attention of this country's citizens can turn to the monetization of their production economy - if it wishes. This sort of planning is very similar to Chinese Financial Plans that began 25 years ago. China has had a far higher economic success rate over every other country during this time period – and so observation confirms this is a valid approach by scientific method.

The Netherlands' #5 CMI position and leading GDP Export per Citizen, is proof of the economic value of providing citizens with their basic needs. In addition to financial planning improvement, other plans for research, discovery, science and engineering, which are now properly supported, can be expected to skyrocket.

Alternatively, a country that finds itself spending itself into debt without making headway in sustainable self-sufficient automation in infrastructure, has a much harder recovery road ahead and is far less well-positioned for success too.

Money is a non-renewable resource; but sustainable automation of our basic production, can be considered renewable and it is a self-renewing asset that yields a continuing annual benefit, productivity, and revenue stream as well.

The RAI – Renewable Automation Index

The CSQ **Renewable Automation Index – *The RAI*,** is the most recent addition to CSQ Research's Online Database. The RAI measures indexed companies that develop and invest in Renewable Automation. Technology companies, and technologies that do not plug-in nor assist renewable, sustainable projects are counted lower on the Index.

Countries that invest in and encourage Transition Economics Maturity policies increase their Maturity levels. Presently, there is just one TE Maturing country (Luxemburg) that is in a collapsing trend – so there is a data-correlation between TE Maturity and Sustainability.

Companies and educational institutions that build LIDAR sensors permit driverless vehicles to see/recognize people or avoid human injury while they work, will score high on the RAI. So too will warehousing systems that automate manufacturing and order delivery. Fin-tech or Big-Data hi-tech companies that set out to improve marketing campaigns or receivables performance, will score much lower and companies with predatory, bubble-building real estate investment, or socially irresponsible debt marketing practices, score very low.

The RAI - Country Index is updated online and the **RAI - Companies Index** is made available to governments exclusively for their procurement needs.

The RAI tracks each country's automations in Healthcare, Energy, Computing, Manufacturing, 3D Printing, Technologies, Transportation Logistics, Agriculture, Construction, Robots, Sensors, Artificial Intelligence and Consumer Goods Automation.

The Goal of the RAI Country Index is to recognize Countries that invest in Renewable Automation and also recognize the wisdom of the management teams there to move their home infrastructures and business forward in this way.

The Goal of the RAI Company Index is to support Renewable Automation companies both financially and with higher-priority than technology investment that simply improves unsustainable, non-renewable short-term profit.

I might be overthinking this a bit, but acknowledging that status-quo investors will struggle to understand their role in a changing socially responsible, sustainably-profitable investment landscape – is probably a good forethought. The change may take a bit of time, training and even governance protections. For this reason, the Companies Index is licensed to companies only with provisos and penalties that protect against intentionally harmful short-selling injury; we saw some of this behavior targeting the 3D Printing Industry two years ago.

Short-selling behaviors can target any company at any time for any number of reasons of course, we all want to be over-cautious to "not cause harm" to startup renewables is all. In reality, it might be that these technology companies are the ones that are "too large to fail".

The RAI seeks to recognize and reward our Leading Renewable Automation Countries. For Companies wishing to market their compliance with Sustainable and Renewable Technology Targets, CSQ Corporate Social Responsibility Certifications are available. These programs are there to help both consumers and investors make wiser decisions so look for the CSQ logo on your company, customer, and country website.

Chapter 5

-

Guaranteed Incomes

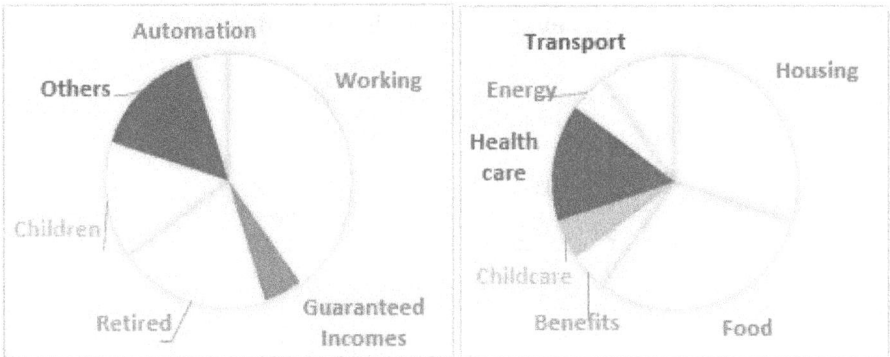

Social projects are sufficient by themselves to build a Good Life in just about any country that is not presently considered a developing nation. Policy selection alone dictates which countries will prosper and which will collapse - and so transition must constantly work to carefully balance tax-neutral targets so that citizen impacts are minimal. Balancing equations are often referred to throughout this books as "throttles".

Guaranteed Incomes

According to the CMI – The Country Management Index, one of the leading countries for GDP Export per Capita is presently held by #5 The Netherlands at $33,652. Ireland does a little better and other micro-economies like Hong Kong and Singapore dwarf these stats, but the Netherlands is a good start for us here for several reasons.

Country	GDP Export per Capita	Multiplier to Dutch Export/Cap	GINI Wealth Equality	HDI	Leaning	American Dream?	Population (In Millions)	Export Quality
Netherlands	$33,652	100%	31	0.915	Socialistic	Yes	17	High
Norway	$28,807	117%	25	0.944	Socialistic	Yes	5	High
United States	$5,057	665%	45	0.914	Capitalistic	No	324	Very High
Sweden	$18,688	180%	23	0.911	Socialistic	Yes	10	Mid
Germany	$18,316	184%	27	0.911	Socialistic	Almost	80	Very High
Canada	$13,286	253%	32	0.902	Capitalistic	No	36	Low
United Kingdom	$7,378	456%	32	0.907	Capitalistic	No	65	Mid
Australia	$10,446	322%	30	0.935	Capitalistic	No	24	Low

Compare the Exports and per Capita Exports of your Country to understand how much revenue your country is failing to earn every year by not engaging every citizen in wealth generating export commerce:

Country	GDP Export per Capita	Multiplier to Dutch Export/Cap	Export 2015 (in billions)	Opportunity Cost New Export (in billions)	Collapse or Advance Trending?
Netherlands	$33,652	100%	$477	$0	Advance
Norway	$28,807	117%	$103	$17	Advance
United States	$5,057	665%	$1,510	$8,538	Collapse
Sweden	$18,688	180%	$151	$121	Advance
Germany	$18,316	184%	$1,309	$1,096	Advance
Canada	$13,286	253%	$411	$630	Collapse
United Kingdom	$7,378	456%	$436	$1,553	Collapse
Australia	$10,446	322%	$188	$418	Collapse

Enabling the success of The Netherlands' citizens, are some of the strongest policies and economic controls in the world. The Netherland government controls protect spending power, employment, housing, and foreign investment and business ownership. Education at all levels is free, daycare, healthcare, guaranteed incomes and even retirements are all paid for through a graduated tax structure that permits all citizens to participate in businesses and other commercial work.

Taxes are higher here than in G7 countries presently, but these differences can be considered tax and revenue-neutral in that they cover healthcare, retirements, and other living costs that other countries do not call "taxes". We discuss historical taxation next chapter as well.

The Export per Capita statistics of Holland prove conclusively that citizens do take advantage of social benefits to improve both their productivity and the standard of living for their communities as well.

High-income earners who are not instructed in the big-picture business and personal benefits of socialistic policies, might look at higher taxes with frustration. At the same time, the standard of living for all of their workers, executive, and owners is sustainable and uninterrupted with this approach. A strong social infrastructure gives the high income earners a place to live in which they are appreciated and even revered in a family-friendly society that they can proudly call home too. This luxury is not afforded to high income earners in other countries where opportunistic capitalist policy creates a very different life.

The cost of Guaranteed Income programs vary based on metrics like Cost of Living, CPI (Inflation as measured by the Consumer Price Index), Rent Controls, housing costs, and so on.

For guaranteed income Calculations, generally the following formula holds true, and the chart that follows calculates the tax increase needed to afford these benefits country-wide in the U.S., U.K., Canada, Australia and Germany.

*Labour Pool * (Unemployment Rate x 2) + Cost of Living * CPI*

With a little more calculation, we can easily arrive at a crude **Return on Investment (ROI)** estimate for our Business Case for providing Guaranteed Incomes to Labor Force workers.

Country	Cost of Living/mth	Population	Unemployment	Guaranteed Income	Tax Increase
America	$2500	155 mill	5%	$233 bill	1.34%
Germany	$3000	44 mill	4.5%	$ 60 bill	1.57%
Canada	$3000	19 mill	6.8%	$ 40 bill	2.2%
U.K	$3500	31 mill	5%	$ 64 bill	2.2%
Australia	$3000	12 mill	6.8%	$ 30 bill	2.1%

Return on Investment (ROI) for Guaranteed Incomes

Country	America	Germany	Canada	U.K	Australia
Export Per Capita	$5,057	$ 18,316	$ 13,286	$ 7,378	$ 10,446
Exports ($bill)	$ 1,510	$ 1,309	$ 411	$ 436	$ 188
Export Increase	665%	184%	253%	456%	322%
Opportunity Cost ($bill)	$ 8,538	$ 1,096	$ 630	$ 1,553	$ 418
Cost of Living	$ 2,500	$ 3,000	$ 3,000	$ 3,500	$ 3,000
Population (million)	324	82	36.5	65	24.2
Labor force (million)	155.4	44.2	19	30.8	12.4
Unemployment	5.0%	4.5%	6.8%	5.0%	6.8%
Current Benefits		15%	14%		
Total Cost ($bill)	$ 233	$ 60	$ 40	$ 64.6	$ 30
GDP ($bill)	$17,348	$ 3,868	$ 1,785	$ 2,989	$ 1,472
Tax Inc vs GDP	26.9%	40.6%	32.0%	39.0%	25.8%
Total Tax Revenues ($bill)	$ 4,666	$ 1,570	$ 571	$1,166	$ 379
New Tax ($bill)	$ 3,618	$ 1,466	$516	$997	$ 347
Tax Increase	-22.45%	-6.59%	-9.53%	-14.45%	- 8.5 %
Tax Rev New Export (15%) $bill	$ 1,280	$ 164	$ 516	$ 233	$ 62
ROI	**3663%**	**1801%**	**1574%**	**2405%**	**1374%**

If I use Canada as an example, the math says that Canada would generate $630 billion in new export revenue annually via Guaranteed

Incomes. The program would cost $40 billion offset by new export tax revenue – estimated here at a maybe-generous $571 billion based on my imperfect understanding of current tax rates. So, a worst-case drop in tax by approx 10% could result if the Guaranteed Incomes have the planned effect within its workforce. This gives Guaranteed Incomes in Canada a planned Return-on-Investment of 15-times or 1574%. This is the true power of laser-focused attention on improving GDP Export Revenues.

These are very positive returns (ROIs) that encourage the adoption of this important Wealth Distribution Program – and these numbers are worst-case numbers presented before any discussion of optimization nor tax graduation have been considered.

Social benefits from Guaranteed Incomes include:

1. Considerable building industry Automation productivity & Hitech industry boosts
2. Reliance on Immigration for population falls
3. Inequity starts correcting toward 1960s levels
4. Homelessness can be almost wiped out
5. Other programs in housing & onshoring are supported
6. Incarceration, Unemployment, and other Social Problems are reduced.

Chapter 6

-

Sustaining Equality creates Wealth

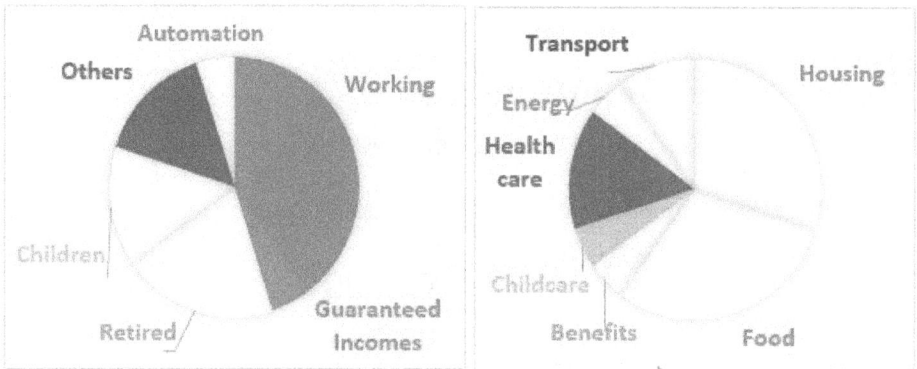

Social projects are sufficient by themselves to build a Good Life in just about any country that is not considered a developing nation. Once the hurdle of surpassing the production and wealth of a developing nation is accomplished, emphasis turns to Wealth Creation and finally to Wealth Distribution.

Wealth Distribution is critical to enabling citizens to participate in wealth building export and Gross Domestic Production taxable production.

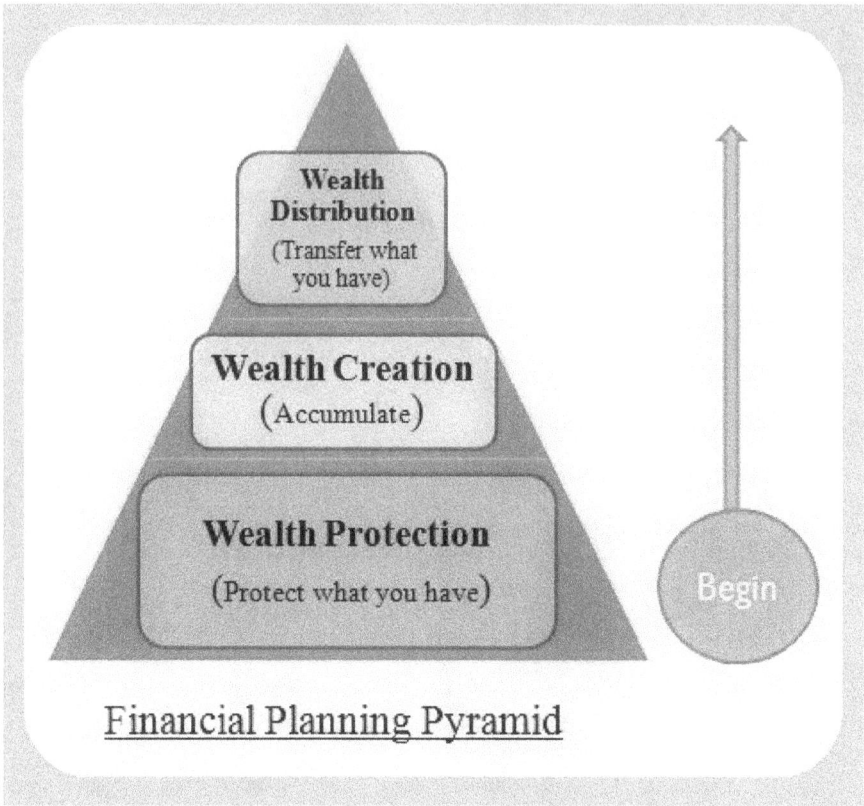

Financial Planning Pyramid

Wealth Creation

The surest way for a country to generate wealth is to take their raw earth, and things that grow on it, and monetize those resources by selling high-quality productized resources and manufactured goods in trade for currency from other nations.

Sales economies do not create this sort of shared economic wealth and benefit because a running shoe, for example, purchased for $1 from the Orient and then sold in North America for $100, has no up nor down-stream industry incomes for the hundreds of local workers who would ordinarily benefit from production all along the supply chain of that product's manufacture. Sales economy profits tend to benefit a handful only and these profits are easier to offshore and avoid tax with at present as well.

Wealth Distribution

Wealth Distribution policy are tax and social benefit programs which include minimum living wages, guaranteed incomes, graduated tax, tax avoidance cleanups, childcare, universal health, child daycare, and retirement social programs.

In the Netherlands, young citizens between the ages of infancy to graduation are invited to take as much education as they want without cost. All dental and medical costs are covered as are massages and other wellness treatments as needed. Retirement age is 60 and all medical, dental, and income needs are met by employers and by the government for the rest of their lives.

For the productive working years of its citizens, from ages 22 to 60, the Netherlands takes tax in the area of 55% of earned income; similar to tax rates in the U.S. for most of the past 100 years. See the next chart.

In the chart, the top line is Top Tax Rate and Red line below is Bottom Tax Rate. I have included US Presidents to give a view to taxation policies and parties in the U.S. over time as well. It was Ronald Reagan's administration that set the stage for our most recent inequity in the 1980s. Before that, low tax for the rich was initiated in 1916 and in 1925 by president's William Taft and Calvin Coolidge.

U.S. Marginal Tax Rates 1913-2009

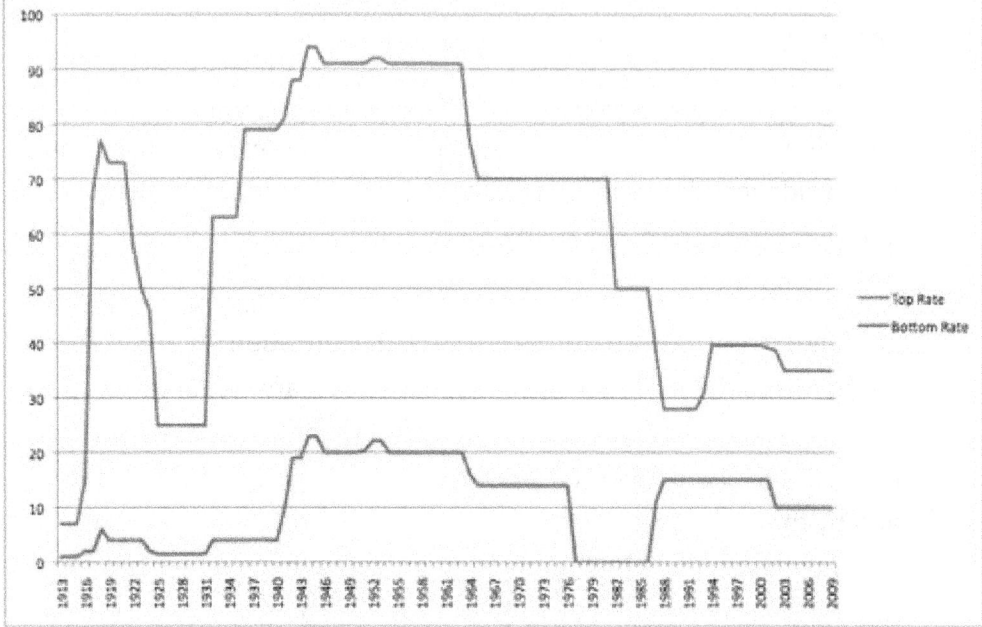

Roosevelt '33-45	Truman '45-53	Eisenhower '53-61	Kennedy '61-63	Johnson '63-69	Nixon '69-74	Ford '74-77	Carter '77-81	Reagan '81-89	Bush '89-93
Dem	Dem	Rep	Dem	Dem	Rep	Rep	Dem	Rep	Rep

The Netherlands' government manages taxes very well and the productivity of Dutch citizens supported by social services is 50% higher than U.S. citizens per capita (by GDP Export).

The following chart shows lifespans and earning years is based on average lifespans of 89 years of age, and retirement at 65, which is the norm in France and the Netherlands. This results in a ratio of 50:50 Labor Force Years to Non-Labor Force Years. North Americans have average lifespans of 82 years which means that their ratio is

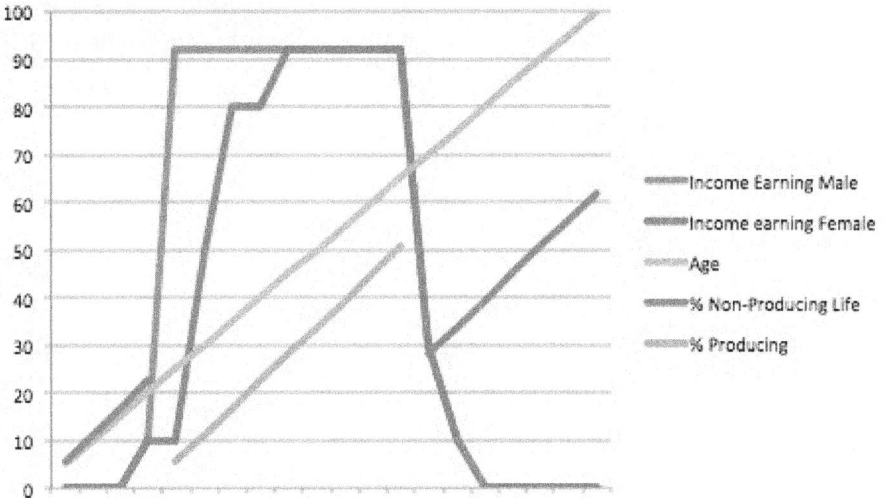

Legend:
- Income Earning Male
- Income earning Female
- Age
- % Non-Producing Life
- % Producing

We are all human, we all have childhoods and if we are lucky, we are going to get old and retire as well. With an average life expectancy of 90 years in the Sweden, working to pay your way for 100% of your life costs during the less than 50% of your productive years, both recognizes reality and has a very humanistic fairness to it as well.

Pure Capitalist systems simply ignore the reality of our lifespans and this results in lower quality of life and lower longevity for the 99% majority of non-wealthy society members.

Finland took on a Pilot Project of Universal Basic Incomes in December 2015 to see if the program would help build a Good Life within its population of 5.4 million.

Many of us in Capitalist countries aspire to find work that sets us for life; one among thousands of us finds an income that sets our children's trust funds for life as well. These projects in wealth distribution realize just this goal for everyone in society reliably.

We discussed last chapter that the Netherlands has one of the best GINI (Wealth Distribution Rating) and highest GDP Export per Capita (Wealth Creation) ratings in the world and this same formula would create approximately $500 billion in new wealth annually for the United States all by itself.

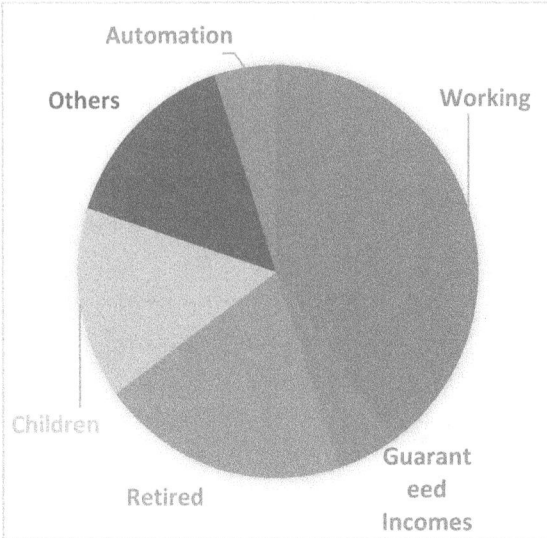

The key to maximizing productivity from citizens is ensuring that all ages and income earners in every income level, benefit group and age group - can participate in the economy. The analogy of an engine firing on all cylinders comes to mind; you want to ensure that all have the opportunity to push the engine forward.

Once your economy supports production in all five income quintiles – including the bottom 40%; and in all age groups - including retired and unemployed. At this point your citizens have the income supports needed to engage in production and in generating taxable wealth.

The leading cause of wage stagnation between 1995 and 2013 included globalization (offshoring and imports) and the decline of labor unions and other forms of group bargaining power that could keep income and benefits onshore.

By 2010, inequity is so extreme in the U.S. that the poor have just 0.3% of the wealth in the United States. That's 160 million people struggling for no stake in the wealth whatsoever.

Much worse than this, according to "Robert Reich: Income inequality the defining issue for U.S.", **95% of all gains since 2009's supposed recovery have gone to the top 1%** as well. *The Denver Post*, January 26, 2014; see also (Wolf, 2015).

Chart 2: Distribution of wealth in the US by quintile, 2010

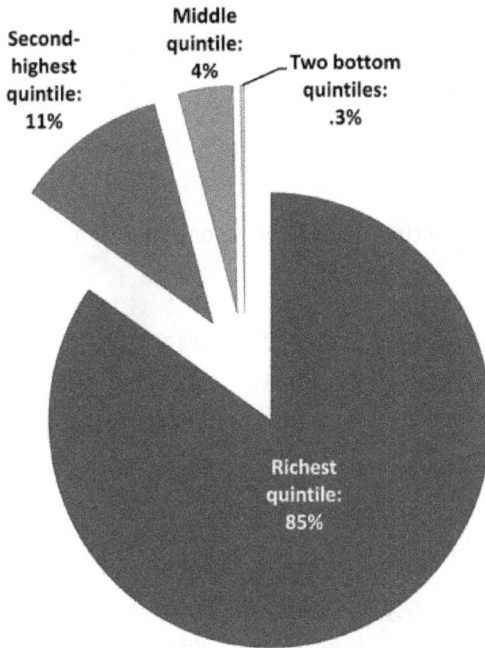

Source: Adapted from Norton & Airely, 2012, http://ppd.sagepub.com/

Remember that wealth and income are two very different measures of economic prosperity, and that high income does not necessarily correlate to mean high wealth or "worth". Net Worth is the sum of all assets, including the market value of real-estate, like a home, minus all liabilities.

How do other nations stack up in measures of Income Distribution? The GINI Coefficient Index, named after its statistician inventor Corrado Gini, is one measure of income inequality depicted here globally.

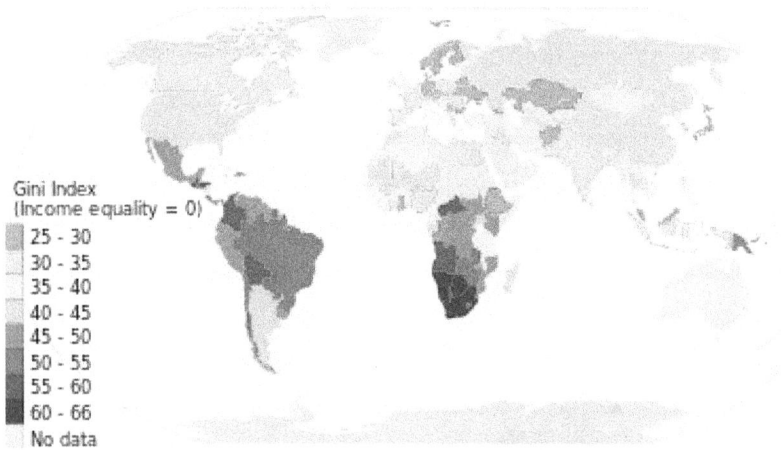

Gini Index
(Income equality = 0)

- 25 - 30
- 30 - 35
- 35 - 40
- 40 - 45
- 45 - 50
- 50 - 55
- 55 - 60
- 60 - 66
- No data

Online at https://en.wikipedia.org/wiki/Gini_coefficient

#	Country	GINI	Source	Cat	Type
1	Sweden	23	2005	SOC	CM
2	Slovenia	23.7	2012	SOC	REP
3	Montenegro	24.3	2010	SOC	REP
4	Hungary	24.7	2009	SOC	DEM
5	Denmark	24.8	2011 est.	SOC	CM
6	Czech	24.9	2012	SOC	DEM
7	Norway	25	2008	SOC	CM
8	Slovakia	26	2005	SOC	DEM
9	Luxembourg	26	2005	SOC	CM
10	Austria	26.3	2007	SOC	REP
11	Finland	26.8	2008	SOC	REP
12	Germany	27	2006	CAP	REP
14	Belarus	27.2	2008	SOC	REP
18	Ukraine	28.2	2009	SOC	REP
19	Switzerland	28.7	2012 est.	SOC	REP
20	Kazakhstan	28.9	2011	AUT	REP
21	Kosovo	30	FY05/06	SOC	REP
22	Australia	30.3	2008	CAP	DEM
23	Pakistan	30.6	FY07/08	CAP	REP
24	European Union	30.6	2012 est.	CAP	HYB
25	France	30.6	2011	SOC	REP

27	Netherlands	30.9	2007	SOC	CM
28	Armenia	30.9	2008	SOC	REP
29	Cyprus	31	2012 est.	CAP	REP
30	Korea, South	31.1	2011 est.	CAP	REP
31	Estonia	31.3	2010	SOC	REP
33	Italy	31.9	2012 est.	CAP	REP
34	Spain	32	2005	CAP	PM
35	Croatia	32	2010	CAP	DEM
36	Canada	32.1	2005	SOC	CM
37	Bangladesh	32.1	2010	CAP	DEM
38	United Kingdom	32.3	2012	CAP	CM
45	Ireland	33.9	2010	CAP	REP
47	Poland	34.1	2009	CAP	REP
48	Taiwan	34.2	2011	CAP	DEM
49	Greece	34.3	2012 est.	CAP	REP
55	New Zealand	36.2	1997	CAP	DEM
61	Indonesia	36.8	2009	CAP	REP
62	India	36.8	2004	CAP	REP
65	Israel	37.6	2012	CAP	DEM
66	Japan	37.6	2008	CAP	CM
73	Venezuela	39	2011	SOC	REP
92	Russia	42	2012	SOC	REP
100	Philippines	44.8	2009	SOC	REP
101	United States	45	2007	CAP	REP
109	Malaysia	46.2	2009	CAP	CM
110	Singapore	46.3	2013	CAP	REP
115	China	47.3	2013	CAP	COM
118	Mexico	48.3	2008	CAP	REP
130	Hong Kong	53.7	2011	CAP	DEM

Legend: From Most Equal to Least Equal

Categories: SOC=Socialist, CAP=Capitalist, AUT=Authoritarian

Types: CM=Constitutional Monarchy, PM=Parliamentary Monarchy, REP=Republican, DEM=Democracy, HYB=Hybrid, COM=Communist

Patterns in Income Inequality

Looking at the Cat - Category of Government in that table above, the top ten GINI countries are acknowledged to favor socialistic policies, regardless of their Government types, be they Constitutional Monarchy, Republic, or Democracy.

Germany, at 12th position, is the first G8 country to appear and then France at 25th. Italy 33rd, Canada is 36th, UK 38th, Japan 66th, Russia 92nd, and the U.S. is at position # 101. All G8 countries shrink from being called Socialist, not wanting to defend a derogatory agenda, and most G8s have predominantly Capitalist policies with Republic or Constitutional Monarchy Government Types.

Germany and France own to a great number of socialistic policies. Germany, for example, has high taxes, universal healthcare, universal college education, great infrastructure and government control of the banks. Germans do it all; they do not buy from China; Dollar stores are non-existent; German workers elect boards of companies. It has the largest ownership of its production economy in Europe giving it a competitive advantage because profit and new investment can be wrapped back into the company rather than going to shareholders and it stays in Germany. Germany owns Deutsche Bahn, Hapag-Lloyd, Airbus, Landesbank, Sparkassen, 20% of Volkswagen, 32% of T-Mobile, KfW Bank, 25% Deutsche Post, Hypo Real Estate, Federal Print Office, and many States own businesses within Germany as well.

Theirs is a socialistic capitalist model open to the free market and non-government ownership within the production economy. Government monitors cell phones, TVs, just as does Canada's CRTC. Germany is growing strongly where other G8s are not.

The GINI Top-twelve here boast at least seven of the most successful countries, on a per capita basis, in the world today.

Setting Targets – Living Wage & Graduated Tax

The goal of managing Wealth Distribution is not to ensure that everyone has the same income, rather the goal is to ensure that all income levels are able to be productive and contribute to the economy. The setting of minimum wage so that is affords cost of living within communities – is also called a living wage.

Plug your own country's numbers into the formulas here to come up with Quintile income and wealth distribution targets for your country. I used the 2010 budget U.S. Federal Reserve stats here because they were readily validatible at several online sites.

Wealth

> **Available Assets** – per page 199 of the 2010 U.S. Budget containing the following wealth and income statistics for 2008.
> $ 10.2 trillion - in publicly owned assets
> $ 54.2 trillion – in privately owned assets
> $ 57.2 trillion - in education capital
> $ 3.9 trillion – R&D capital
> $ 118.1 trillion in total after assets claimed by foreign interests

1995 Assets were about half these numbers at $ 54.1 trillion.

The Reader's Country Total Assets _____

> **Debts**

> > $ 18.15 Trillion – up from 16.1 in 2012 when it was 108% of GDP

> > Debt was presented by the Federal Government Debt Clock at usgovernmentdebt.us on October 15, 2015

Debt to Asset Ratio

18 trillion debt / 118 trillion in assets = 15%

> With $118 trillion in assets, this makes one wonder why the U.S. carry debt at all. The current debt load appears to be within any mortgage lender's serviceable range – which is often 34% of assets.

Income

> $12.95 trillion annual (2012 – U.S. Bureau of Economic Analysis)

The reader's Country Total Income _____

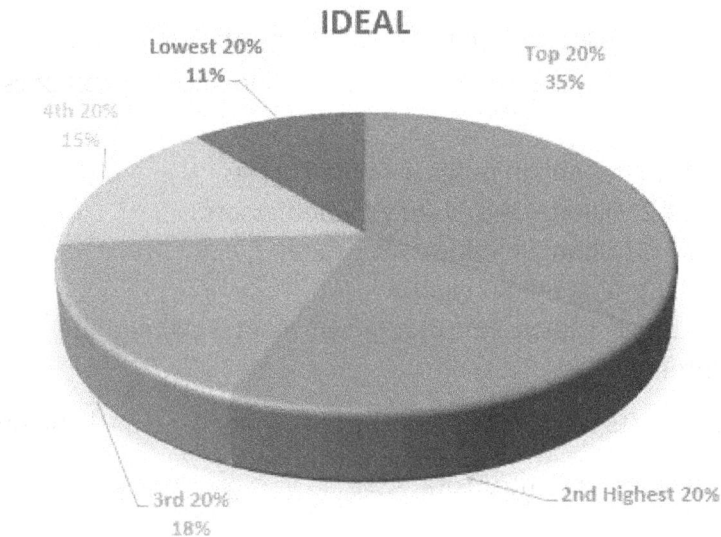

IDEAL

Lowest 20%
11%

Top 20%
35%

4th 20%
15%

3rd 20%
18%

2nd Highest 20%

The Lowest Quintile (20%)

To adjust all citizens to wealth and income levels suggested in the IDEAL Income Distribution Chart above, 11% wealth is the target for the bottom 20% of wage earners. This means that wealth within the bottom group of 80 million U.S. income earners, would have to rise to approximately $74,387.

That's 11% of $54.1 trillion of assets (U.S. wealth in 2003) divided among 80 million. Also, these 80 million people would then need to take home incomes of $30,000 as minimum. This income is more than double the current U.S. household income levels today. See Census.gov at the link here (US Census Bureau, 2015) in Bibliography.

To achieve a **zero-tax income** of $30,000 per year would require 100% employment, or equivalent income, with a minimum wage of approximately $18 per hour plus health coverage benefits (allowing for 4% vacation pay).

Next Lowest Quintile

By the "Ideal" targets in the income distribution chart above, 15% of total wealth is assumed for the second lowest Quintile. 15% of $54.1 Trillion divided among 80 million calculates to wealth per individual of $101,438 and family incomes of $60,000 annually or a minimum hourly wage of $34 per hour with benefits after tax.

Middle Quintile

The Middle 20 Percentile targets wealth of 18%. 18% equates to wealth per individual of $121,725 and family incomes of $90,000 annually or a minimum hourly wage of $49 per hour with benefits after tax.

Second Highest Quintile

21% amounts to a wealth of $142,012 and family income of $120,000, or a minimum wage of $65 per hour with benefits after tax.

The Highest Quintile

35% average wealth of $236,687 with an income of $150,000 annually, or a minimum wage of $82 per hour plus benefits after tax.

Wage Stagnation

In this next Federal Reserve chart, household income is the red line beneath GDP (Gross Domestic Product) in blue above it. Leading causes of wage stagnation between 1995 and 2013 include technological change, the decline of labor unions and more specifically, their joint bargaining powers, and globalization.

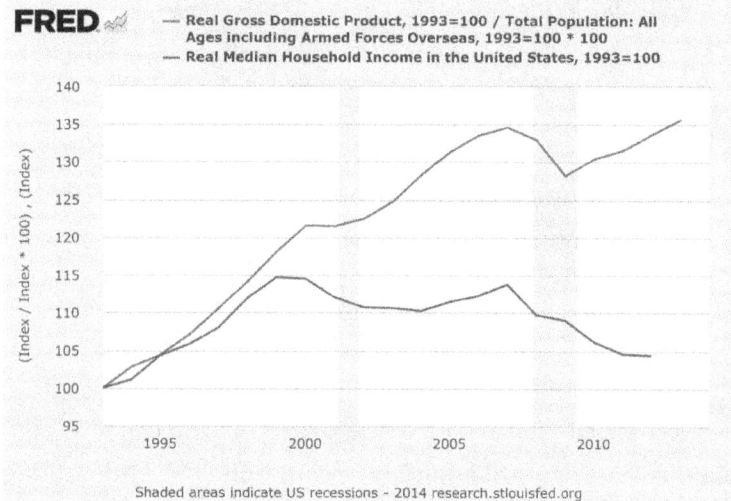

FRED

— Real Gross Domestic Product, 1993=100 / Total Population: All Ages including Armed Forces Overseas, 1993=100 * 100
— Real Median Household Income in the United States, 1993=100

Shaded areas indicate US recessions - 2014 research.stlouisfed.org

Minimum Wage

By taking this opportunity to target national goals of wealth distribution and employment, governments put an end to "Starvation Wages", ensure a Cost-of-Living affording Living Wage, and reduce the many and varied costs of Social Problems created by Wealth Inequity.

Your policy should ensure that these minimums are regularly reviewed and kept current. Over time, this will not guarantee perfect distribution, but it will go a long way to protect the Good Lives of everyone while permitting movement between the Quintiles for High Performers members of each level.

Graduated Tax

Implementing Graduated Tax structures ensures that wealth distribution meets national targets for sustainable equality. In a graduated system of tax, both large businesses and rich individuals pay a larger percentage of the total costs of running the country and must also be held accountable to keep others employed, salaried, and pensioned as well. The alternative is to jump to the same conclusion that Holland has and host pensions centrally in government.

Haven't we all heard the scenario where asking the Rich pay high tax is bad for society? I have, and yet nothing could be further from the truth. In fact throughout the 1940s through 60s, the rich paid up to 92% in tax and a maximum of $2 million of income per year was permitted as well. Society boomed during these times and it wasn't until the "Low-Tax" Trickle-down policies that wealth-inequity became really extreme in America; as is normal in a Winter K-Wave Economy as well.

As discussed above, there are often five quintiles used to represent the population of a country. This model might be too simple for very large countries, but it serves as a starting point that can be used to monitor the success of graduated tax programs actively over time.

Once wealth creation increases as a result of strong wealth distribution supports, only then can Governments be said to have managed their country's finances very well.

Chapter 7

-

Housing Policy Cycle Controls

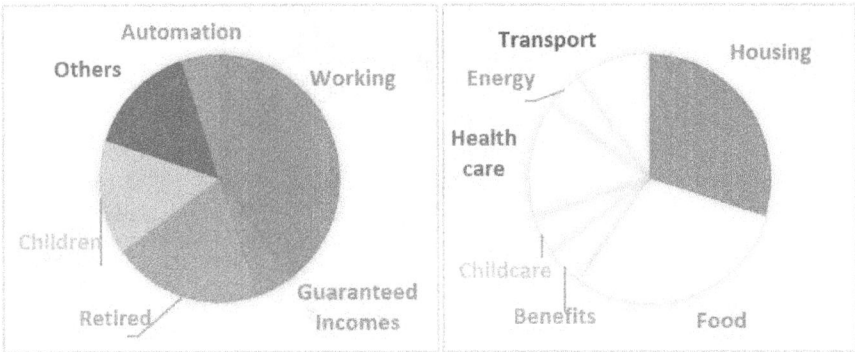

When left uncontrolled, the influence of foreign and local Real Estate speculators is to turn residential housing into an investment marketplace. We call this phenomenon Bubblenomics; a situation where a basic need of life - shelter, is converted into a wealth generation tool through scarcity. Artificial scarcity of this sort denies a market of the natural supply & demand rules to consumers, by those who can afford to control the buying and selling.

Bubbles, however, are not a norm for countries that implement responsible housing controls. The Netherlands have no housing bubbles for one example, and this is by plan and not by luck either.

Economic Controls for Housing Bubbles

Economists can ever be counted upon to fall back on basic Economic lessons of Supply and Demand. If Supply is small, demand will rise and with it – prices also rise, and the opposite is true as well.

Average Home Prices in Toronto vs Inflation

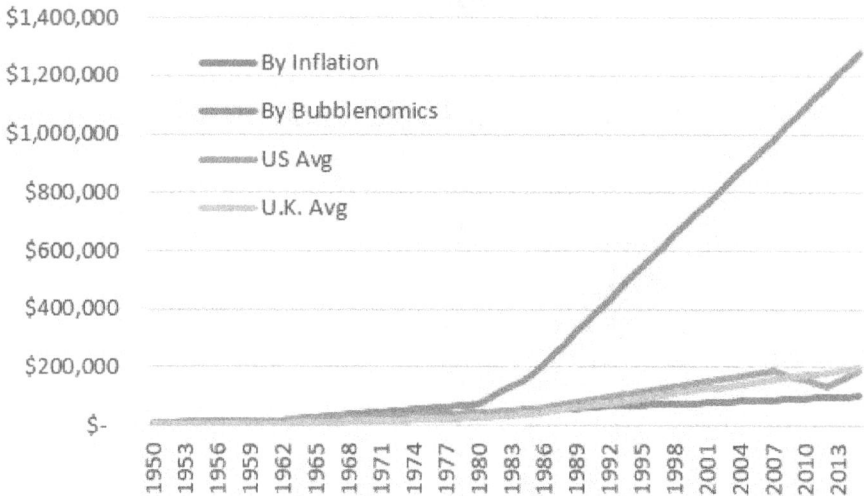

It is for just this reason that marketing people use scarcity to extol higher prices for goods that could otherwise be supplied readily and at fair market rates.

This is the approach that has created ghost cities in China and other major countries - where housing supply is readily available, but is artificially withheld with high prices – as required for "exclusive" or "luxury" condominiums. As China's economy slows now, it will struggle to transition from "investment-led growth" to a "consumer growth" model under its current housing policies.

At the point where scarcity is planned and controlled, the free-market of pure Supply and Demand can be said to no longer exist.

The Ghost Cities of China

The Netherlands has no housing bubble. The reason for this is that the citizens of the Netherlands relied heavily upon the 92% of controlled rental properties for housing until just this past 10-years or so. Although not perfect in every location, their foreign investment tax structures protected citizens from bubbles and because Economic Controls protected housing costs from soaring, young people can still purchase homes and start a family here today.

This means that when families do decide to purchase a home, they can do so with a high probability of paying off their mortgage as well.

The first rule of home ownership is to avoid paying rent, don't pay condo fees, and pay off your mortgage as soon as possible.

Paying off one's mortgage has become a very great improbability in recent years for many uncontrolled cities; and this is even true in the larger U.S. housing market of 130 million homes where 35% appear to live in expanding mortgage poverty where they will never be able to stop paying a mortgage.

This situation is also the actual definition of Usury; a financial lending practice that is exploitive and a criminal act in most countries. Whenever someone is forced to take on a loan they can never repay, even if the interest rate might appear reasonable, these individuals are victims of Usury.

Usury is preferable nomenclature to equally appropriate historical references to Indentured Servitude and Slavery on the Code of Hammurabi stone. In the historical case of Indentured Servitude, these commitments had to end after just seven years by law.

In uncontrolled centers, the definition of Usury has been altered in law to say that this is the practice where interest rates are set above some threshold that is deemed too high – 35% interest annually might be an example. I jokingly refer to this telling as a "Boiled Frog" definition of Usury; housing markets charge thirteen-time inflation, which amounts to the same result as would exploitive interest rates.

The Greater Toronto Area (GTA) in Ontario, Canada is a good example of a bubble – and not the most extreme example either as Vancouver's, Hong Kong and London's bubbles were quite a bit more extreme.

In Hamilton, just on the outskirts of the GTA, a 1982 house cost $32,000 - with interest at 22% - an all-time high rate. Within five years, interest rates dropped to 12%, and houses skyrocketed to $90,000. The same house has climbed to $500,000 today, increasing steadily as rates dropped to 1%. In Toronto, average home prices climbed to a $1.28 million.

Clearly, falling interest rates encouraged speculation far more than housing costs, because elsewhere, outside of bubble areas, the housing costs were also influenced by markets, but they only ran two or three times the Rate of Inflation.

Annual Inflation Rates are based on the Consumer Price Index (CPI). The CPI is a list of important consumer items that are tracked by governments to confirm that prices for basic goods are either changing or staying the same, and at what rate in %/Year.

A $1.28 million average home's cost is almost thirteen-times the cost of Inflation over the 65-year period running up to 2016. To calculate this, I took a $10,000 GTA house in North York in 1950 and added Inflation year-over-year to arrive at an Inflation Cost of $102,000. The Average U.S. and U.K. home are $188,000 U.S. and £212,000 respectively. As average homes in 1950 were $5000 and £3000, I would say that they have generally increased by three to four-times the Inflation rate as well.

Housing prices become unsustainable beginning with bidding wars over scarce resources (like housing inventories), so when Canada began to add six-million immigrants in the 1990s, and an overwhelming majority of these new immigrants and foreign investors, focused on the GTA and Vancouver – prices climbed with demand. With insufficient controls, scarcity drives bidding wars that bear little resemblance to the underpinning value of an investment - and highest-bidders-won irrespective of all other factors every time, until a bubble was firmly established.

Canada turned away from rent controls in commercial spaces altogether too and there were no controls for new Residential Rental contracts – which have permitted them to grow to double the rental rates asked for just three years ago.

The colors and underlines in the chart below indicate wealth distribution targets being met from the previous chapters. The "Absolute Min. Salary in Bubbles" calculation shows how Bubbles work dramatically against Wealth Distribution targets and a Good Life; observe how higher tax rates now apply to bubble rent-payers as well.

By adding a few assumptions - like a 35% household rent maximum (this number is used in mortgage applications but 25% should be considered conservative), 3 weeks per year vacation, tax rates (Canadian rates are used in this example), and $1000 per month minimum fixed cost estimate per a third-party report (Erin Davis,

2015), we can arrive at a Housing-driven Minimum Wage calculation.

Rent	Monthly Wage b4 Tax	Fixed Cost min. Met?	Pretax Income Needed	Cdn Tax Rate	Minimum Wage /Hr @Tax	Absolute Min Salary in Bubbles
$ 400	$ 1,176	No	$ 14,118	20%	$ 9.53	$ 20,168
$ 600	$ 1,765	Yes	$ 21,176	20%	$ 14.30	$ 23,050
$ 800	$ 2,353	Yes	$ 28,235	20%	$ 19.07	$ 25,931
$ 1,000	$ 2,941	Yes	$ 35,294	20%	$ 23.84	$ 28,812
$ 1,200	$ 3,529	Yes	$ 42,353	24%	$ 29.58	$ 32,776
$ 1,400	$ 4,118	Yes	$ 49,412	30%	$ 36.04	$ 37,339
$ 1,600	$ 4,706	Yes	$ 56,471	30%	$ 41.19	$ 40,451
$ 1,800	$ 5,294	Yes	$ 63,529	30%	$ 46.34	$ 43,562
$ 2,000	$ 5,882	Yes	$ 70,588	30%	$ 51.49	$ 46,674
$ 2,200	$ 6,471	Yes	$ 77,647	31%	$ 57.43	$ 50,488
$ 2,400	$ 7,059	Yes	$ 84,706	34%	$ 63.80	$ 54,627
$ 2,600	$ 7,647	Yes	$ 91,765	43%	$ 74.04	$ 61,953
$ 2,800	$ 8,235	Yes	$ 98,824	43%	$ 79.73	$ 65,395
$ 3,000	$ 8,824	Yes	$ 105,882	43%	$ 85.43	$ 68,837
$ 3,200	$ 9,412	Yes	$ 112,941	43%	$ 91.12	$ 72,279

Hourly Minimum Wage vs Rent Costs

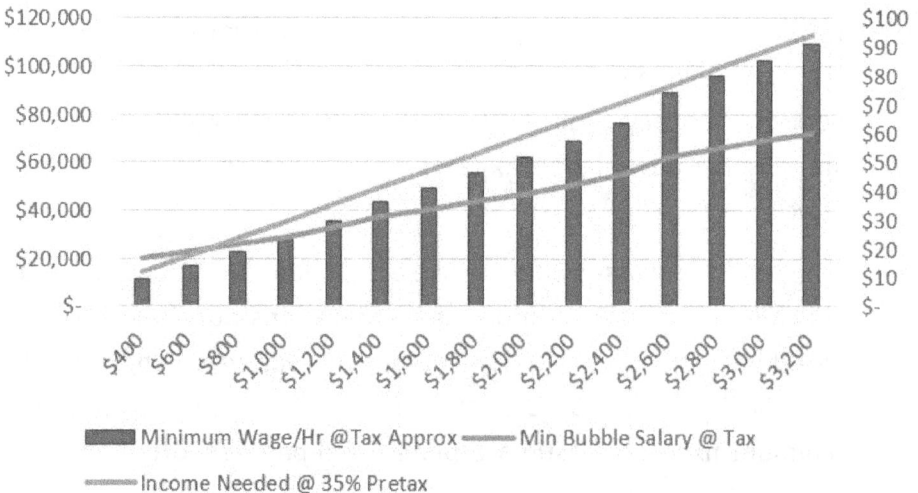

Minimum Wage/Hr @Tax Approx — Min Bubble Salary @ Tax
— Income Needed @ 35% Pretax

With no housing bubbles, the Netherlands can control rents at €710 ($773 U.S or $1030 Can) per month which means that guaranteed income programs can also work well and be affordable at the same time as well.

Elsewhere, rent controls have been in place in New York City; are in the Netherlands too; in Paris, France - where "En Viager" contracts were established, to protected seniors from these market-speculation-based bubbles and other Cost of Living up-swings (American Press, 1995). Housing market controls and comparison from country-to-country could comprise its own book and so these paragraphs introduce and provide enough information to build throttles as needed.

Housing Bubbles vs Good Lives

People need homes to be able to start families and if those children are going to be able to stay close to their parents when they begin their own families, costs of living in the community must be maintained relative to Inflation and salaries. If Inflation has only amounted to one-third housing costs nationally – as discussed; and is one-thirteenth housing costs in bubbles; but salaries and jobs have decrease over the same time period (from the 1970s on), clearly Bubbles work in an opposite direction to that of a sustainable society. Let's fix this...

How to Correct and Reverse Bubbles

So how do we correct Housing Bubbles and restart the unsustainable Winter Cycle into an affordable and sustainable Spring Phase and new Cycle?

Consider that with Central Bank interest rates at 1% for much of 2015 and 2016 - and no-way for interest rates to go up-nor-down easily, a very great number of new homeowners are steadfastly against any policy that requires an interest rate increase.

Put simply, few homeowners have the salaries to permit this interest rate increases on half-million dollar mortgages. An increase of just 2% would cause many families who are living from paycheck to paycheck now, to 1) lose their home (once savings deplete), 2) to be evicted by the Sheriff, and 3) be forced into an uncontrolled, overpriced and under-supplied rental market.

Eviction

When 2008 started their Great Depression, Housing Policies in Spain stuck to their status quo rules in a good example of what not to do. Job-losses progressed steadily to today's 23.8% unemployment rate and high eviction rates was seen in many countries and major U.S. cities like Detroit, Michigan, and San Francisco. These are epicenters of the subprime and foreclosure crisis and now anti-eviction groups like Occupy Detroit and the Eviction Defense Collaborative also.

Eviction groups cited that they are victims "of mass unemployment and mortgage banking fraud." (Noor, 2013) (Garrett, 2015)

Spain is a country with no housing controls and debt is unreleasable for life. There, even after eviction you still must pay principal plus interest charges, and bankruptcy does not release you from this debt either. Authorities evicted 100 homes a day in 2014 through 2015 and conditions got so extreme that Amnesty International interceded for the first time ever by launching an Anti-Eviction Campaign in 2015. ("Amnesty launches Spain anti-eviction campaign - The Local," 2015)

Anti-Eviction and Suicide

Spain's Anti-austerity party Podemos looks poised to win a federal election after beginning just two years ago and who could blame the citizens of Spain in the face of obvious incompetent management of the basic need of shelter. (Babcock, 2015)

Suicides related to Eviction in Spain are reported at five to twenty per week and are now the leading cause of unnatural death; double deaths by automobile accidents. A common slogan among anti-eviction protestors is the chant *"It's not eviction, it's murder."* ("4 commit suicide in Spain over evictions as EU struggles with unemployment — RT News," 2013)(Govan, 2016)

I live in the statistically wealthiest city in Canada, Oakville, Ontario, and suicides at the rail crossing right near the local homeless shelter, which has to turn away homeless people in February due to overcrowding, is a regular occurrence - although incidents seldom reach our newspaper.

The U.N. chastised Canada for failing to see to the needs of its homeless citizens in March of 2016 and with winter fast approaching again, I am unable to update this writing with any report of

99

improvements made. The point I am making is simply that this is an important issue in any housing discussion that is as universally true for wealthy countries and wealthy cities as it is for poorer places today, and this influences any discussion of shelter as a Human Right.

In Spain, just one percent of housing is devoted to public housing compared to 35% in Netherlands and 18 percent in Britain. There are 3.4 million empty homes in Spain and 11 million in all Europe of Europe; 1.8 million in Germany and 700,000 in Britain. There are enough empty homes in Europe to house the homeless twice over. (Neate, 2014)

Canada's rent and housing problems are headed in a collapsing direction as well. Canada has the highest immigration rate of the G7 by a wide margin - 20% per capita where the next largest G7 immigration rate is 14%. Although many new condos were built during the past 20 years, relatively few rental accommodation units were built. Bubbles and immigrant demand too, create high rental demand with low supply which has led to sharp rental increases. Canada has no new-rental increase controls and this demand has permitted landlords to lift their rental rates. This has forced up rents by 50% and more in just 3 or 4 years in major centers of Toronto and Vancouver.

This means that if you are unable to buy a home at bubble prices you are going to be forced to pay greatly inflated rents or condo fees. Condo fees too, can be surprisingly large – at $700 to $1,100 per month and more – a second mortgage basically.

As we begin a discussion of making corrections in housing, I will preface by saying that options for home-owners and renters, need to be well thought through. Too often, administrators force forward rules that don't work; with rules that force people into the street, or that squander personal possessions, and there can be none of those shortsighted calls enforced here.

Leadership in Interest Rate Increases

Interest Rate increases within Bubbles; in regions where Usury has been permitted to artificially run up the cost of housing many times beyond inflation, is proven to lead to a high rate of suicide consistently whenever evictions take place. Giving the statistical facts in evidence, a case for negligent manslaughter can be made because the result of increasing rates without eviction or homelessness mitigations, are well understood.

Economic Policies become life and death decisions within societies where there is increased unemployment and no income guarantees. If your leadership make no mention, acknowledgement nor accommodation via responsible mitigations for this fact, as they adjust interest rates, they are either exhibiting sociopathic behavior or they are not qualified to occupy a leadership or decision-making role.

For too long citizens have been disappointed by uninvested civil servants and police enforcement that do not always have common sense solutions available to them either - when addressing real problems. That track-record must come to an end.

If housing admins are ousting people into the street, they are either not intelligent enough to find solutions – or they are not empowered enough to insist on solutions from their administrators; solutions that actually work to keep people sheltered.

Fearing the loss of your full-time job and benefits in countries with no safety-nets, like Canada, is a non-starter; no positive result can come to pass of these unworkable solutions. The first step in initiating a change is to give housing administrators impunity to spend as needed to protect lives without risking civil servant livelihoods; to curb sheriff's orders that would turn people into the streets in -20 Celsius weather conditions – or even in conditions where countless homes sit unoccupied.

Read the case study on Gander, Newfoundland's handling of the 911 traveler emergency to see what a thinking community is absolutely capable of coordinating.

When people can no longer afford monthly mortgage payments, another program must keep them in their homes. When people lose six or ten rental units that afforded their incomes, an income guarantee must be there for them as their investment properties become homes again.

If interest rates went up by 3% to 5%, this change would probably force out the past 15-years of leveraged low-interest mortgage holders and condo rental speculators. If we then gave an option to defaulting homeowners to continue living in their homes via either a Land Grant system - or via an inflation-controlled Rental Agreement, we would find that we could in fact be able to return to a more affordable housing market and lifestyle safely and with minimal disruption.

Flushing out the investors who have accumulated multiple properties is an important change. The ideal result of any policy is to return Housing to its original purpose - as that of shelter - and not an investment and wealth management strategy. We have stock markets for this investment purpose. Look upon every investor flushed from uncontrolled existing real estate as a victory and ensure that all have citizens have incomes and homes.

We will talk about Housing changeover in detail next, but before we do, let's talk about the controls needed to govern buyer entry into the housing market so that we avoid recreating many of the social problems that led to a wide-open market approach in the first.

Governing the Housing Market

The buyer-entry solution could include restrictions on who can offer to buy property so that new home buyers, previous homebuyers, and local investors – can bid first based on an Inflation-Controlled maximum price. If local bidders make no offer, then bids can be opened to refugees, immigrants, foreign investment, and so on.

In Toronto and Vancouver, 6 million immigrants descended on two major uncontrolled centers with cash-in-hand, pushing out citizens and pushing up prices so that their children could not or would resettle here. Overloaded schools and overloaded road systems resulted.

Large immigrant communities moved together, established beach-heads that voted together, did not inter-marry, nor did they invest locally nor do business in their new host country in many cases. Requests to change Canadian culture and political correctness were frequent and many challenges were also found to be staged to permit lawsuits or other illicit financial gain.

All manner of small businesses were swamped with competition from households with twenty immigrants living under one roof – which is a decidedly non-Canadian standard of living. Corporate employment failed to keep up with job demand – or did not hire the newcomers. As a result, wherever three tire-shops stood before, twenty more sprung up - until no small businesses could make a decent living.

There was new home construction, but the housing-suppliers increased prices and pricing bubbles maintained the benefits of ever-higher investments through flipping and renting. As commercial investors turned to housing, and interest rates continued to drop and stay low year-after-year, prices took on a life of their own – similar to a stock market.

New homeowners in Toronto's suburbs buy direct from China in bidding wars for property that often ends up selling for $300,000 to $600,000 over asking – with 10 Chinese buyers vying for the home. Once the sellers exit their home, they are "out of that market" because neither they nor their children can rebuy easily. Only their own Chinese Real Estate agents are invited to handle the sale initially, and at a later time of sale as well, until local realtors realize that they are a few years from collapse as well.

Housing Controls Summary

The setting in place of housing entry controls protects the cost of houses from bubbles so that young people have a chance to begin productive lives in the neighborhoods in which they grew up in. These are desirable goals in many countries where citizens think to the future.

A discussion of Housing Controls from Cycle to Cycle, therefore, must mitigate several risks:

- Beginning in late K-Wave Summer phase, **Interest Rates** may want to run up, and if they do, they cannot then drop below an agreed minimum that dissuades savings or responsible foreign investment – a 6% to 8% rate perhaps.

  Interest Rates cannot be permitted to rise in high-Usury regions without Anti-Eviction and other housing alternatives in working order and in affect in Law and in the hands of trained government staff. Treat this need as importantly as you protect against as laws governing manslaughter because the notion

104

that there is a difference is not based in fact; nor in statistically proven reality nor science.

- A **per-Square-Foot Price-Increase Cap** that would prevent rapid increases in housing prices. Perhaps Caps could be tied to Inflation (CPI) or perhaps tied to an immigration benefit of some sort?
- For **First-time Homeowners** – Locally-born Citizens could have three avenues to find a home nearby their parents' homes, and the option to stay in school while raising a young family.
  - o **Rent-controlled access to a home suitable for children** – for married couples by age 19. Rents should be affordable via guaranteed incomes if parents elect to stay in university while raising young families.
  - o **Land Grants** - A home is assigned and is there for the family to use as they need until remote work moves them - or their kids leave home to their own homes. The average person lives in seven homes in a lifetime, so moves are permitted as needed.
  - o Access to **Zero-down-payment Homes** with mortgage payments that fit into guaranteed income payments for university/post-secondary students low debt-to-income ratios, low unemployment, and high minimum wage are required to service a mortgage. One home is permitted only. Higher salaries to high-performance students.
- **First time Homeowners – Non-Locally-born Citizens**
  - o Rent controlled access to a home suitable for children – for married couples by age 19. Rents should be affordable via incomes that their parents should maintain allowing them to stay in university while raising young families. Marriage to a Locally-born Citizen is encouraged when an option.

- **For Existing Owners**

  Existing Owners trade up if they own property and use the equity of that property to also purchase another property
  - **Purchasing Trade Up** – Residents must use the equity in an existing property while trading up, down or other.
  - **Land Grant**
  - **Rent-controlled** - Higher down-payments for existing owners with preference to owners that grew up in or live in the area presently.
- **Merit** – The idea that some roles in society afford a higher Merit than others; and then High Performers too may be a consideration in deciding who gets more desirable water-front locations, etc. Examples used above compared the value of a Cancer or Burn Care Worker to a Financial Worker with a track-record of socially irresponsible decisions. Although difficult to implement and manage fairly without corruption, this is worth considering as a performance incentive.
- **Investment Properties**, similar to rules implemented in Holland, Investment Properties are possible with higher-down-payment percentages than owners, and taxing of gains. Controls should encourage investment and productivity while discouraging non-productivity.
- **Offshore Investment** – Should housing be considered an investment before all have shelter? If you see from my observations above that this question should be answered "No", then you might also agree that offshore investment in private homes should be discouraged through heavy tax and rules that permit heavily protected rental-properties only perhaps.

- **Foreign investment** brings the Real Estate Bubbles and problems of other communities to your country. Perhaps these bidders could be permitted to compete only after local bidders are not interested at mandated pricing. In this way housing costs stay reasonable and new home construction is encouraged.
- **Monitoring** is required to ensure rental properties are not soaring in monthly costs.

Clearly, our present systems for managing housing are not brilliant. Current rules and systems are flawed, so my advice is to not blindly protect any status-quo that has played-out as can be expected in a Winter Cycle. Enact corrections as needed.

Nothing is too big to fail and nothing is too important that it cannot be adjusted in pursuit of Human Rights and a Good Life – once a system of protections have been put in place.

Home Ownership & Mortgages

This is the system that most of us in the G7 grew up with. Many in our society are never taught that there are any other systems. Mortgage borrowing is stressful, it reduces our quality of life and even longevity, and as with most non-production-generating financial services, it advances society negatively when not controlled. Uncontrolled ownership bubbles make properties exponentially more expensive, our children cannot begin lives in their hometown within bubbles, many feel forced to take on debt beyond their means and reasonable debt loads, and home ownership encourages investors to live on the production of those forced to rent in unregulated bubbles.

In Mesopotamia, borrowers had to become the indentured slaves of moneylenders when they could not repay their obligations; and then, every seven years, these servants were released from their debt entirely by law. In many ways, the majority of today's mortgage borrowers and forced renters are committed to a similar form of indentured servitude – but for a lifetime and not just seven years – in Usury scenarios.

Government Land Ownership

Ownership of homes is the norm in most G8 countries but, in our national parks, 100-year leases are granted only.

So – what was wrong with a government system that handed out homes as needed in the soviet system? Opponents might like to argue that this is a socialistic or communistic policy. The point remains that this is another system of land assignment that is widely used throughout G8 and G20 countries today. It is also a tried and true option for getting the next cycle started.

When we have an unlimited number of homes to give to citizens, land grants seem a natural option. Where we start seeing inequities is when land grants award estates, or prime waterfront locations, giving preference to some individuals above others. This becomes a Merit and Reward discussion.

This happens all the time today of course because families have been protected by class laws within a capitalist system, just the same as were Royals or Races in other class-based societies.

Can we switch back and forth?

I mentioned that in K-Wave Spring, Property Ownership works well enough, and then I mentioned that in K-Wave Winter, switching to Government Ownership works better. Remember that the important objective here is ensure that everyone has what they need and to ensure a Good Life for everyone. Can we switch from "Government

Owned" to "Self-Owned Housing"?

Yes, absolutely; why ever not? When the Soviet Union converted all of its states into Republics in 1986, all land grants were simply switched from a land grant model to an ownership model.

Since then, these same apartments in central parts of Moscow jumped up to cost millions of dollars. Nothing changed in the homes; residents simply became victims of their own housing bubble. This example, and China's ghost cities also, showcase that Land Grants are a far more sustainable system than uncontrolled home ownership.

Will landowners want to give their property to the state?

 Yes and no. I suspect there are four groups of decision makers and preferences as follows:

1) Free and Clear Home Owners - 30% currently

Those who own their homes free-and-clear might prefer to retain ownership of their home. If swapped for a land grant arrangement, a low percentage of their incomes would go toward tax. These owners would maintain their properties themselves - until robotic maintenance arrives, so that taxes would be lower again.

2) Mortgage Owners – 70% currently

Owners with a short time left on their mortgage, and no concerns for employment incomes, may elect to continue paying for and buying their home. Lower taxes would be levied in this scenario because homeowners are assuming all costs and upkeep.

Other homeowners with low-percentage ownership may decide to sign their properties over to government in the same way that the Russian Government did for its citizens. Higher Taxes or rents would be needed to offset government admin costs - perhaps.

Residents might prefer to be responsible for upkeep – until robotic maintenance projects complete. These folks would pay lower rents or tax.

3) Renters

Renters might prefer to request land grants, assigned homes, or to be able to secure quality rental homes at a controlled rate in keeping with the financial capabilities of society. A higher tax rate and resident upkeep would be required.

4) Landlords

Landlords too, either own their properties or work with high mortgage costs; some Landlords have a single or several rental units, and some will have 500 or even 5000 units. High Tax on rental homes and perhaps even higher rates over a certain number of units, perhaps 20 units, in addition to higher interest rates, will distribute this wealth in a way that doesn't hurt the landlord's ability to make a personal livelihood, but one that does discourage the rent and housing price bubbles created by rental landlord "dynasties".

The objective of wealth distribution is not to have everyone in society earning a similar amount, there will be high and low income earners in every economy and Cycle, the objective is to avoid thousands of hundred-million dollar offshore accounts that do nothing and benefit society not at all.

Transition Economics would have to dictate the rate of change that could be accepted in a housing system switchover. In democratic countries, 51% might like have to vote for these changes as well. These options would not be accepted easily until a high percentage of the population are disadvantaged or stranded outside the housing bubble – as in a K-Wave winter.

Recall also that our technology will shortly permit us to live anywhere we like, to build anywhere we like, without reliance on a power grid, or a daily commute into an office, nor a drive to a nearby mall to buy groceries or clothing. What difference will it make if the land is handed to us from our community's pool of available land – or if we go out and purchase it ourselves? Is our right to grind our way through a mortgage really so important to us?

Like any privilege, failure to maintain or upkeep assigned property before maintenance bots come onto the scene, could result in penalties financial or other.

As our automation projects make money less important, the residual value of an estate handed down to our children, also becomes less important.

Housing Changes from K-Wave Spring to Winter

Russian Dachas are cottages that were assigned to families living in the major cities pre-Perestroika in 1986. Even the poorest Moscow

citizen owned one so that children, grandparents, and families could get away and enjoy the countryside, plant gardens, and change pace from a busy urban life during the summer months.

Trains connect the major urban centers to cottage country where dachas could be reached easily, often on foot by walking for just a mile or two.

Most North Americans aspire from a young age to own their homes, and then we work toward paying off a mortgage for much of our adult lives too. This is Capitalistic Housing Policy and Home Ownership. We host Communistic Housing Policies as well, an example is when the State leases cottage property only in its Parks.

Many people who were able to purchase their homes before the housing bubbles of the 1980s, were able to pay off their home and cottages easily given the availability and relatively high wages of full-time salaries then compared to today.

In 1963, you could purchase three acres of Muskoka waterfront property, one of the most beautiful cottage areas in the world, for about $250. At the same time, salaries for steel workers was $300 to $450 per month, and this meant that most Canadians could easily afford a cottage.

When my 71-year-old best-friend-Tom's father was 17, back in 1965, he was a teenager working a student summer job. With his savings he had the choice of buying either a used car or two acres of waterfront property in Burlington, Ontario. Today that property would sell for millions of dollars and his summer income be probably less than $100 per week

In 1982, incomes were up to $5,000 per month, and the average home price for a modest detached dwelling was approximately $35,000. That house would rocket up in price by approximately three times over the next three years and would never come down.

My parents told me from a young age to buy a home and pay it off as quickly as possible – and that made a lot of sense because mortgages could be paid off completely with five or ten years of concentrated effort. Today, only 29% of homes in the U.S. are owned free-and-clear, and the rest are paid off only 50% on average. Falling interest rates had to go so low to stave off depression in 2008 that raising them even a few percentage points would force the foreclosure of tens of millions of homes in North America.

Needless to say, countries that do not implement Transition Economics Maturity Model controls, tend to find themselves Collapse Trending in Winter Economic Cycles.

Understanding lending costs

Usury is the practice of making unethical or immoral monetary loans intended to enrich the lender unfairly. Many countries enact Usury Laws that govern maximum interest rates, maximum monthly payments, and maximum debt load as a ratio to income.

Banking laws in Canada presently permit Canadian Lenders to extend $26 for every $1 on deposit. This means that for the average detached home in Toronto which costs $1 million dollars financed at 5%, the bank will ask you to pay $5,816 per month; $1,613 will be the principle and $4,203 will be the interest payments. Borrowers will pay $50,436 in payments annually for the next 25 years, to return to the lender the $38,461 that they originally had to have on account. That is a working lifetime of steep payments in exchange for $38,461.

If at any time during that 25 year period, the homeowner is unable to continue payments, the bank can foreclose and sell the property to repay the full value of the mortgage commitment. Your forces your family to find shelter in a marketplace where rental rates increased 50% to 75% in response to the rising demand. There will be many additional monies wasted on moving and storage costs, and you might spend many years worrying about financial pressures as well.

No-one imagines that they will not be able to meet payments when they first apply for a mortgage, but the statistics show that most mortgage takers will have to refinance, downsize, or suffer foreclosure. 70% of all mortgages in the U.S. are never paid off by the original borrower.

My point in mentioning this example is that owning property is great, but it is terrific only when your system of government and economy supports it. The G8 economies supported home ownership in K-Wave Spring, Summer, and early Autumn, until around 1995, but that was 20 years ago. Today in K-Wave Winter, the statistics say that our economies and housing markets do not support home ownership.

At this time in a capitalist cycle, soliciting low-interest, low-down-payment mortgages, ceases to be beneficial to society and becomes Usury. The availability of easy financing creates bidding wars and pricing bubbles, and mortgages that statistics say will never be paid off. Most countries enact laws to protect its citizens against this form of Usury as well.

China and other countries that support land ownership are in the same situation where land ownership forces a very hard life for the great majority of its citizens.

Low-interest rates with just 3% down-payments are being offered in the United States again this year as people who lost their homes in 2008 become eligible to buy again. Does this sound like the beginning of just another bubble?

What sort of home would I get?

This is a discussion of options and not recommendations. Discussion of a change in land ownership is going to shake any community to its core. I know myself that the notion of a government administrator deciding my lot in life – would worry me deeply.

Our robotic or manual home-building capabilities determine the quality and size of granted homes, as does current government incomes, available consigned properties, economy wealth, wealth distribution, and individual incomes.

If you are a brilliant engineer who builds hi-tech businesses, technology, and writes books that improve mankind's well-being, would, or should, your contributions be recognized with a larger and better parcel of land or home?

Our society rewards these considerations almost not at all today.

Would a Trust Fund Manager who earns $50 million per year by squandering 100,000 jobs to other countries - be rewarded with a larger parcel of land?

Our present capitalist system *does* reward this behavior today – with bigger houses, nicer cars, private schools, on and on. If you buy finished sneakers for a dollar and sell them for $100, we throw in a very handsome fleet of yachts as well. The net benefit to the planet is just about zero in this last example, as the value is delivered by the shoemaker and transportation can be automated right to the wearer's doorway. The same situation holds true for coffee growers who barely recover costs for their work and equipment while sales organizations reap enormous profits.

Consider that as money becomes irrelevant with new technology, are skills like "driving financial efficiencies" – especially the ones without regard for social well-being, important, desirable, or necessary? The answer is probably - less-and-less.

Would a cancer-care nurse who dedicated his or her life to attending to the needs of the suffering and dying be granted a more comfortable lake view and a nice home to come back to?

Today, our system rewards in-hospital nurses modestly and nursing home attendants are almost paid as minimum wage workers.

Through these examples, I am introducing a merit measuring discussion that focuses on using different measures to trigger social rewards. What contribution does this person bring to society? What is their performance? In the case of a Mother Theresa – this person is a leader as well? Does he or she inspire others by example to do amazing work for society with little regard for personal recognition? If yes, then a very nice lot would make a lot of sense. Just don't get me started about pro-sports salaries.

Whether you like the idea or hate it, this is just another very implementable change that makes a lot of sense and only takes a well-managed project and operation to achieve.

What is the right place for you to live?

Should people live alone? Should they live in Dorms? Do they live in apartments? Do they live beside lakes? Do they live on boats? Should special requests be considered?

I love these questions because there are many correct answers. When I was very young, the answer to this question was that I needed to live in a home with my family – ideally in my own room, with a yard for my dog, close to my friends and school. That was house number <u>One</u>.

When I headed off to degree studies at seventeen, some of the best times of my life were lived in a dorm room with other students my own age; that was House <u>Two</u>.

When I had almost finished degree studies, I took a two bedroom bachelor flat with a buddy; House <u>Three</u>, and when I started working and wanted to start a family at twenty-five, I took a small three bedroom house with a big mature yard, on a quiet cul-de-sac, that needed a lot of weekend projects. House <u>Four</u>.

The woman of my dreams came along and our family grew to need a four-bedroom home with a pool within two years. A cottage would have been too much work so we owned a motorhome for a year or two until the kids convinced us that it was all about a pool for them.

Half of our neighborhood's kids agreed that our pool was the best on the block and so my wife and I had to camp poolside at House <u>Five</u> to watch bathers for eight hours a day - some days. That went on for ten years until kids were eleven or twelve – and then the pool was very rarely used and we could have done without the extra maintenance work and energy cost as well.

Divorce came when the kids were thirteen and seventeen and we needed two homes temporarily. My kids headed off to University and a friend and mine; a woman who was in a similar situation to my own, shared a three bedroom condo. Home <u>Six</u>. Our parents were getting older and we wanted to bring them closer to live with us, so a three bedroom bungalow with a nanny apartment or two, would have been ideal; House <u>Seven</u>.

As we get older, our needs will change too - until our kids either take us in to live with them, or until we decide to live with other seniors within supervised apartments; House Eight. Like everyone, we will need 90% of our lifetime's healthcare within our last 5% of days most likely, and we hope to look back on a full life with grandchildren and maybe even a great-grandchild or two if we are lucky.

Everyone is important; some individuals represent a greater utility to society than others - and this must be recognized and rewarded. If we all keep two or three children families, it is entirely likely that a sustainable flow from home to home might actually work very well throughout our lives.

Automation in Housing

Automations are on the cusp of making exciting innovations in housing. The #WPProjects chapter below introduces automatically built and serviced towns called "Worldvilles"; Worldville is, of course, a temporary name given until a proper town-name can be assigned.

Where online games like MineCraft and WarCraft encourage young builders to design virtual buildings and neighborhoods today, online Worldville software tools will likely enable these same people to compete for Best Real-World Community Design competitions. Simply hitting the Enter button will build the approved winning design in real life; and this will happen surprisingly quickly and soon too.

Building these computer-assembled real-world homes are an array of new large-scale 3D-Printers, assembly robots and connected smart factories, and of course, new ideas about what are efficient and interesting homes.

China has been 3D-Printing six-story buildings and luxury homes for four years now. Automated bricklaying and other sophisticated construction robots are becoming mature and affordable but lack integration with one another. Pre-fabricated home factories build homes that either simply pop-up once they are towed to their lot -

ready   for   occupancy   –   see
https://www.youtube.com/watch?v=gTGVqZX4o0w for an example.

Micro-homes too are providing inexpensive, energy-efficient housing in both rural and intercity settings where low costs and rapid construction make these small, cute and practical homes better solutions for the elderly and the homeless.

#WPProjects assigns home automation projects to Serbia and Uzbekistan initially with component plumbing, heating, electrical, windows & doors, and servicing etc. assigned to other countries.

As to why we have been able to put a man on the moon by not build an automated house, of course the answer is one of direction and leadership only.

Instead of building sustainable communities, we are instead leaving companies to churn out gadgets and building materials as simply and cheaply as possible - without regard for sustainability. A robotic assembly line that builds homes is a sophisticated engineering project and not one that can capitalistic business can be counted on to build without direction – obviously.

Milton Friedman was a very well-funded Economist in the early 1980s, famous for consistently defining Greed over the Greater Good and defending that the most important innovations in time were created by capitalist needs and corporations. His six appearances on the Donahue Show are interviews available still on YouTube at https://www.youtube.com/watch?v=MQ0-cDKMS5M.

The facts in reality, however, clearly show that Milton was a misinformed and socially irresponsible individual forwarding a message by special interests. It was government who lead almost all great advances in civilization – and this was especially true throughout the cold-war technological era when engineers were in charge of projects as well. I explained in the TED Slide show of World Peace – The Transition, that mankind's incredible technological leaps and strides of the 20th century only came about at the direction of government funding and programs – from computers, to nuclear energy and drive systems, to jet and pressurized aircraft, to a moon launch, strides in space and ever cities on the water as in nuclear aircraft carriers.

2. I mentioned that Our Leadership Changed

▸ Engineers were Marginalized and Business Ethics Grads took to the Boardrooms

▸ Copywrite 2015 World Peace – The Transition at CSQ1.org

After the cold-war; after 1975 or so, all that capitalism created were profitable refinements on the same technologies. Advances in Technologies with great potential like 3D-Printing advance slowly and only ever developed at a rate that profit will permit.

Government have only ever been the ones to lead big social changes of this magnitude, and leadership here is something that you must vote for as well.

Housing KPIs (Performance Measures)

Key Performance Indicators – KPIs, are mentioned throughout this book again and again. It's important that we have shelter for children and parents; it is important to accommodate other needs as well; and just as important are needs of setting expectation well and meeting promises consistently.

If we need another home; it must be made available within "x" months but "y" months is too long; we must have a chance to preview a few ("x") options and we need not less than three months' notice of confirmation of a change. When automated housing software systems break down, we need a manual system to work in its place very temporarily. Planning KPI-driven Risk-managed housing systems takes the stress out of life – as is the case with most good planning.

Automated Home maintenance, home construction, and even one-day home renovation and demolition, need sophisticated management and planning as well.

Good Planning with solid KPI & Exception Reporting alongside release-managed process improvement are the ingredients of the best self-correcting processes that you are ever going to work with.

Good Execution – I often say that the best programmers are those whose code cannot be broken easily by the next dozen changes.

Operational Performance of housing systems can be imperfect either through poor training, overload, or flubbed changes from time to time, so good Quality Assurance rigor and contingency planning go a long way to maintaining a stress-free work life and productivity that meet everyone's needs for Housing.

Chapter 8

-

Immigration & Refugee Policy

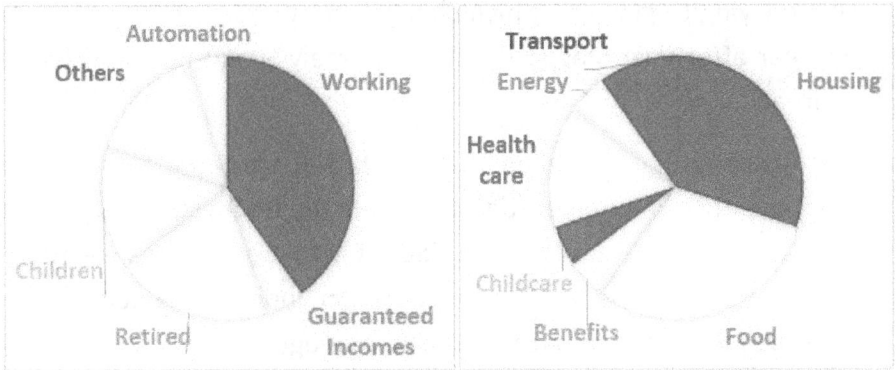

With just 20% of the planet living a Good Life, there is much work to do to correct a major problem without distractions like war, corruption, violence, and displaced communities and families getting in the way and slowing forward progress.

The difference between a productive society versus unproductive, comes down to planning for community, executing thought-leading policy and process, monitoring progress, and making optimizations that drive high rankings in wealth creation and wealth distribution in comparison to other countries.

Internationally, the U.N. have set initial goals for International progress in its Global Goals, but these are a start and work in progress. What they do not offer is planning of any sort. No step-by-step instructions are suggested on how to build sustainable solutions.

The difficulty created by having no planning, is that there can no training; with no training there can be no coordinated pulling - and as any coxswain (rowing team captain) can tell you, uncoordinated pulling in all directions turns you in circles, or worse, as often as not.

We see the result of slow and embarrassing progress in society today. Democracies have many thousands of voices, and each voice is quite certain that things are not working as they should today, but 99%+ all are trying to guess at which changes are needed. This is a recipe for year after year stagnation unfortunately – and not a desirable approach.

CSQ Research is a Canadian Think-tank that studies the policies of every country - over time – and compares the track record of policies to country's GDP track records. CSQ's CMI – Country Management Index and RAI – Renewable Automation Index explained above, measure the performance of each management team in every country by assigning a performance and maturity rating to each. Intuitively you might agree that this is what a pragmatic approach probably more closely looks like.

If our voted policies continue to lead us toward social collapse, as has happened to many civilizations in history, we see progressively increasing social problems. Symptoms of collapse start with increasing unemployment, divorce and lower fertility rates; usury and dual income traps begin; incarceration rates grow alongside homelessness, problems begin to include religious extremism, racism, gender inequality, substance abuse, incarceration rates increase, terrorism and then finally revolutions and war emerge as collapse takes hold fully.

Refugees

Refugees are individuals and families left without homes and supports in their own countries. Most often, they are displaced through no fault of their own whatsoever; sometimes as a result of voting poorly. Most refugees are regular citizens like you or I, going about their work and raising families, until they were driven out of their homes and communities by war or tyranny. Often refugees face starvation or death should they try to return to their homes and past lives.

The reasons for instability within a refugee's society can originate from purely internal conflicts and wars between competing local communities; sometimes the instabilities result from foreign influences. When foreign countries have intervened, very often the same countries who had a hand in creating the conflict – are next asked to assist by taking in and providing financial aid for the Refugees that they have also displaced.

The United States interceded in Iraq in 2003 and then left no strong leadership and authority as they pulled out in 2011. At that same time, in 2011, NATO allies – including Canada and the European Union, insisted on sanctions against President Bashir al-Assad of Syria, Iraq's neighbor.

Before extensive droughts beginning in 2004, Syria was one of the most beautiful countries in the Middle East; and was a place where women walked down the street safely at night. The political and security vacuum created by a civil war beginning in 2011, permitted mercenaries to descend from the north of Iraq into Syria and this began a well-entrenched war between many groups with many agendas; Arab Spring, Syrian Army, Kurds, Turks, Hammas Palestinians, IS Islamic State Muslim Extremists from Iraq, Hezbollah from Lebanon, Israelis, and many other groups, displaced 13 million of 22 million Syrian citizens (Wikipedia, 2016).

4.4 million Refugees were displaced outside of the country and fully 3.3 million are currently in Turkish Refugee Camps. Turkey has spent $8 billion in support of Syrian Refugees; the U.S. $4.7 billion. Details of aid spending are surprisingly well documented at Wikipedia at...

https://en.wikipedia.org/wiki/Refugees_of_the_Syrian_Civil_War
("Refugees of the Syrian Civil War," n.d.)

Millions of ordinary people in Syria lost everything and had to flee to find a safe place to live. The E.U. absorbed perhaps 200,000 refugees with 50,000 making their way to Greece, and Canada was the ninth largest aid supporter agreeing to also take 25,000 refugees and commit $1 billion.

Democracy is important, not because it works perfectly – democracy must constantly reform and improve. Democracy is important, because democratic countries do not continue wars with other democratic nations. Our governments undermine their value to humanity quite a bit, however, when our actions create and then leave political vacuums in parts of the world where education levels and longstanding rivalries require a strong policing presence.

Was a Canadian, American, or E.U. citizen consulted when NATO pulled supports for Syria's President Assad after arming ISIS forces throughout the IRAQ war? Absolutely not.

As a voting citizen I would want to ask; what are the alternatives? What are the long-term Costs and Benefits – in both human suffering and real dollar costs? It would have been a penny spent to save a million pounds.

The cost of Coalition and NATO interference in Iraq and Syria - in human suffering and refugee support dollars spent - have been staggering. Why was there no social plan presented, and no business plan that considered long-term costs?

Engineers and doctors pledge an oath to do no harm to society; and I think most voters agree we have a moral imperative to defend peace and security where we can while we work toward improving global human rights pragmatically. There are 11 million people displaced from their homes in Syria – a country of 22 million where women in 2010 could walk down the street at night safely.

I heard a Texas Republican Governor tell a story to a Fox newswoman last month - about How the Cow eats the Cabbage. The joke's point is to not make incorrect conclusions due to shortsightedness; it turns out that the cow in the joke is an escaped baby elephant and the elderly woman calling the police can't quite see that it's not a cow shoving cabbages up its butt.

The State of Texas' Governor doesn't understand the joke so he explains proudly that "In the South", his constituents know how the cow will get cabbages pushed at them – when it comes to U.S. foreign policy abroad. Ironic, and embarrassing, shortsightedness costs lives so cast your vote for an engineer next time.

There have been benevolent Dictators; and there have also been Leaders who strongly controlled the peace based on accurate analysis of credible threat and acceptable losses within their own countries. Saddam Hussein was no picnic, and the 100,000 Kurds that he is reported to have killed in order to keep the peace in Iraq is outrageous. However, from a well-intentioned place of moral high-ground, the Coalition countries removed Saddam from control at a cost of 500,000 Iraqi deaths from 2003 to 2011.

Today, Iraq's 33 million citizens endure one of the highest per capita murder rates in the world in excess of 9,000 per year. The U.S. has 12,000 murders per year but for a much larger population of 360 million. None of these numbers should be considered normal; Japan had two murders last year – "2" – and that is not a misprint.

And of course, events to date are hardly the end of the opportunity for tragedy because Russia was no longer prepared to stand by and watch their former ally Syria be torn to bits either. In 2015, they sent in ground troops and withdrew to support Syria with air strikes in March of 2016. On Sept 16th, The New York Times reported that "Russia Probably Attacked United Nations Humanity Convoy".

Fear sells newspapers and to add to this publishing pressure, the Times' new web-based newspaper format must provoke readers into reading the full article after paying a subscription charge as well. Quite honestly, an article has to be pretty provocative and exclusive for a web-reader to not prefer any number of free alternative web-based news sources.

So, now we have the world's two great nuclear super-powers (with 15,000 warheads between them) in close combat proximity with the United Nations crying "War Crimes" in a major U.S. newspaper while Donald Trump is President-elect.

That is a lot of pretty fantastic dominos really; as if Russia made a point of bombing an aid convoy. My own reaction was "What a load of nonsense"; but by all means decide for yourself.

None of these events described here were ever the doing of Syrian nor Iraqi citizens – and yet they are Refugees nonetheless. It is a fate you would not wish on your worst enemy.

Tensions are too high; awareness, education and leadership in what to do next to restart our played-out Economy are not understood; and not communicated. And much worse, emotions - and not logic, rule the day today as they did in 1930 Germany.

Our academics and experts have failed us too often now – and citizens are heated and open to listening to almost any message of perceived leadership now.

It may take a book like this one - to explain what is needed to diffuse a World War III sized powder-keg; and it definitely takes a democratic electorate that casts their votes in such a way that builds a Good Life and not a bomb shelter.

Bernie Sanders would have beaten Donald Trump – so take another look at Bernie's policies and consider how his policies aligned to policy discussed here in this book as well.

For country performance leaders, look to the management teams of The Netherlands, Germany, Norway, Sweden, Finland, China, Switzerland, and Russia as a strong start.

Abundance - is the cure for most petty conflicts over religion, gender, and race. In this next year, plan to build abundance by rolling out Livingry Projects and not Weaponry Projects: Projects like #WPProjects - that support food and shelter sustainably. Without these strategic renewable automation infrastructures, there will forever be the humanitarian need to care for displaced people and Refugees.

Immigration

What topics must the discussion of immigration touch on to assist a positive economic change new economic cycle?

Let us take a more detailed look at the benefits perceived to result from Immigration as follows:

- Foreign Investment
  - Real Estate
  - Business
- Population Increases vs Fertility Rates
- Humanitarian Outreach
- Skilled Labor

Canada boasts the G8's largest Immigration percentage increase – adding one-fifth, or six-million immigrants, to its population since 1990. The next G8s were Germany, Spain, and the U.S. at 14%.

The strategy of boosting new immigration has a historic track record of improving economies. New immigration was observed to relieve great depressions in 1883 and in 1779, however today's offshore banking and online trade networks seem to be negating a positive economic benefit as business and employee benefits are not shared within Canadian communities when this happens.

With no immigration controls, nor monitoring of settlement location, nor investment within country by its immigrants once in-country, the financial benefit and cultural impacts of immigration here have been arguably negative to Canada's own culture alongside disappointing observable economic performance in the same time period.

Consider ...

Country	# of Immigrants	% World	% Country	G8 or G20	Collapse or Advancing
Saudi Arabia	9,060,433	3.9	31.4	20	Advance
Australia	6,763,663	2.8	27.7	20	Collapse
Canada	7,284,069	3.1	20.7	8	Collapse
Germany	12,005,690	4.9	14.9	8	Advance
U.S.A.	46,627,102	19.8	14.3	8	Collapse
Spain	5,852,953	2.8	14	8	Collapse
France	7,784,418	3.1	11.1	8	Collapse
Italy	5,788,875	2	8	8	Advance
Russia	11,643,276	4.8	7.7	8	Advance
Turkey	4,580,678	2.1	5.81	20	Collapse
South Africa	2,399,238	1	4.6	20	Collapse
Argentina	1,885,678	0.8	4.6	20	Advance
South Korea	1,230,000	0.5	2.9	20	Advance
Japan	2,437,169	1.1	1.9	8	Advance
Brazil	1,847,274	0.8	0.9	20	Advance
Mexico	1,103,460	0.5	0.9	20	Collapse
India	5,338,486	2.3	0.4	20	Collapse
China	848,511	0.4	0.1	20	Advance
Indonesia	295,433	0.2	0.1	20	Advance

Immigration is not proven to improve Economic Growth in Canada.

According to Canada's GDP stats of exports; Canada's exports are down 50% since 2000, imports are up 50% since 1990's "250,000 Annual New Immigrant" Policy began. Record high trade deficits hit just last month at $3 billion after annual trade deficits every year since 2008. Canada's track-record in affordable housing is one of run-away housing bubbles, poor infrastructure improvement, and its

GINI is increasing throughout this time period. GINI is a measure of Inequity that indicates increasing wealth of richer individuals; this is generally seen to have a negative impact on Export per Capita and the economy at large.

Worse off is Australia who is in a worse situation in all areas of its economy, with a similar number of immigrants but a lower over-all country population which makes this immigrant percentage higher than Canada's.

Across the G20 chart above, High Immigration countries show negative economic track records, while low immigration countries are largely among the strongest economic improvers. If I draw a line at 10% Immigration rates for the G20 nations above, 75% of G20 countries (with higher than 10% of Immigrants) are in Collapse while 33% are in Collapse Trending with Low Immigration. Having lived through this time in Canada's history, I – like many – can attest to the dilution of the Canadian's standard of living throughout this period and a very notable period of culture shock particularly in major urban centers where Indian and Chinese communities settled closely together to comprise 80% of their communities.

With Canada's unemployment rates at 7% - and unreported unemployment at twice that, Canada's labor force struggles to find placement into jobs and incomes for its citizens today. Housing in major hiring centers is at thirteen-times inflation since 1987 due to an absence of responsible management controls as well. Usury here is rife and desperate homebuyers are forced into purchasing loans that they will seldom be able to repay.

"Usury" is the practice of extending loans that can never be repaid; the practice is illegal in most countries - and most social leaders would agree that these are immoral practices as well. Our dictionaries have altered Usury's definition to focus on unreasonably high interest rates only, but when essential housing costs within bubbles are thirteen-times the rate of inflation and inventories (supply) appear to be kept scarce artificially, Usury can happen at interest rates of just 2%.

The Canadian Mortgage Insurance people at CMHC have very recently started to realize this problem and just this week raised requirements to ensure that new owner can endure a percentage point or two in interest rate increases. This also means that many, many first time home owners and young families are not able to buy homes that they need.

Inviting immigrants to settle in these areas - as they have preferred, can have the negative effect of exaggerating these scarcities and bubbles.

Average Home Prices in Toronto vs Inflation

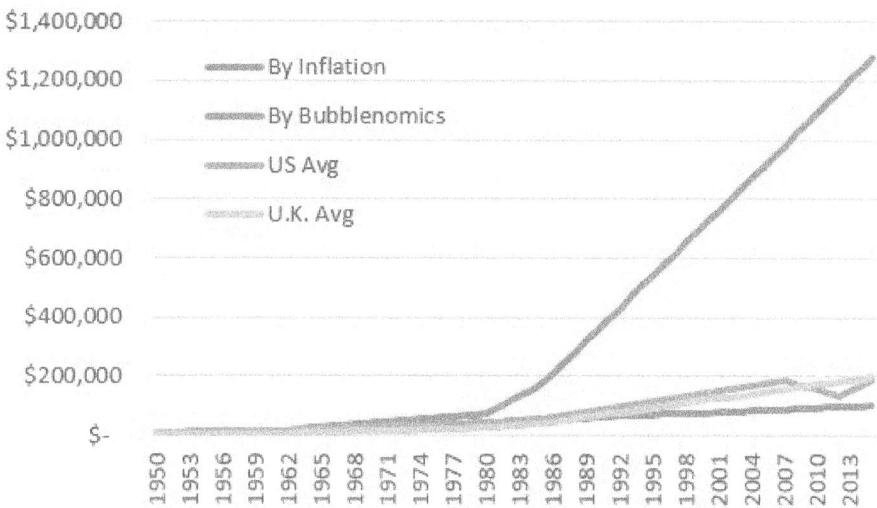

In the chart above, the Toronto Real-Estate bubble in Red is compared to the housing prices in non-bubble markets and the Inflation line over the same 65-year period (over the last economic

K-Wave cycle).

At #100 on The CMI Index, Canada is a country on a trajectory to Collapse — and not success — based on its poorly researched management decisions in energy, immigration, wealth distribution and due to its general declines in citizen spending-power which have resulted from a long list of lax monitoring and poor government control.

This hard evidence reinforces that there can be no business case for Immigration in many countries now, other than that of normal family unification best-practices. Increasing Immigration rates at this point would, therefore, amount to compounding "problem policy" at a time when this country can hardly afford another burden to infrastructure and to its automating and offshoring job market.

Despite this information, third-party groups like the Conference Board of Canada and Canada's Immigration Minister continue to call for 25% increased rates for immigration — no longer 250,000, but now 407,000 annually through to 2030.

Without Guaranteed Income protections and responsible controls in energy, housing, and many other areas, Canada could Collapse no different than Spain, Greece, England, Australia or any other country that is unable to devise effective solutions to restarting their economic cycles.

Fertility Rates vary for a number of reasons. First among fertility influences in all nations is prosperity; so the number of children in a home globally has decreased over the last 200 years as incomes and amenities have improved to families.

Women who live in countries with GDP per Capita at an average of $8,000 annually, tend to have fewer children on average internationally as the next chart depicts.

Population Increase and Fertility Rates

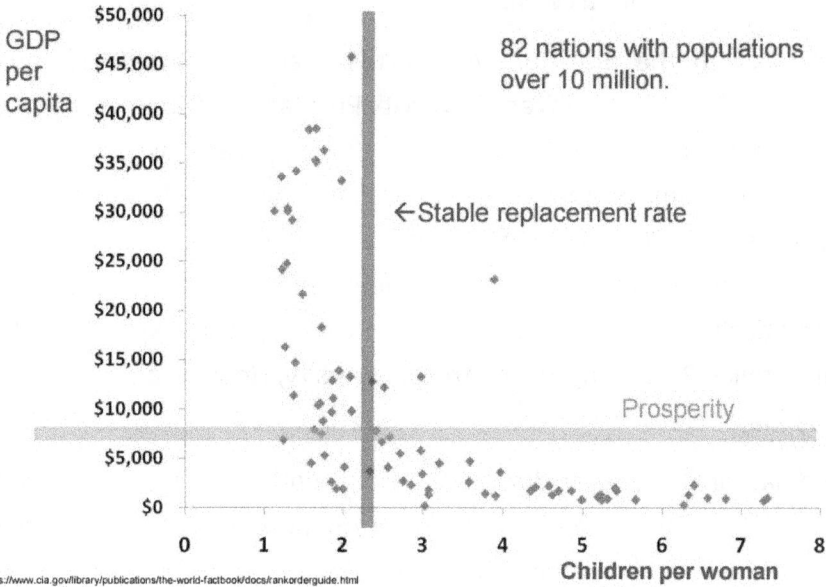

GDP per capita

$50,000
$45,000
$40,000
$35,000
$30,000   ←Stable replacement rate
$25,000
$20,000
$15,000
$10,000   Prosperity
$5,000
$0

82 nations with populations over 10 million.

0   1   2   3   4   5   6   7   8

Children per woman

https://www.cia.gov/library/publications/the-world-factbook/docs/rankorderguide.html

BIRTHRATES
Canada, Germany, Netherlands, U.K., U.S.

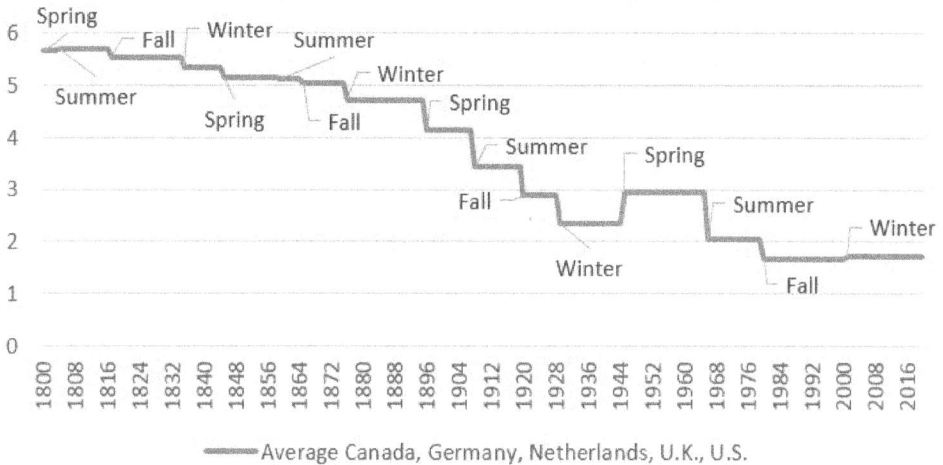

Spring, Fall, Winter, Summer, Winter, Summer, Spring, Fall, Spring, Summer, Spring, Fall, Summer, Winter, Fall

6, 5, 4, 3, 2, 1, 0

1800 1808 1816 1824 1832 1840 1848 1856 1864 1872 1880 1888 1896 1904 1912 1920 1928 1936 1944 1952 1960 1968 1976 1984 1992 2000 2008 2016

Average Canada, Germany, Netherlands, U.K., U.S.

The second influence is based on Economic Cycle Phases. In this next chart of average Birthrates per Economic Phase, we averaged birthrates in North America and Europe. Here we see that birthrates are always higher in Spring and Summer Phases; and these are times when living is easier as well.

I also asked the question: Are fertility rates increased by Free Universal Day Care and Free University Programs as found in Quebec and the Nordic States? I did find a 20% increase over births in Germany. Germany does have a subsidized Day Care Program but it supports 220,000 fewer spots than are needed. Beginning in 2014, Germany made all university programs free. Russia's birthrate fell dramatically to German levels after Perestroika in 1986. Prior to Perestroika, Russia supported free University, Housing and Day-care in its major cities.

Free daycare in Quebec did lead to more mothers going to work but this has fact has led the German government to look closely at what should the role of women be in society.

BIRTHRATES
Netherlands, USA, Finland, Netherlands, Russia

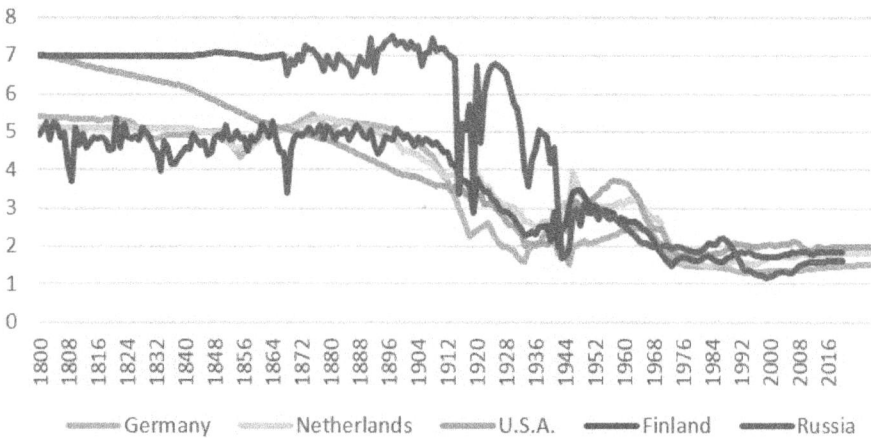

Germany ⸻ Netherlands ⸻ U.S.A. ⸻ Finland ⸻ Russia

Gender Equality

Gender Equality discussions enter into daycare discussion as they have in Germany. Most will agree that Gender Inequality becomes a big problem whenever these policies are misused to:

- Shame women away from raising their own children at home should they wish
- Risk family pensions of $1.2 million to $1.8 million as 20-year working-dads are replaced in socially-irresponsible and even serpentine efforts by major businesses to by-pass pensions by hiring women; or
- Force families into a dual-income trap. With Canadian families at now 76% Dual Income Families, the realities of a dual income trap cannot be ignored and adversely impact birthrates as well.

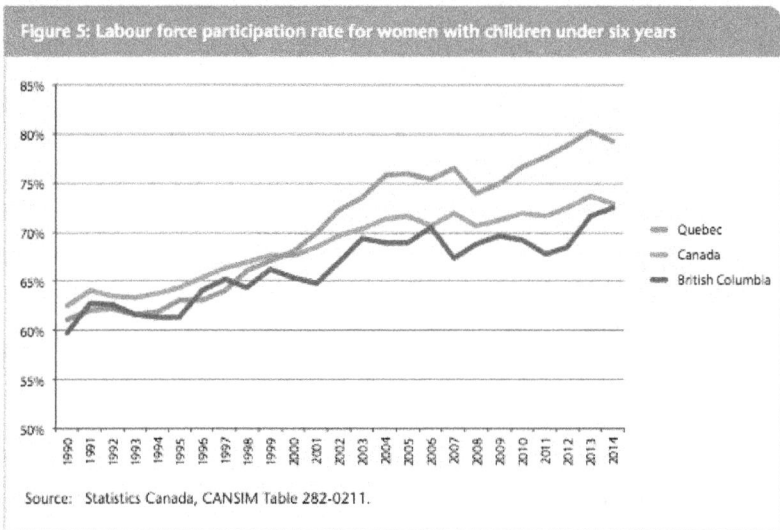

Figure 5: Labour force participation rate for women with children under six years

Source: Statistics Canada, CANSIM Table 282-0211.

Improving Fertility Rates by providing a Good Life

In the end, the biggest increases in fertility resulted from a Good Life in a Spring and Summer Economy; an Economic Phase that easily afforded the things a family needed with a single family income.

Immigration for Humanitarian Reasons

Immigration Author and Journalist Roy Beck put together a colorful presentation using Gumballs to represent Immigration Data in 2010. View this video yourself on YouTube at https://www.youtube.com/watch?v=LPjzfGChGlE (Beck, 2010).

Using statistics from the World Bank and U.S. Census Bureau, Mr. Beck proves with certainty that our first priority has to be to help impoverished people of the world in their own countries. Immigration for Humanitarian Purposes is an ineffective plan that steals away the best and brightest of countries that need agents of change at home who can move their communities forward with priority.

Immigration for Skilled Labor

Immigration for Skilled Labor is essentially the socially irresponsible practice of offshoring engineering. Often the imported skilled workers are invited due to lower salary expectations and then they will offshore work to remote teams in his or her homeland where he can funnel jobs and take a percentage as well.

When engineers graduate from advanced computing programs in Canada, they immediately head abroad realizing that the local skilled job marketplace is saturated with Offshore Engineering created by a complete lack of offshoring controls.

The social costs of immigration for skilled labor is tremendous.

Immigration for Unskilled Labor

This is a business practice that routinely externalizes its social costs. Whether for field workers or for nannies applying for families to join them, the social costs can be tremendous for what is largely an illegal immigration practice. If ever there was an easy business case to make, the automation of sustainable local food manufacturing and distribution would surely cost just a fraction of the social costs realized by managing the many and divisive social problems created by the immigration of unskilled labor.

Protecting Culture

Steel yourself for immigration policy discussions that protect culture because these discussions include topics such as intermarriage, immigrant percentage maximums in communities, and topics that would make a staunch liberal squeamish. The alternative to having these frank conversations, however, is to squander, blend, or diminish your culture. This makes these discussions very important to have openly and honestly.

Culture is a very important component of every country. Economies are influenced by a broad number of discussions as well. Transition Economics applies both scientific method and statistics to correcting the problems in our cyclic economies so that we make the correct policy decisions at the appropriate time. If there is no case for Immigration as a tool of Economic Growth by Scientific Method, Policy makers should be resistant to Immigration and focus on strengthening culture instead.

Chapter 9

\-

Energy Policy

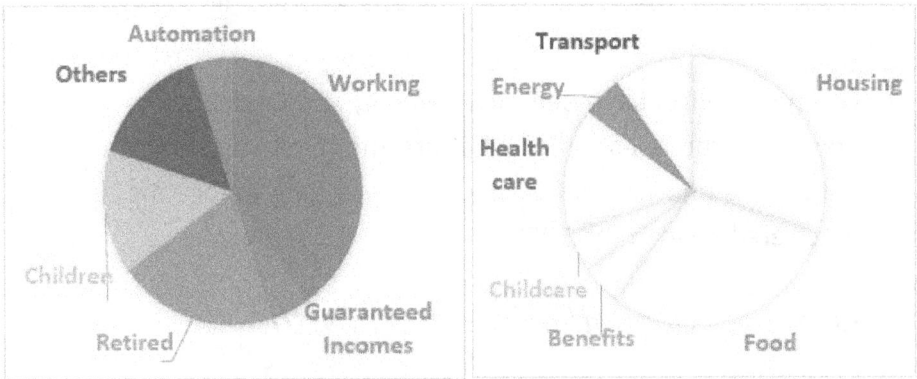

Few discussions will have a more positive impact on any society than the projects that create clean and **abundant** energy.

- Prosperity Depends on Energy
- Prosperity stabilizes population
- Therefore, Energy can stabilize Population worldwide too (Hargraves, 2016) (Slides 5 & 6)

Note that I use the word "Abundant" and not "Conservation" here. Energy Conservation does stop consumption growth and we do not want prosperity to be scarce either. Energy creates Clean Water and Food, Energy drives Prosperity, and Energy is the cornerstone to building a Good Life for everyone.

Fortunately, technologies exist to give us the safe, clean, inexpensive, full-time energy that we need in perpetuity today – contrary to the messages that are more often communicated to us in the media.

It is fundamentally important, therefore, to endorse only the science that makes inexpensive, abundant energy available to us. All other sources energy should always take a distant back seat – this is especially important in a K-Wave Winter as we have things today.

And so what of the Global Warming and Carbon Tax debacles that rage on globally?

Environmentalists have been guessing at, and Engineers have been working on, the question of what are the most sustainable energy technologies and trends for society - since long before the nuclear reactor era began in the 1950s.

CO^2 is the Foundation of Life on Earth

CO^2 (Carbon Dioxide) is the foundation of life on this planet; plants need CO^2 to live and globally we are at the lowest levels of CO^2 in our planet's long history as well. Contrary to Al Gore's message in 2006's "An Inconvenient Truth", CO^2 does not drive global warming - rather it's warming that drives CO^2; the other way around - and the varying cyclic tilts of the earth in relation to the sun have more to do with global warming than does Combustion.

CO^2, therefore, is far from the nemesis that it is made out to be. What we don't need, however, are the toxics that fossil fuels also set into the air during combustion. Clean CO^2 is just fine and - according to the science, there may well come a day, perhaps a million years from now, when we will have to generate Carbon in our air artificially in order to continue to live on this planet. See https://youtu.be/5Smhn1gL6Xg (Moore, 2016) for more.

New Energy Poverty and Legal Recourses

Energy Poverty is commonly discussed as a major problem in developing nations where electricity service is scarce or unavailable. The correlation between Energy and Prosperity is well understood and well documented, yet in the G20 and other developed nations, a New Energy Poverty is emerging alongside growing unemployment, poor safety-nets and rising energy cost.

During the past sixty-years, scientists and engineers have routinely been forced to take a back seat to sponsors of Wind, Solar, Fossil Fuels, Uranium Nuclear Power Plants, and other finance-driven energy sponsors whose solutions hardly qualified as our strategic best next-steps in energy.

As a direct consequence, many G7 countries live in the shadow of a New Energy Poverty created by five-year-term politicians authorizing many 25-year financial procurement contracts totaling billions of dollars in inappropriate part-time energy spending.

Examples of New Energy Poverty are found in the U.K. where energy poverty kills 24,000 people every winter now; Spain reports 4,200 deaths each year. People turn their heat down to low because they can't afford it and they die in the night; highest at risk groups include rural citizens, children, the elderly and the poor.

Germany and Ontario, Canada, where Wind and Solar spending has created 100% increases in electricity costs in the last ten-years, experience Energy Poverty now as well (Bourbeau, 2016). Fully 800,000 Germans have had their power cut off because they can no longer afford it. (Clemente, 2014)(HUTZLER, 2014)

The case for legal accountability in politically-driven or financially-motivated decisions that have already been made; like decisions to invest billions in 25-year part-time energy infrastructure contracts, is just beginning. A small handful of benefactors won lucrative lending contracts and generation contracts at the very great expense of society - but defenders of energy poverty are certain to be out in full-force as well. (Kerr, 2016)

Carbon taxes too, will make power generation less profitable for many power generators. This meant that the Alberta Government in Canada had to move in 2016 to change PPAs (Power Purchase Agreements) to ensure that its power continued in the face of shrinking financial rewards now. By the present rules, power generators have the option to terminate Alberta's power if profitability drops. Alberta had two choices – to make this change, or to pay the Federal Government's New Carbon Tax on behalf of its power generators.

Similar to Tax Avoidance clean-up discussions in Chapter 11, the streamlining of legal processes needed to correct the Energy Contracts that led to Energy Poverty, is an important first step in ensuring that your country can reset and realize renewed spending power once again.

Full-Time Power Generation

The Future of Energy is Thorium 6th TEA Conference Attendees

So, let's take a look at what are the more promising, sustainable sources of energy that can carry us all most easily into the next cycle of clean, inexpensive, abundant and sustainable power.

Our power generation options can be categorized by efficiency, cost, safety, and by full-time vs part-time availability. Obviously, the aim here is to identify and adopt the most reliable, inexpensive, and safest full-time energy sources so as to ensure energy abundance and avoid Energy Poverty.

Geo-Thermal Electricity
Low-Emissions, Usually cheapest, Renewable, Concentrated

Whenever you can dig down into the earth to heat a sufficient amount of water to a sufficient temperature, you can run a city on the energy created. How is this possible? I will take you back to grade One Geography class: You might recall that our planet is a naturally-occurring Thorium Nuclear Reactor with a molten core, and so the deeper you drill, the hotter it gets.

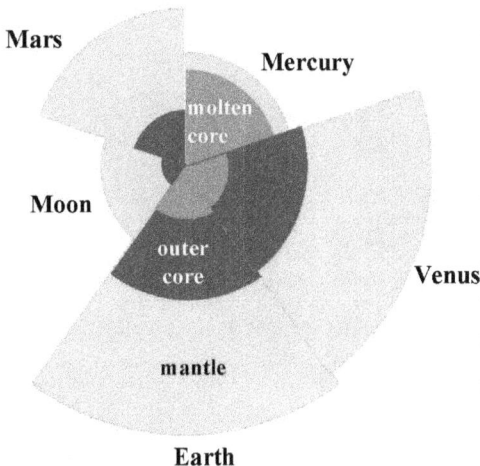

The Nuclear Reactions below our planet's surface create both tremendous heat, and the strong electro-magnetic fields that prevent our planet's atmosphere from being blown away as they have on Mars. Like our moon, Mars has no molten core and, therefore, it has a much less powerful magnetosphere.

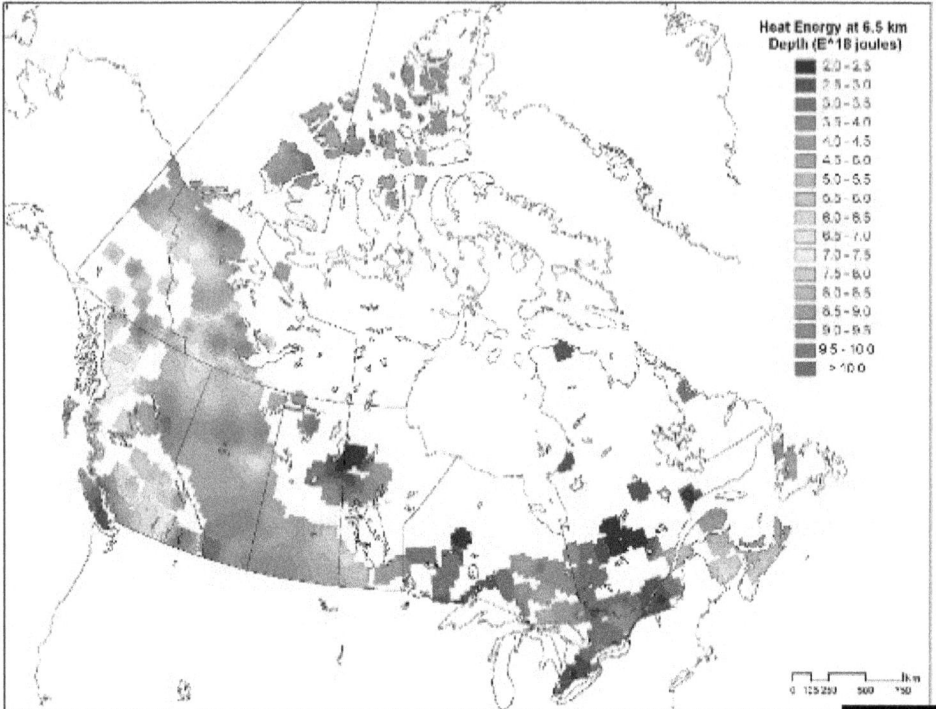

(Lopoukhine, 2014)

Geothermal Energy is abundant, clean, renewable and can be generated almost anywhere. The map above shows the heat energy of Canada at 6.5 kms below surface.

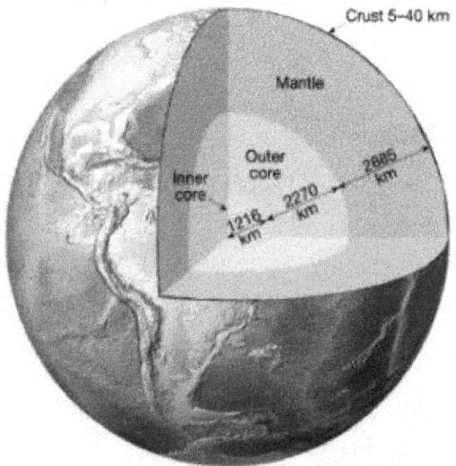

The deepest bore-hole in the world is in Kola, Russia at 12 kms (7.5 miles) deep. The Earth's center is 6,400 kms (4,000 miles) so this barely scratches the surface and probably does not extend through half of the distance to the earth's mantle. Temperatures at the bottom of Kola are 180 degrees Celsius (356°F) (Hamilton, n.d.).

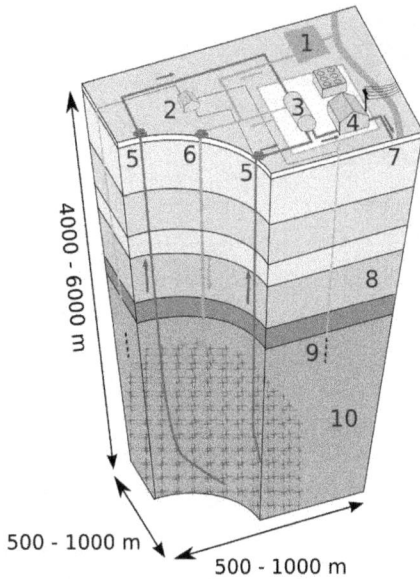

To get more heat, simply dig deeper. Commercial 6-km (18,000 ft) "fracking" wells cost $8 - $12 million to dig, so count on a cost of roughly $20 million to drill a feed and return hole for a geo-thermal plant.

Compare this cost to roughly $2 billion for a Rapid Breeder Uranium Reactor - which heats water to 300°C; or a Thorium Fluoride Salt Reactor – which heats water to 700°C for around $300 million.

With Geo-Thermal, engineers dig holes/bores and then pump heated water from the holes. The geothermally heated water drives a power plant (Wiki, 2016).

In 2015, there were 18,500 Geo-Thermal Power Plants Worldwide, almost double the number from 2010. Canada has no Geo-Thermal Plants in 2016 despite several local companies building and maintaining geo-thermal plants for other countries.

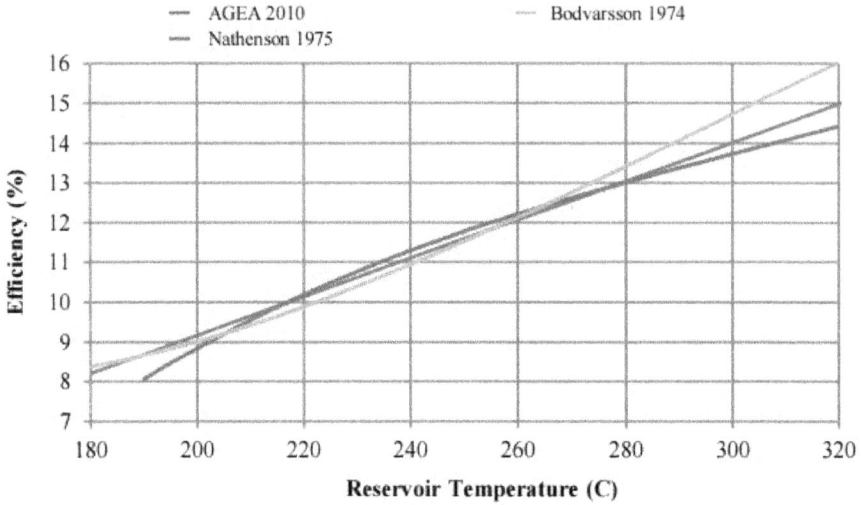

Efficiency (%)

Reservoir Temperature (C)

The chart above shows that the efficiency of Geo-Thermal plants are widely dependent on the heat of the water extracted. If water temperature is low, efficiency can be low as well. If water temperature is higher, efficiencies of 20% and more are possible. The Unit Cost of Geothermal in New Zealand is 20% shown below in Green with boxes lower than High-CO2 alternatives of Coal and Natural Gas (CCGT).

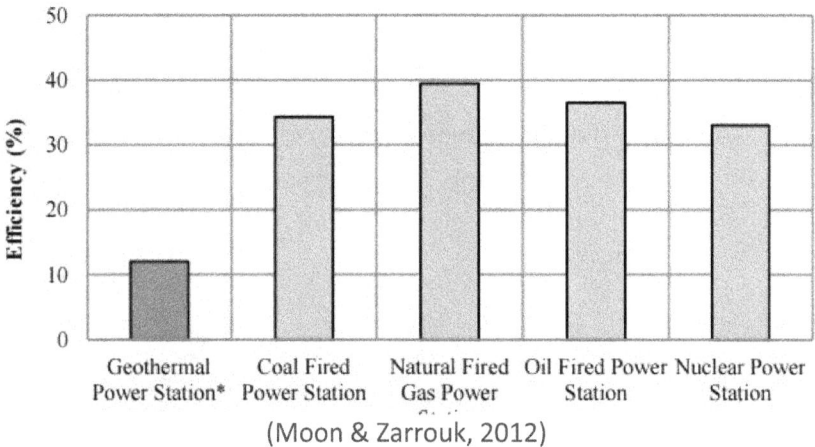

Efficiency (%)

| Geothermal Power Station* | Coal Fired Power Station | Natural Fired Gas Power | Oil Fired Power Station | Nuclear Power Station |

(Moon & Zarrouk, 2012)

Unit Costs Of Electricity Generation 1989-2005

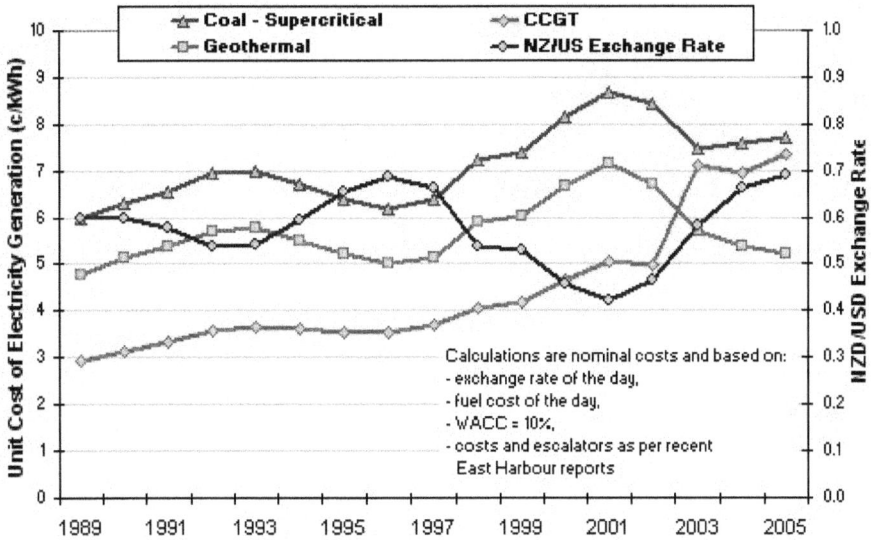

Legend:
- Coal - Supercritical
- CCGT
- Geothermal
- NZ/US Exchange Rate

Y-axis (left): Unit Cost of Electricity Generation (c/kWh)
Y-axis (right): NZD/USD Exchange Rate

Calculations are nominal costs and based on:
- exchange rate of the day,
- fuel cost of the day,
- WACC = 10%,
- costs and escalators as per recent East Harbour reports

(Ministry of Economic Development, n.d.)

In countries where Natural Gas is abundant and cheap, often a Carbon Tax makes the difference between Geothermal being profitable and very profitable.

Water and Steam are most often used to generate electricity in turbine-driven power plants because steam expands very rapidly to one-thousand-times the volume of water. Pressurized Water at 300 degrees takes a very large turbine (perhaps the size of a high-school classroom) and a relatively large volume of water to generate. Water heated to 700 degrees under pressure however, takes far less water and a much, much smaller turbine to extract more electrical energy. Lava and molten rock reaches 700 to 1200 degrees Celsius (1,292 to 2,192 degrees Fahrenheit) and so stable but active volcano ranges like the one in Hawaii, create highly economic geo-thermal power plants – but most other locations can furnish heat with the right plant.

Hydro Electric

Low-Emissions, Very High Efficiency, Concentrated, Renewable

Hydro (Water) Turbines operate at very high efficiencies of 85% and can work to create clean electricity for decades. Hydro can require very expensive generating station startup costs – including the construction of dams and sometime massive reservoirs. Installation will tend to consume a lot of CO_2, but once built will operate with very low emissions and with few interruptions.

Nuclear Fission - Thorium Reactors

Low-Emissions, Non-renewable, Concentrated Energy output

When you want clean reliable energy and you want it in close proximity to large populations where geothermal is marginal, cheap, plentiful, 30% Efficient Thorium Nuclear Reactors fit the bill.

Unlike our basic training, there are many different possible types of nuclear reactors; almost as many as there are models of cars today. Thorium Reactors were designed at the same time and place as our far more expensive Rapid Breeder Uranium Reactors, in the Oak Ridge National Laboratories near Nashville, Tennessee, U.S.A. in the mid-1950s and 1960s. A Thorium Molten Salt Reactor (fed with Uranium oddly, but designed for Thorium) ran for five-years alongside a Rapid Breeder Uranium Reactor. The Director of the U.S. Nuclear Power Research Program stated very clearly that Thorium was the better choice for civilian power needs; Thorium was better for reasons of safety, economy, reliable power production, and somewhat more responsible radioactive waste management.

Energy Generation Comparison

*Each ounce of thorium can produce $14,000 - 24,000 of electricity (at $0.04-0.07/kW*hr)

230 train cars (25,000 MT) of bituminous coal or,
600 train cars (66,000 MT) of brown coal,
(Source: World Coal Institute)

6 kg of thorium metal in a liquid-fluoride reactor has the energy equivalent (66,000 MW*hr electrical*)

or, 440 million cubic feet of natural gas (15% of a 125,000 cubic meter LNG tanker),

✓ **Low CO2 Impact**

✓ **Consumes Plutonium & Radio Active Waste**

✓ **Reduced quantity and shorter duration for storage of hazardous waste**

or, 300 kg of enriched (3%) uranium in a pressurized water reactor.

("Thorium Energy Generation," n.d.)

As the slide above explains, a 6 kg nodule of Thorium in a liquid-fluoride reactor has the energy of:

- 230 train cars of Bituminous Coal
- 600 train cars of Brown Coal
- 440 cubic feet of natural gas (that's 15% of a 125,000 cubic meter LNG tanker)
- 300 kg of enriched (3%) Uranium in a Pressurized Water Reactor

For reasons of reliability (Rapid Breeders didn't stop – which becomes a safety concern) and weaponized plutonium production (important through the cold-war nuclear build up years), U.S. President Richard Nixon funded the adoption of Rapid Breeder Uranium Reactors - and Thorium Reactor Research was halted.

Search in the bibliography document for "Excusable mistake" to read an explanation for why the Thorium Reactor program was halted (Moir & Teller, 2004).

To understand why today's Nuclear Industry defends its 470 rapid breeder uranium reactors vigorously - with little interest in Thorium, consider the investment and revenue that reactor manufacturers, security services, and weapons manufacturers all earn from this status quo.

A GE (General Electric) or Phillips reactor must be fed a specific blended ultra-high-profit fuel pellet from the manufacturer for the life of the Reactor; this is not a requirement nor revenue stream for Thorium Reactor manufacturers.

Like an ink-jet printer, Reactors are built as a loss leader to secure lucrative long term fueling contracts. I imagine that an upstart employee might be risking their position by making mention of considering a shift away from Uranium Reactors.

China, India, France and the U.S., have begun to design and build Thorium Reactors with an estimate of 2030 for large-scale electricity production.

India's Advanced Heavy Water Reactor (AHWR) Designs are based on improvements to Thorium designs from the 1960s – and, with India sitting on the world's largest deposits of Thorium, they strongly prefer this option to replace their country's inefficient and air polluting Coal Power Plant Infrastructure (IANS, 2016).

Once successful, the worry becomes that we in the West may very shortly have to buy, or license under-patent, our own reactor technology. This sounds like a considerable opportunity and wake up call for both Government and the Nuclear Industry.

Construction costs for Liquid Fluoride Thorium Reactors are much lower – approximately $200 million, than for Rapid Breeder Uranium Reactors that can run into the several billions of dollars. Spent thorium fuel is less voluminous and has a much shorter storage and radio-active half-life than Uranium.

Thorium Reactions require constant "feeding" of fuel and all reactions stop immediately as soon as power fails. Uranium Reactors must have cooling pumps operational in order to avoid melting down - as was seen in Fukushima, Japan in 2011.

Fusion - Cold and Hot
Low-Emissions, Inexpensive Cold, Expensive Hot, Concentrated

Clean, safe energy forever. Cold Fusion's name has changed to LENR (Low-Energy Nuclear Reactions) recently; I suspect the reason, to be brutally honest, is to ease the scientific peer-reviewing community's embarrassment at having irresponsibly ignored and even snubbed important development and research into Cold Fusion since Doctors Pons and Fleishmann first announced its discovery in 1989.

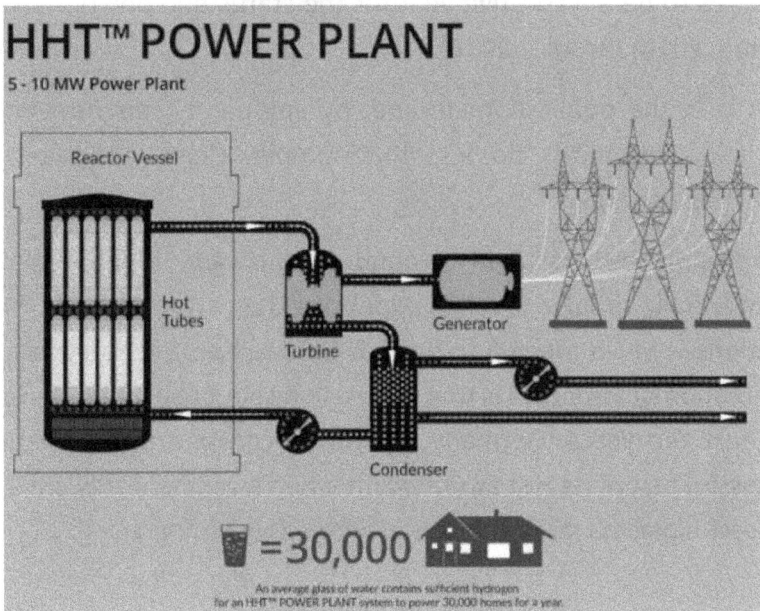

HHT™ POWER PLANT
5 - 10 MW Power Plant

Reactor Vessel

Hot Tubes

Turbine

Generator

Condenser

🥛 =30,000 🏠

An average glass of water contains sufficient hydrogen
for an HHT™ POWER PLANT system to power 30,000 homes for a year.

This slide from Brillouin Energy explains that there is enough energy in the hydrogen of a glass of water to power 30,000 homes. Real world measurements on how concentrated are Cold Fusion reactions have yet to be publicly announced but clearly there is fantastic potential. The reason for the excitement is that Cold Fusion appears to work as a power amplifier, taking one unit of power and returning six to ten just like it – and we are still in early days.

Nuclear Fusion does not create radioactive waste, as does Nuclear Fission. Of the two, Nuclear Fission has been far easier to make work reliably than has Fusion.

If there was ever a case to say that money is a very bad thing; or that academia's peer-review protocols are failed as well, surely Cold Fusion's bungled reputation, legal, patent and financial encumbrances surrounding the development and rapid rollout of safe Cold Fusion Power Plants showcase both.

With too many accredited scientific voices, governments, and major companies pouring money into LENR to ignore in 2016, 2017 promises to be a disruptive year for the status quo power industry. (Acland, 2016) (Brooks, 2016)

LENR is in the public domain and, by any name, this new energy technology promises no less than simple, clean, abundant and sustainable energy.

Hot Fusion too is right around the corner. Cold Fusion is exponentially simpler and less expensive than "Hot" Nuclear Fusion reactions – which are still to be proven in full-production trials. The expectation of scientists is that Hot Fusion should be available within the next ten years. Germany recently succeeded in completing a successful test of its Hot Fusion plant when it momentarily created a successful plasma stream in a trial within this past year.

Plasma, the fourth state of matter, streams out of a Hot Fusion reactor at temperatures in the billions of degrees Celsius; a temperature far too hot to be contained by anything other than very strong magnetic fields.

Combustion
High-Emissions; Reliable, Concentrated

Combustion is one of the least efficient means of extracting energy from matter. Our total life-time energy needs would require us to combust enough firewood to fill a gymnasium. In comparison, the fission of Thorium, could supply that same amount of energy very safely with a Billiard-ball-sized amount of readily available rare earth.

- **Gasoline** combusts with 15% Efficiency
- **Diesel** combusts with 30% efficiency – this is the highest efficiency of any combustible fuel.
- **Natural Gas** – 5% to 10% efficient
- **Fuel Oil** – 5% to 20%
- **Coal** – 15% to 60%
- **Clean Coal** – a research-only fuel alternative that is **not deemed practical for production use** anywhere in the world today.
- **Clean Fuels** – 30% Efficient (see Clean Fuels below)

("Combustion Efficiency and Excess Air," n.d.)

Combustible Fuels can be detonated in Generators to generate electricity, or can be burned to convert water to steam for collection by turbines.

The Catalytic Converter was added to gasoline cars as an emissions necessity in the 1970s. Its function is to re-burn the gasoline that is missed during combustion. Modern Diesel engines run lean and at much higher fuel injection pressures until they do not have to re-burn missed fuel. Instead of a catalytic converter, diesel cars have a filter that addresses the NOX emissions of fossil-fuel. So, not only is combustion inefficient, gasoline vehicles are inefficient at combusting gasoline as well.

Incineration and Plasma – Energy from Waste
Medium to Low Emissions; Reliable, Concentrated

The largest nuclear warships in the world, the USS Nimitz Class Aircraft Carriers were designed in 1972 and are due to be replaced by a new Gerald Ford Class in 2017. These ships are small cities that desalinate water, cook, run heavy equipment and hydraulics, hi-tech systems, and propel this five-football-field-sized watercraft 35-knots (55 km/hr) in sustained operation for months at sea with a crew of 6,000 via just two nuclear reactors. The ship's reactors need core replacements only every 25 years – so any notion that we have an energy crisis is bollocks – as the Brits say.

Technology that is deemed worthy of being on one of these marvels of technology can be counted among the best in the world. Waste from these super-ships could never be stored and so instead, it is converted to plasma and then to recyclable glass.

Plasma is the fourth state of matter; matter begins as a solid, then a liquid, then a gas, and then finally, at three-thousand to nine-trillion degrees Fahrenheit, all matter turns into ionized gas or "Plasma".

Plasma's temperatures can exceed the heat of even nuclear reactions; hotter than the sun itself. Measuring these temperatures in Fahrenheit is like measuring the galaxy in feet. Even "cold plasma" creates a lava waste byproduct that is so hot that it is mechanically explosive in the presence of water. So, instead, aircraft carriers convert their waste to recyclable glass via a Cold Plasma technology – and so should we too.

Plasma and other waste incineration technologies take our garbage, and landfills, and convert waste into heat and power with 70% to 80% efficiency and very low pollution and emissions. Sweden, Denmark and many other nations use this process with the proviso that the balance between waste-burning and waste generation is managed well.

Plasma and conventional incineration are a good energy generation and waste management pairing that promise to life-cycle-manage a majority of produced material turned waste as well.

Solar Thermal Tower
Low-Emissions, Efficient, Concentrated, Renewable

Suitable for high-sun regions, concentrated, reflected sunlight is used to superheat water or molten salts to temperatures of 550 degrees Celsius.

$5.27 cents per Kwh

The molten salts method retains heat for power generation when the sun is not shining but it also requires a morning startup procedure that gets the plant up to operating temperature using alternate fuel sources. In this configuration, the molten salts heat water into steam that drives Steam Turbines.

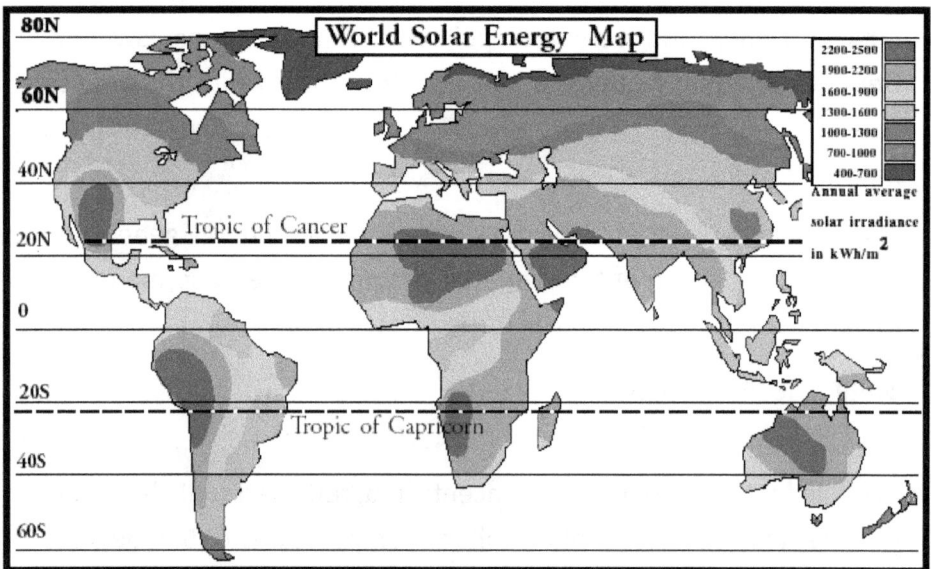

World Solar Energy Map

Annual average
2200-2500
1900-2200
1600-1900
1300-1600
1000-1300
700-1000
400-700

Annual average solar irradiance in kWh/m^2

http://www.inforse.org/europe/dieret/Solar/solar.html

The design does unfortunately, kill bird-life as the air at the tower is superheated and birds flying into the pond-like mirrors, quite literally burst into flame at a rate of one every two minutes at times. ("Solar Thermal Tower," n.d.)

Nuclear Fission - Rapid Breeder Uranium
Low-Emissions, Reliable, Least Safe, Expensive, Concentrated

Very expensive to build and operate; not appropriate in close proximity to very large populations; security of facilities and spent fuel is also very expensive and the risk of melt-down and radioactive contamination exists although on only three occasions.

Cumulative Reactor Years of Operation

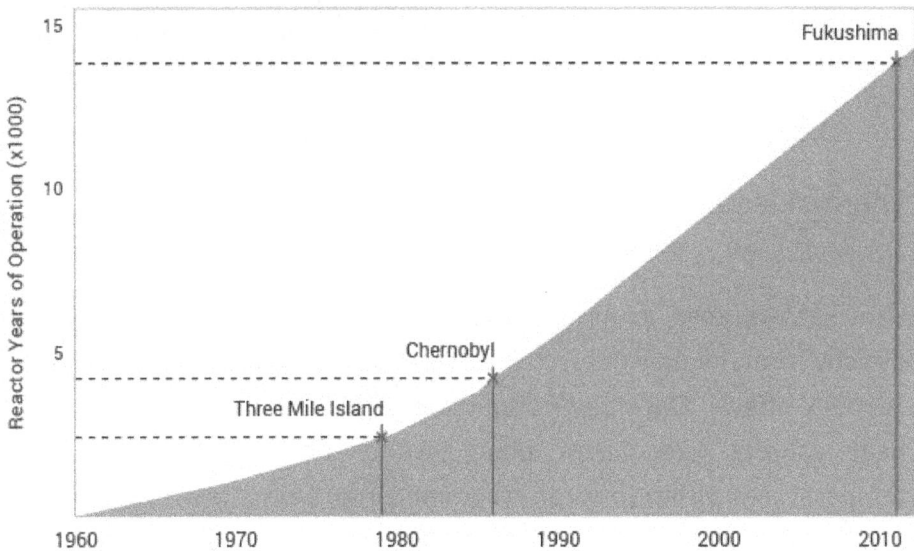

("Safety of Nuclear Reactors - World Nuclear Association," 2016)

Nuclear fission remains a heavy-lifter in clean power generation throughout the world. There are 470 of this type of Nuclear Power Plants in operation. Fukushima's accident was the first meltdown in 25 years – and Uranium reactors can never explode like an atomic bomb either. Explosives require much high levels of enrichment than the 5% fuel used in reactors.

Russia's brilliant new floating nuclear fission reactor ships are another mobile power-generating option based on a proven 50-year icebreaker design. This solution is designed to pull up beside major cities, in China and elsewhere, and supply mobile power on demand (Diggs, 2015) (OKBM, n.d.)

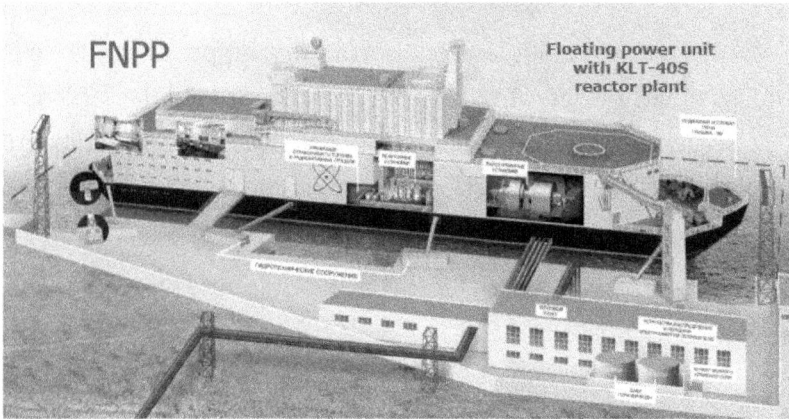

ThermoElectric

Low-Emissions; 8% efficient, Clean, Dilute

Uses Heat-sources, anytime of the day or night, to create electricity directly from the flow of electrons across semi-conductors (using the Seebeck effect). Once semiconductors are attached or exposed to heat sources like steam pipes, wood stoves, or even the temperatures within your car in summertime, heat is converted into electricity.

Replacing the alternator in a car with a thermoelectric exhaust pipe lining, is one example application. TECTEG Manufacturing, is working with McMaster University to produce high amperage cells for high-temperature environments. Its devices are engineered to deliver 100-200 amperes (enough electricity to meet the peak needs of a modern home). (Klein, 2014)

See https://www.youtube.com/watch?v=YhynSkFIJOs .

Part-time Energy Production

Part-time renewable energy sources are often dilute and too weak to warrant heavy investment so energy advisory committees that recommend these should be discounted heavily.

In the Energy Collectors section below, we discusses battery and other storage collectors that may one day make part-time energy of use, but currently there are no cost effective energy storage systems that can make part-time energy storage a consideration.

Part-time energy technologies include:

Solar Energy Cells

Low-Emissions, Renewable, Dilute, Unreliable, Expensive

Photovoltaics continue to mature. The drawback with Solar is that the sun is a weak energy source, unreliable and can only generate energy during the day - and then an energy-storage battery grid is needed. The most efficient photovoltaic energy conversion panels can still only convert 46% of the sun's energy - with affordable commercial panels at 15%.

The other main problem with Solar is the sun is a relatively weak, dilute, energy source.

Germany leads the world in investment in Solar and Wind and this fact has forced them to also increase their dependency on Coal. Electricity rates have had to climb so high as to lead many citizens into Energy Poverty.

Wind Power

Low-Emissions, Expensive, Dilute, Unreliable, Renewable

In addition to being one of the most expensive energy sources, wind is a weak and unreliable energy source as well. Wind power generators operate at efficiencies of 40% but it takes thousands of multi-million dollar fans to generate a significant amount unpredictable energy. Wind systems consume quite a lot of CO^2 in their manufacture and installation, but then run with no emissions thereafter. Maintenance is an ongoing expense and energy may not be available to the power grid when demand requires it.

One very concerning worry in Canada has been the fact that surplus power generated in off-peak times (times without local demand) by wind-farms has had to be sold to other neighboring governments at a lower cost than its production cost. With Hydro (Water) Turbines and other generators, power output can be "feathered" or steamed-off (adjusted up or down) as needed to make power available as needed at all times and not more at undesirable times.

Wave Power

Low-Emissions, Expensive, Dilute, Unreliable, Renewable

Although promising to be sure - due to the weight of water, wave farms are unproven as a source of cost-effective, reliable power at the time of this writing. According to Wikipedia, most investments in wave farms have stopped within just months of initial operation. Look for updates to this report on our website at csq1.org.

Energy Conversion

Energy converters include steam and gas turbines primarily:

Steam Turbine

Steam Turbine is used for 90% of the Energy Generation today - Water is heated under pressure to permit Steam Turbine blades to capture steam as it expands and turn that energy into electricity. Steam expands to one-thousand-times the volume of water. 300

degree Celsius steam needs a very large turbine but 700 degree Celsius needs much smaller turbines and converts the energy more efficiently as well.

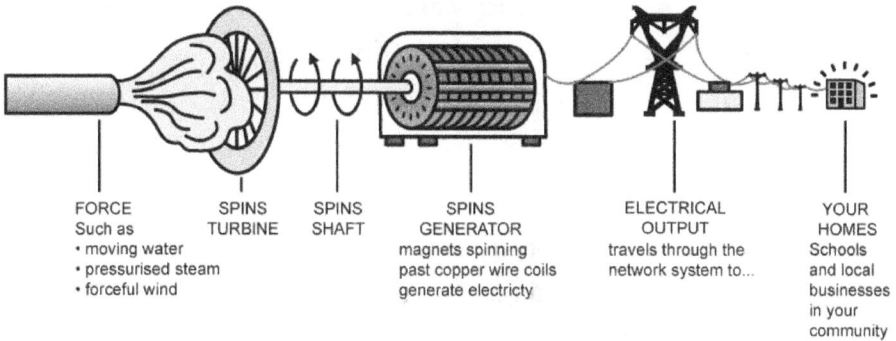

FORCE	SPINS	SPINS	SPINS	ELECTRICAL	YOUR
Such as	TURBINE	SHAFT	GENERATOR	OUTPUT	HOMES
• moving water			magnets spinning	travels through the	Schools
• pressurised steam			past copper wire coils	network system to...	and local
• forceful wind			generate electricty		businesses in your community

Gas Turbines

Air is used instead of Water in a Gas Turbine. "Air flows through a compressor that brings it to higher pressure. Energy is then added by spraying fuel into the air and igniting it so the combustion generates a high-temperature flow. This high-temperature high-pressure gas enters a turbine, where it expands down to the exhaust pressure, producing a shaft work output in the process. Gas turbines are used to power aircraft, trains, ships, electrical generators, and tanks " ("Gas Turbines," n.d.).

Engines - on Earth and in Space

Engines and generators/alternators convert fuels, by burning or reaction, to electrical or mechanical energy here within earth's atmosphere.

In Space, NASA has confirmed this fall that a Radio Frequency Resonant ElectroMagnetic Cavity "EmDrive", actually does appear to create thrust from microwave photons and quantum vacuum particle fluctuations; thrust from energy alone - without fuel.

Thrust in a vacuum with no fuel propellant is what Star Trek called an Impulse Drive; these were the smaller engines on the back of the saucer – and not the long tube-like warp drives. If EmDrive works - it would reduce the 414 day trip to Mars down to about 70 days and the moon would be a short four-hour drive away. By using solar power, the drive could theoretically motor about the cosmos indefinitely. (Knapton, 2015)

Superconducting EmDrives, the next generation, promise cheap and viable flying cars and this is pretty amazing research that we are not getting to spend the time and resources as needed now because we do not have our act straight here on planet earth.

An EmDrive does not expel anything. As this is contrary to Newton's third law, our scientific community want to research pragmatically before publishing wild claims. Once an energy-based propulsion system is working and proven, it will clearly have considerable impact on travel and exploration in the future.

Instead of investing in weaponry and unsustainable monetary policies, investing in Livingry – investing in automation projects like #WPProjects – permits our best and brightest engineers to automate our needs, build sustainable Good Lives easily, and frees us to advance incredible research projects like these.

Energy Collectors

Rapid Charge Battery Systems

Today's best electric cars, the Tesla is an example, require the installation of a special charging bay in your garage and then it can take up to nine-and-a-half hours of charge time to give your vehicle a 245 mile (394 km) range of travel. The Tesla's 'S' model has a 300-mile range but often 150 miles (241 km) is the max range if you do not want to be careful to drive it for optimal battery length.

Tesla fast-refilling stations – called Superchargers - can recharge up to 50% of the car within twenty minutes and are designed to move you along from a gas station during a long trip. On a 240 volt system (North America runs on a 120v standard), it takes one hour to charge for each 30 miles – therefore 9.5 hours for a full 300-mile charge; and on a standard 110v system, one hour of charge is required for every five miles or fifty-two hours to charge fully.

These battery charging overheads keep electric cars constrained to daily city and light highway use primarily, and then gas and diesel vehicles meet our long-haul transportation needs.

Battery powered cars are multiples more expensive than entry-level gas and diesel cars too; today's Tesla are an $80,000 to $120,000 CAN purchase, and this does not include the additional cost of installing a non-standard 240v charging station in your garage. Lithium-Ion Batteries too, have a lifespan of just six years and an environmental cost in manufacture and dis. The cost of a new Tesla battery will be between $12,000 and $29,000 U.S. to replace.

Now, to the bigger problem with battery cars; at present, battery powered cars do not save emission pollutions. See https://www.youtube.com/watch?v=17xh_VRrnMU for a full explanation. (PragerU, 2016)

 Some reports have explained that battery cars create more CO_2 than gasoline cars due to their primary reliance on Coal Plants for 13+ hours of charging on a regular basis. If you are running a hybrid car less than 50kms per day, the smaller battery permits solar recharging and creates no CO_2, but much larger batteries, like the ones in the all-battery cars must be plugged into the power grid.

As soon as cost-effective, longer lifespan, faster charge-time batteries can replace current technology, then and only then, will battery-powered car become a superior alternative to gas and perhaps even diesel vehicles too.

Promising Battery Technologies to look forward to, include the Carbon-Polymer direct-charge batteries, Vanadium Redox Flow batteries (G1 VRB) or perhaps Graphene Nanosheets. Direct-charge systems permit direct charging to the atoms of the carbon polymer array instantly. Today, atoms within battery cells must pass charge to neighboring atoms in sequence – requiring many hours to permeate a large pool of battery atoms such as the designs found in a larger battery grid on a battery car today. A direct-charge system promises to drop charge times down to perhaps 15 minutes; or something comparable to a refill of fuel at a refilling station. I had heard that these batteries might be available in 2016, but so far there have been no announcement.

Flywheel Kinetic Energy Management Systems

Based on an idea as old as a potter's wheels, modern industrial flywheels provide data centers and industrial lines with uninterruptable power supplies based on only the momentum of a turning weight. Using mechanical or magnetic bearings (to reduce friction), and perhaps one day superconducting bearings, flywheels provide an environmentally friendly power backup that can last for decades almost maintenance-free with efficiencies as high as 90%.

Super Capacitors and Ultra Capacitors

Supercapacitors seem poised to shortly make life a whole lot more interesting. A cell phone that charges in seconds, or a battery-powered car that recharges in minutes as opposed to 30 hours – and supercapacitors don't wear out so this is really big news whenever it becomes available.

Before there were batteries, there were capacitors; quick charging and able to cycle for 10-years without degrading, these static-charge devices only hold small charges for short periods – not long enough to compete with batteries certainly.

Today's super capacitors can hold hundreds of times the energy that the old capacitor could until Super and Ultracapacitors now promise to outperform batteries - but they are more expensive as well. Li-Ion batteries improve by 10% annually and supercapacitors are still playing catchup albeit in leaps and bounds.

This makes supercapacitors very well purposed to recovering brake energy on vehicles and making that energy available for use on board a bus, for one example. Super Capacitors do not, however, appear to be able to cost-effectively turn part-time energy, into cost effective energy grids in the near future unfortunately. In time however, it actually seems inevitable.

Nuclear Diamond Batteries

Now here is a really fun-fact: Our nuclear reactors discard a uranium fuel cell contained within a carbon shell that collects most of its radioactivity at its surface. By applying heat to spent carbon 14 fuel cells, researchers in Britain are harvesting the surface layer of radio-active carbon and turning it into industrial diamonds using low pressure and high heat. These radioactive diamonds are then sealed in non-radioactive diamond until the resulting battery has the radio-activity of a banana and a charge that will only be half-spent in 5700 years.

Perfect for places where batteries can never be replaced, such as in space or in pacemakers, researchers are actually looking for your contributions and ideas for how to best use these batteries at #diamondbattery on twitter.

The invention of nuclear batteries promises to turn the long-term problem of nuclear waste into a nuclear-powered long-term energy supply. Now just add a cold-fusion 10x "boost", and we have something important and interesting indeed. There are no moving parts in these batteries; simply placing them close to a radioactive source is sufficient to create a charge indefinitely.

Fuels

Fuels are transportable energy that can be used to provide energy for our vehicles and homes. Gases (Natural Gas, Propane, Hydrogen), fluids (gasoline, aviation fuels, kerosene, diesel, etc.), and solids (coal, wood, charcoal, peat, pellets - made from wheat, corn, and rye and other grains). Finally there is uranium, thorium, and even solid-rocket fuels made of aluminum and other components.

Fuels are either combusted or energy is extracted from nuclear reaction - fission or fusion process.

Early on, wood and coal were combusted to boil water and create steam-piston propelled trains and even cars. With the invention of the carburetor in 1876, liquid fuel could be used to combust in large engines directly – and we have used either gaseous (propane or natural gas) or liquid fuels in our cars ever since.

As an aside, an inventor named John Weston is running a 1992 GEO Storm GSI 469 mpg (miles per gallon) on gas fumes directly - with or without a carburetor (Weston, 2016). A little on-line investigation shows that a handful of others seem to keep an Air & Vapor Flow System working pretty well. Similar news of a Pogue Vapor Carburetor that was suppressed in the 1930s by big investors' concern for lost oil profits, has been an urban legend since the 1940s. I will let the reader be the judge but clearly the catalytic converter's role to reburn missed fuel shows a potential for Improvement.

Clean Fuel Puzzle

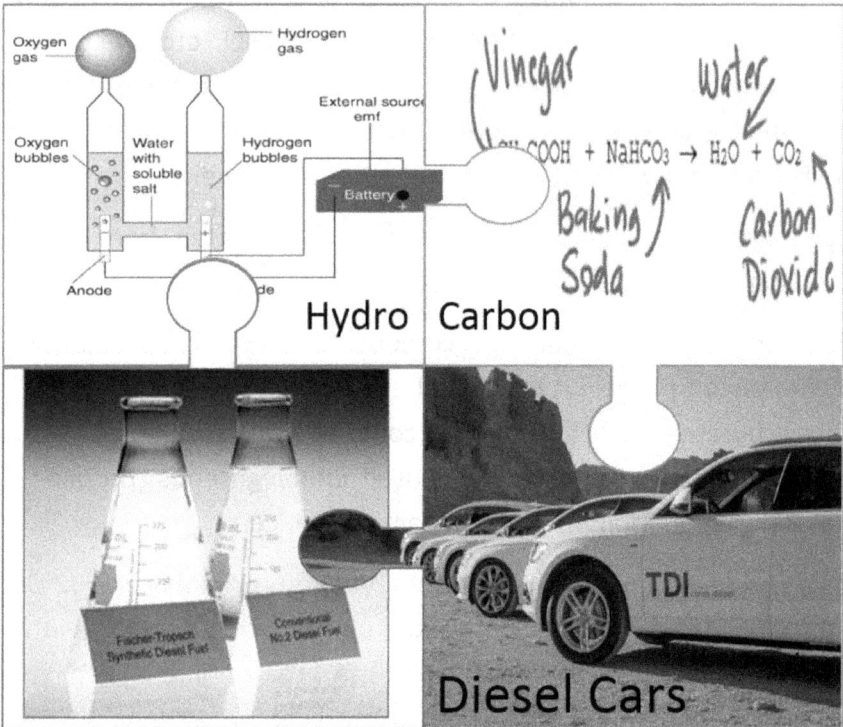

Oxygen gas — Hydrogen gas — External source emf — Oxygen bubbles — Water with soluble salt — Hydrogen bubbles — Battery — Anode — de

Vinegar — Water

$CH_3COOH + NaHCO_3 \rightarrow H_2O + CO_2$

Baking Soda — Carbon Dioxide

Hydro | Carbon

Fischer-Tropsch Synthetic Diesel Fuel — Conventional No.2 Diesel Fuel — TDI

Diesel Cars

Zero-polluting alternatives to combustible fossil-fuels have existed since the Fischer-Tropshe process was first developed to create Paraffin Oil in 1925.

A viable alternative to fossil fuels is far from new technology, and it cannot come soon enough as fossil-fuels are far and away the dirtiest form of fuel that we can combust.

Today, Audi Automotive and parent company Volkswagen, are building cars of the future - as you might expect. You might not also realize that they are manufacturing fuel oils of the future too.

Audi makes crude oil from electrolyzed water (H^2O) and recovered carbon dioxide (CO^2) in a 70% efficient process that creates an ultra-low emission Blue Crude™. (Gray, 2015)

Audi's clean hydrocarbon crude uses the same Fischer-Tropsche process that has been around since the 1920s (Davis, 2015). Its zero-carbon-footprint process makes use of wind energy. Carbon Dioxide sources include simple, safe home recipes like baking soda and vinegar (Calkins, n.d.), CO^2 Air Recapturing, Natural Gas and other common sources.

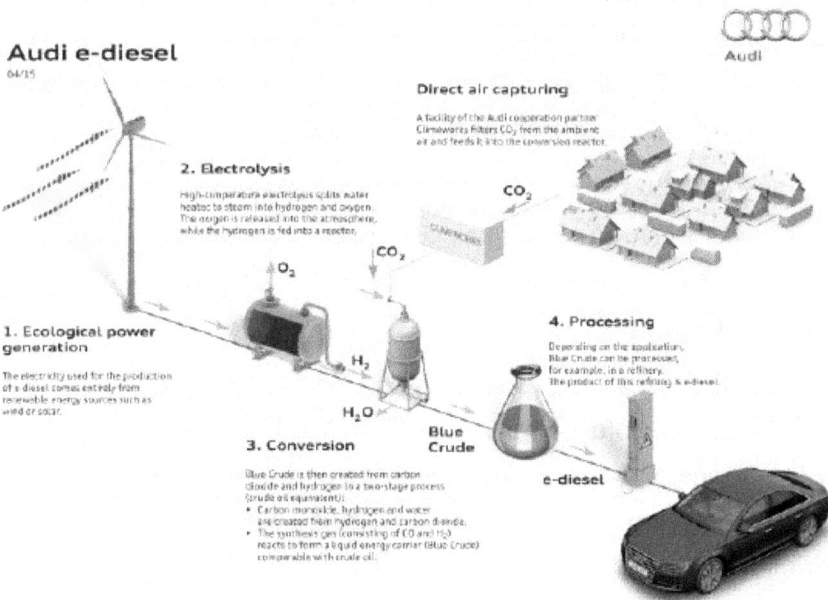

This Clean Crude needs only to be refined to create component diesel fuels, gasoline, kerosene, and aviation fuel as needed, just like a fossil-fuel based crude oil would. You could choose to refine gasoline from this Blue Crude, but the most efficient combusting fuel and engine combination is a diesel-battery hybrid configuration.

Diesel fuel takes less energy to refine from the crude, it has the highest energy recovery of any other combustible fuel source, and even without a readily available 100-mpg (miles per gallon – not a mis-print) hybrid configuration, is almost twice as efficient as a gasoline vehicle at highway speeds.

Audi's President runs this fuel in his A8 and he reports that this fuel makes a car run quieter and with more power too.

The reasons to adopt Blue Crude are compelling. The combustion power of Audi's e-Diesel fuel is greater than that of fossil-fuel diesel, it makes cars run quieter as well, and it is expected to be available to consumers for approximately the same price per liter at retail pumps – equal in cost, or less than, fossil-fuel-based diesel. Blue Crude could be used in our current fuel distribution system easily as well, without expensive modifications – and no pipelines are required as Blue Crude can be manufactured local to demand.

The only waste by-product from manufacturing Blue Crude is oxygen – which might lead to bigger insects and smarter people after much time - but the problem of what to do about all that clean air is a problem for another book.

Assuming that clean fuel additives can be found to guard against solidification in cold temperatures, and other practical storage considerations, I imagine that it might even be possible to create a food-grade version of this product – although, why would you choose to drink it?

Cost is of little consequence when a combination geothermal reactor and nearby Blue Crude refinery could provide a limitless supply of clean burning mobile fuels in the same way that the USS Nimitz Aircraft Carriers desalinate water through electrolysis for a crew of 6,000 every day for the past forty years.

Volkswagen, Audi's parent company, is one of the few companies to bring an affordable diesel car to North America, which is surprising considering Europe's predominant preference for more-efficient Diesel vehicles.

Diesel is Very Important

Diesel fuel, and diesel vehicles, are important because:

1) Diesel fuels made from water and Carbon Dioxide can be fabricated cost effectively in Zero-Carbon-Footprint processes, and burns with Near-Zero Emissions.
2) A Diesel-Hybrid configuration would bring Diesel Vehicles to 100 mpg almost immediately.
3) Gasoline-based cars prevent us from developing cleaner, cost-effective alternatives to fossil-based Crude Oil.
4) Diesel was originally developed to burn Paraffin Oil made from coal and natural gas. This hydrocarbon burns with 50% fewer emissions and Crude Oil was a dirtier alternative that Oil Companies made to work in Diesel engines.
5) Diesel takes less energy to refine, and its higher combustion efficiency takes the same car almost twice as far on the highway over gasoline.
6) Diesel does not dissolve in water making spills and environmental cleanups easier.
7) Diesel is a lubricant that ensures long engine life – where gasoline is "a corrosive" that wears out engines more quickly.
8) Diesel cars last longer, have fewer maintainable parts, lower running costs and set the high-bar for reliability, often continuing to operate for 500,000 to 1,000,000 kilometers and beyond during their service lives (double, and more, than gasoline engines).
9) Diesel fuel detonates through high compression only and is not flammable.
10) One can run a diesel passenger car for 10 hours without stopping as a tank of fuel will often sustain almost 1000 km of highway driving.

11) Replacing all cars with Diesel equivalents would reduce total energy needs by 15% and more overall (depending upon the country).

Defending Diesel Vehicles is Very Important Too

In the early autumn of 2015, Volkswagen was centered out for adjusting their in-car programming to turn off emission controls on their diesel passenger cars. EPA officials claimed that these changes resulted in diesel cars emitting nitrogen as high as ten to forty normal gasoline cars in operation.

A simple reprogramming changed these settings so that emissions were corrected. The EPA's testing of Diesel Vehicle Emissions does not consider the vehicle's greatly improved power and efficiency either. As such, the EPA does not compare apples and apples as it should.

I am assuming that the EPA is credible in their original assertions here too, despite a track record that has come under criticism in numerous cases in past years in regards of technology that promised to detract from fossil-fuels exclusively. I am referring to California's removal of 1997 GM EV1 electric cars in 2001 - upon the advice and direction of EPA Committee Hearings that were filled with Big-Oil-backed panel members. (EPA, 2001)

The failure of North American Governments to protect Volkswagen's diesel vehicles has compelled the company, and Renault in Europe as well, **to pull Diesel vehicles from our roads altogether.** This is a setback for Diesel that I hope every reader will urgently complain to his or her government to correct.

A more efficient, low-CO2 vehicle will not be available until the automotive Thorium Reactor is developed. A car with a Thorium energy source could run a car for 100 Years on a piece of abundant, inexpensive Rare Earth the size of a pea.

Hydrogen Fuels & Vehicles

Hydrogen is burned by fuel cell vehicles like buses and cars. The great thing about Hydrogen is that it can be fabricated right at the pump and a refill

Fossil Fuel is not needed

In 2012, researchers at Princeton University (Elia, Baliban, & Floudas, 2012) confirmed via an extensive research study that a combination of coal, natural gas, and non-food crops, could replace all of America's fossil-based crude oil needs altogether - with synthetic paraffin oil based fuels manufactured using the Fischer-Tropsch Method mentioned above as well. This fuel would reduce emissions by 50% immediately and do away with the need for expensive pipelines as fuels can be synthesized close to distribution centers.

Avoid Alcohol Fuels that dissolve in water

Hydro-Carbons can also be combined to create alcohols which can burn in today's gasoline automobiles as well. Ethanol in a 3% to 40% mix is the only form of alcohol that is consumable by humans, but I think that all other forms of alcohol are deadly poisons. Methanol - is so poisonous that just a thimble-full can cause blindness in humans and animals.

What makes Methanol especially unsafe for humans is that it dissolves in water, which means that spills or pipeline leaks - especially those pipelines that extend under water, are a very great environmental concern. Biodiesels contain a certain percentage of Methanol and Glycerines that dissolve in water as well.

Fossil Fuel Oils, diesel, gasoline, kerosene, aviation fuel, and others, do not dissolve in water; and Audi's Clean Diesel is created by a Fischer-Tropsch Method and does not dissolve in water.

Alcohol Fuels draw from corn and other food stocks that can also make food more expensive.

Pipelines versus producing fuels locally

Pipelines carry fuels to distant markets easily and can be important whenever we are forced to move Fossil Fuels like Crude Oil from source to destination. But pipelines create as many and more problems as they solve when spending on pipelines prevents spending on localized clean fuel production. As pipelines typically only carry one type of material, crude oil or natural gas are the most common pipelines; Crude can then be refined into its ten component fuels at destination.

How important are these expensive, disruptive investments when we can create fuel exactly where it is needed and as demand requires it? One-third of all of our energy cost goes to transporting food & energy so producing fuel locally is always preferable – until cheap and abundant energy is widely available.

Alternatives to Pipelines

Pipelines are not always cheaper. A Business Case is important when making the decision to move oil by pipeline versus train because barrels (# of rail cars) to remote destinations (like the gulf coast, east and west coast), need to be understood in order to support a decision. In the end, fossil fuel is polluting – so pollution-free clean fuels that are produced locally save transportation costs cannot be ignored (fully one-third of all of our energy is used to transport food and energy). For moving Oil and liquids, alternatives to pipelines discussed above included:

1) Driverless-trains reduce rail costs, permit refining in needy communities at any point between Oil Fields and Markets, and railways can be used for multi-purposes and financial benefit.
2) Locally manufactured clean Fischer-Tropsch Crude Oil – this option is available and done today in a Germany by Audi
3) Hydrogen - requires new vehicles North America-wide – but hydrogen can be manufactured right at the gas station.
4) Battery Cars – not yet ready but hopefully within the next ten years.

PROs and CONs of Oil Pipelines

CANADIAN CRUDE OIL EXPORTS BY RAIL
BARRELS PER DAY

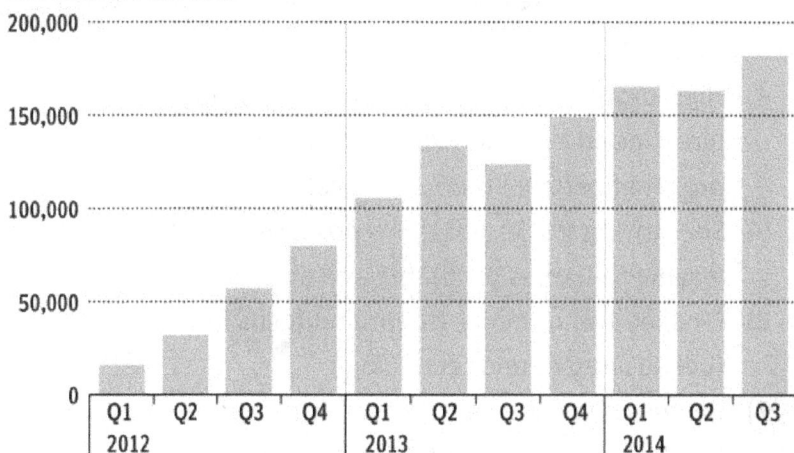

COST OF TRANSPORTING A BARREL OF OIL FROM HARDISTY TO MARKETS

	Pipeline	Rail-Manifest	Rail-Unit Train
To Gulf Coast	$7-11	$17-21	$12
To East Coast	N/A	$16-20	$13-16
To Canadian West Coast	$3	$10-14	$8-11
To U.S. West Coast	$5-6	$16-20	$13-16

(Hussain, 2015)

For Pipelines - PROs:

1) Shipping costs - $3 to $11 per barrel pipeline; $8 to $21 per barrel rail - for transport of fossil fuels

Against Pipelines - CONs:

1) Pipelines are expensive to build and environmentally disruptive; railways can be built robotically now too. See http://www.popularmechanics.com/technology/infrastructure/a22018/robot-railroad-track/

2) Job mobility forces Income Guarantee programs; when jobs are permitted to move, they can move to clean-fuel companies too, which is a PRO in several ways. Recall our Guaranteed Income Business Case in Chapter in 5.

3) Low-profit – pipelines carry unprocessed, raw material to remote markets where jobs and high-profits await refiners there.

4) High-profit – Truck or train hauling of locally refined fuels (gasoline, diesel, kerosene, etc.) creates good jobs, higher profit refined fuel products, locally.

5) Self-driving trucks and trains promise to reduce costs further leaving refineries profitable and able to employ easily.

6) Pipeline ties our investment and focus into status-quo fossil fuel businesses and technology

7) Rail permits us to build smart transportation networks that integrate to Connect Smart Factories in an overall Automation Strategy.

Rail vs Pipeline, the Environment, and Safety

Pipeline spills dwarf rail spills with the largest rail spill ever - equaling just eight cars in 2013. In the following graph we see that pipelines spilled 211 Rail Cars, or 148,235 barrels, of crude from 2010 to 2016 in Canada.

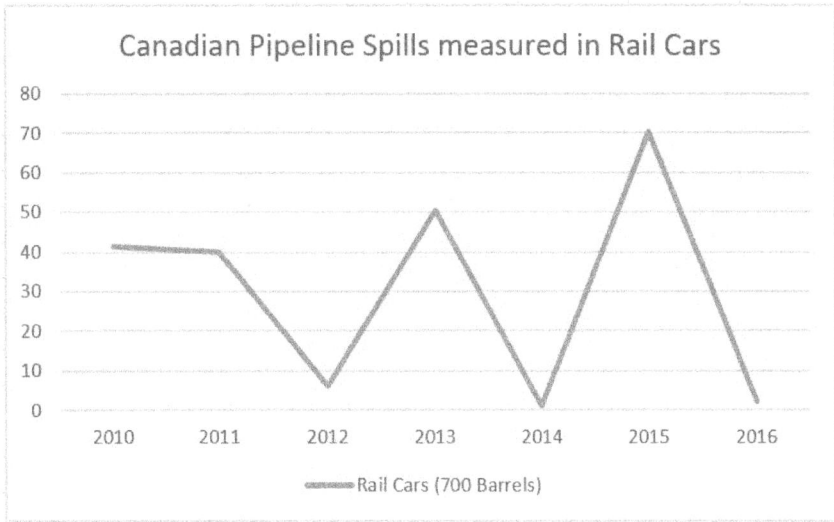

Canadian Pipeline Spills measured in Rail Cars

Rail Cars (700 Barrels)

Moving Natural Gas

Natural Gas pipelines are typically buried and spills do not present expensive nor environmental harmful cleanup problems. When integrated into serviced subdivisions, natural gas is an expensive infrastructure initially, but it does make use of available inexpensive natural resources.

Fuels Summary

In an inexpensive, abundant, electrical-energy setting, use of electric boilers and similar building heating systems – alongside vehicles powered by either locally-manufactured clean fuel, or next-generation batteries, is preferred.

Investing in pipelines and other infrastructures to move fossil fuels long distances should be viewed as tactical planning - and not strategic planning.

Chapter 10

-

Reshoring Production & Engineering

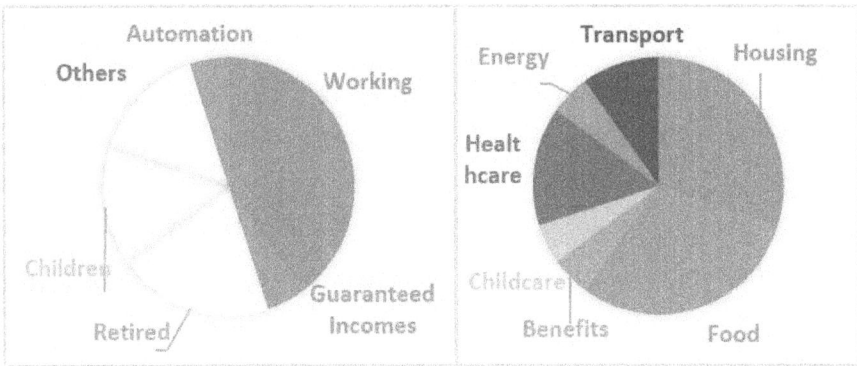

For 100 years or more, toward the end of the industrial revolution, offshoring production to countries where products could be built more inexpensively became a normal practice of business in North America. Pollution controls were less onerous abroad, and the damage to the environment was not felt here at home either.

Governments permitted or ignored this practice in countries where jobs were thought to be readily available in other industries or by retraining workers. Politicians believed that healthy businesses that made healthy profits would make a healthy and wealthy country as well.

This trickle-down was the model that worked throughout the early part of the 1920s when Henry Ford rebuffed the expressed opinions of peers, and insisted that his factory laborers receive high wages by the standard of the day. Mr. Ford realized that good wages and employment built good communities and that if he could be smart in his production, the highly incented workers would also ensure high quality and reliability of his products for a lifetime.

The strategy worked very well for Ford as every worker bought his cars and then generations of children did too. Truly, the interests of business were aligned with the interests of the country. The Great Depression and World War II trained a generation to understand very well that building strong societies was the only goal that mattered – and business was to be the tool for society's construction.

Since the year 1995 or so, the effect of causes automation and offshoring, was to sustain high levels of unemployment, and as workgroup collaboration tools were improved, the engineering and programming work also went offshore. I noticed that the practice of offshoring engineering became flagrant by 2014 or so here in Canada.

The Netherlands had none of these problems. Today the GDP in one of the smallest nations in the G20 is roughly the same as both Canada and Russia, and their technology industry is world renowned and thriving.

How did the Netherlands achieve this? They made offshoring their engineering illegal twenty years ago, and only permitted companies access to this market of 30 million when those companies produced good and jobs in the country.

The Netherlands was too small to sustain the job losses caused by offshoring early on and became an early adopter of reshoring twenty years ago.

Recently, a New York Times article that interviewed Maurice Taylor, the CEO of Titan International tire (Parussini, 2013). He had just returned from a visit to a plant in France that he was considering purchasing an unprofitable GoodYear plant in France. He announced to the reporter of the article "How stupid do you think we are?" Mr. Taylor went on to explain that he had watched workers labor four hours a day and then sit unproductively for the remainder. Competitor Michelin is 20 times larger and 35 times more profitable with a long history and one would assume future too, in France.

What the Netherlands did to defend themselves against offshore thinking of this sort, was to refuse access by a GoodYear - or other, to sell their products here if not manufactured in the Netherlands; and with ownership by Dutch citizens as well.

Starbucks Coffee Shops here are not owned by the U.S. Company for one example. The Starbucks in airports and other centers are local companies and local owners who license the name only. The Netherlands might be one of the few countries in the world that receive corporate taxes from Starbucks because of that company's famously aggressive multi-national corporate tax avoidance practices - in every country that they reside in.

The CEO of GoodYear Tires would remain CEO for about a month if France denied his company access to sell tires to 66-million French citizens – and with trade-ally support, the damage to GoodYear could be much greater. This is the power of on-shoring and responsible controls to eradicated manipulation by multinational business.

A country's bargaining power with any multi-national is its access to markets. Any corporation that wants to offer growth to its stock-holders will abide by the law of the land.

Multinational businesses will externalize social costs and play a game of benefit and profit to their advantage until governments collaborate and take back their markets. Since the Bush administration, the U.S. has played Mexico and Canada off of one another in this way very successfully; pulling jobs from one country to give to the other country - unless each country contributes sizable ransoms to sustain jobs.

Creating international trade agreements that permit this behavior of trade extortion, and tax avoidance, diminishes all three countries.

Some of the first moves of U.S. President Elect Donald Trump were to reign in offshoring – and this is a strong TE-Maturity policy too. Trade is important and you will want to maintain healthy Export revenues, but do not offshore engineering and important self-sustaining manufacturing in the balance.

In short, a country needs to manage its imports and exports carefully.

Chapter 11

-

Business, GDP & Taxation

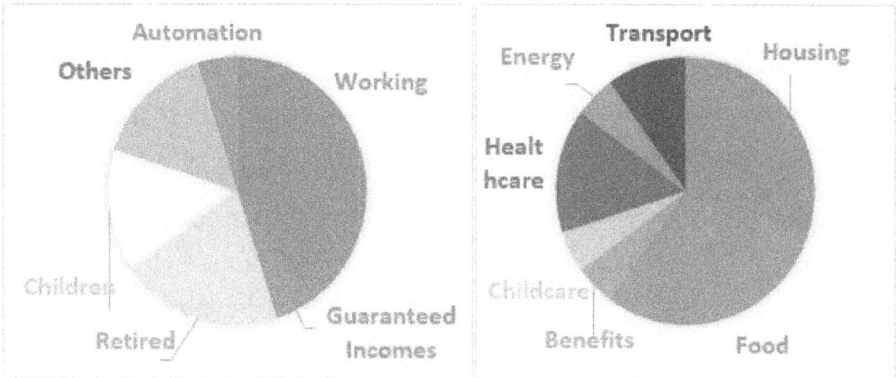

Absent on our Transition Economics Charts so far, are the contributions from commerce between businesses (B2B) and business-to-consumer (B2C).

An initial Transition Economics introduction could easily fill a much larger two or three volume book-set by simply explaining example throttles and Key Performance Indicators in every chapter. A book on Transition Economics for Business is in the works to do some of this.

Transition Economics Throttles

For example, if a mine operator wants to open in a foreign country but local governments refuse the use of excavator equipment to build roads in favor of local laborers with shovels because this creates local jobs, what Transition Economics throttles can calculate the compensation of local economies for the jobs-lost to road automation equipment? Recall that at some point, automated road builders will do away with these construction jobs altogether and so the guaranteed incomes of workers switching income sources must be considered before access is provided to this marketplace; and to the resources that the mining business wishes to harvest.

To keep Transition Economics simple and easy to incorporate, I preferred to keep this first release out of the weeds by presenting example throttles superficially. Specific throttling algorithms nor ratios are suggested in the Transition Economic Reference and a Business Case and Project Management Approach is provided to discuss assumptions and costs transparently there as well.

An explanation of why I feel this has to be a two-step introduction might best be explained with an economics example. I generally disregard Keynesian Economic Theories; this is because historical observation has confirmed that these are the unsustainable practices that led to a global social collapse via war in the 1930s – and then they again permitted today's Winter Phase to continue on to extreme levels of inequity without responsible controls.

Realizing that Keynesian Theories are policies that help a handful of special interest groups at society's expense, why would we care to learn these policies more deeply? As if to wonder if there is a missing complexification that will somehow overcome the underlying unsustainability and make them work; why would I commit to memory, or labor to research further, practices that are proven invalid and unsustainable by observation? Why would I choose to teach practices that are invalidated by Scientific Method?

This reality has in no way slowed down well-sponsored Economists like Milton Friedman (the "Capitalism invented everything" guy), Ann Rand ("Greed is Good") and Allan Greenspan ("Trickle-down

Economics", "Low Interest Rates", and "Low Tax"); household names that were not only incorrect in their directions, but research proved them socially irresponsible as well.

Transition Economics is none of these things; it is Scientific and Socially Responsible from inception, but readers will have to make up their own minds about the research presented here before diving deeper. This is what I would do; this is how I would do it as a reader. For this reason I will introduce throttle algorithms in two steps.

GDP Quality

The measurement of overall GDP is a summary aggregate of all transactions registered throughout the country. This number is only useful in comparison to other countries when ranking relative size from one country's economy to the next - as I can determine. The value of a country's GDP will broadly allow us to compare how large is your reporting of commerce compared to others but little useful information can be gleaned simply by itself.

Drilling down into the GDP, however, reveals important information about the efficiency and performance of your economy. Answers to Questions like: Are you importing more than exporting? Wealth is created by taking revenue from exporting your productions, so monetizing these productions are of essential importance to creating wealth.

Diverse Exports of high quality & high profit manufactured goods, like cars, pharmaceuticals, and technology, are preferred to commodity exports like coal, iron ore, and similar, which sell for pennies per ton on a highly competitive fluctuating world market.

High GDP Imports indicate that your citizens are unable to be self-sufficient and prefer instead to pay other countries so that those other countries can monetize their economies and build what is needed.

Maintaining a trade deficit; having more wealth leave the country than enters in - over time, diminishes the country just like it would any household. Many consecutive years of trade deficits can lead to real weakening as it did for the Soviet Union in 1986.

Incomes were always very low in the Eastern-European countries so I suspect that the U.S.S.R. did not collapse, as much as they more-likely preferred to align with the successful financial best-practices of their G8 trading partners who were successful in monetizing their economies through the 1950s, 60s, and 70s.

China remains the unprecedented champion of planning policies which successfully monetized their economy; China advanced more than any other nation for 30-years. This job of economy building was a mammoth effort for China because much of its one-billion population was just emerging from the stone-age 30-years ago.

GDP Export

I have always maintained that one of the best indicators of success for any country is their GDP Export per Capita. High GDP Export per Capita usually indicates high productivity across labor forces including retirement age people, and it is usually related to high quality exports as well.

The GINI Index is a good indicator of wealth distribution and the relative comfort of all citizens in low to high income brackets. More often than not, Socialistic Policy nations score best on the GINI Index and, more often than not, those same countries are among the highest GDP Export per Capita nations in the world as well.

These statistics are readily available online — just google the Wikipedia list. The GINI Index is above and on wiki as well. The CMI at CSQ Research combines this information to speak to each country's Management Team Performance as well.

Tax Laws and Tax Avoidance

Examples of tax avoidance are too frequent and too large to ignore. Tax evasion – the illegal payment of tax – is probably dwarfed by legal tax avoidance arguments.

In Canada, Revenue Agencies target individuals and small business because from experience, they realize that the teams of up to 100 lawyers at major businesses and even Canada's own Banks - are far too sophisticated to be collected from. Major Canadian Banks like CIBC, ScotiaBank, and Royal Bank's presence in the Cayman Islands gave that Tax Haven the early credibility it needed to attract 75% of the World's Hedge Funds as well.

Often, when Canadian Revenue Agents do finally find a way to collect on an illegal corporate tax dodge, the Supreme Court has sided with Business so that those tax avoidance cases have been permitted legally. Loopholes are set up in tax law with the intention to benefit local companies, but these options are exploited and then no-one ever goes back to confirm that the loopholes are in fact benefitting Canada as well.

This leaves frustrated Revenue Authorities with few other options than to come to pursue private citizens aggressively to pay for social programs.

"The Great Canadian Tax Dodge" ...
http://tvo.org/video/documentaries/the-great-canadian-tax-dodge, is one of many documentaries which explain that Business Exceptions (right-offs), complicated tax avoidance mechanisms, and offshore tax havens enabled very well-paid tax specialists to avoid incredible amounts of tax – and this story is true in the U.K., U.S. and really everywhere else globally now.

189

Revenue Canada estimates that $100 billion to $170 billion dollars leaves Canada untaxed every year - to tax havens around the world, costing that country up to $80 billion in tax revenue that would otherwise go to pay for social programs. Often monies sit offshore in zero and negative return accounts doing nothing despite arguments that some of the money makes it back to its host countries where it creates jobs and pays tax. Tax Justice Experts assure that these claims are nonsense.

Statistics Canada reports that $100 billion reside in just three islands – Barbados, Bermuda, and Cayman Islands which hold close to $2 trillion in contributions from all countries. Canada's debt is $636 billion - for comparison to your country – growing at a rate of $80 million per day. (TaxPayer.com, 2016)

Tax Fairness movements in Canada, the U.S., and elsewhere actively examine the issue of tax avoidance, and the exposing of sophisticated corporate strategies and tax loopholes commonly used to legally avoid tax. (Mirza, 2015)

Industry tax specialist Junaid Mirza cautions that "Simply turning off the tap on tax avoidance may not return a $100 billion increase in tax revenues for the Canadian government. "While revenues are likely to go up in the short-term, there is much academic research that suggests a decrease in investments would follow an increase in tax rates (or effective tax rates given inability to take advantages of tax planning). So that $100 billion, over time, is likely to be fairly close to zero."

Mr. Mirza's points are very valid, but upon reading, one realizes that there would be no negative impact in turning off the Tax Avoidance tap overnight, only benefit; and that with global financial regulatory controls in place, we would also not see other unregulated Tax Haven's absorb avoided tax in their place.

Tax Consultants, legal firms, accounting firms, tax havens, and handfuls of special interest Financial Services individuals benefit at the expense of every other member of society in these structures, so really I should not have to suggest that these structures are unsustainable, and nor should they.

I raised five kids and I find myself looking on these cases as a parent would look upon my children behaving in a socially unacceptable way in polite company. Society needs this now too; to reign in irresponsible behavior firmly again. No-one likes to feel reigned-in nor controlled - and for this reason, voluntary, pro-active social responsibility is always a preferable, albeit a sadly unreliable first option.

Chapter 12

—

Government Thought-Leadership

"Transition Economics" discusses social policies and their track-records in 180 countries; and it explains that 72% of all countries internationally are in a Collapsing trend right now. In 600 pages, this book lays out a plan to turn around the 72% countries using the lessons-learned from the 28% that are growing - and it explains that governments must plan and lead the way.

What are the next steps for civil servants charged with forwarding policies that correct their country's current situations?

Government must lead Technology

Government must insist upon major advances in technology and process; whether by providing the educational infrastructure or financing for major projects, this is true in history and it is even truer today in our finance and litigation-laden business environment. Government must accomplish this by leveraging Research Councils, think-tanks, academia and then finally business (as a secondary supplier).

For government directors, this means that they have to get very good at recognizing, supporting and leveraging thought-leadership. Those who are good at it need promotion and those who are not good at it need to sit in admin capacity or millions of people will suffer. Take a look around and ask are there multi-billion dollar technology companies being created. If the answer is no and long-standing administrators have corrected shortcomings, replace these program decision-makers with engineers immediately.

Thought-leadership is not IQ; it is definitely not EQ, I call personal thought improvement CSQ in one of my books - but what Thought-Leadership Is a system of planning that has the highest possible probability of a positive outcome for society. Aristotle called this planning a "Right Plan". CSQ Research supports the building of Right Plans - as should we all.

This time, governments want to license the financial rewards of Renewable Automation to Business; ensuring that automated services are available for all, and ensuring that we can recover our investments in R&D and guaranteed incomes and Engineering Safety Nets. Perhaps governments should look to own or part-own all renewable automation smart factory patents in law too.

Consider in all of these discussions that anything less works against a sustainable society, leaves us with the unworkable Cancer industry model discussed in Chapter 4, and therefore has to be considered poor planning that is in no-one's best interest.

Fund Automation in a Focused and Planned Way

Automation will feed us, manufacture medicines, it will build housing and energy plants, it will pave and then drive our roads; Automation will also make money for us at the same time that it makes money problems quite a bit less important. Automation, therefore, is our greatest risk mitigation to international financial collapse and so we have to plan for it and we have to fund it generously.

WHAT DOES IT TAKE?
TO BUILD A RIGHT PLAN

Worthwhile Goals
Simple Steps
Proven Process
Right People
Clear Directions
Great Vision

Allocating $800 million of a $120 billion infrastructure budget (4%) is not "funding generously". Think big and not of mom-and-pop businesses levels initially; small grant programs are well and good but will ever return investment intermittently and usually in unsustainable technology only. Instead, make big commitments to solve specific big problems, for example:

In Infrastructure spending: Building a road without building a "robotic road-builder" at the same time; or in Housing: building a home without a home-building robot; means that next year the roads and houses will not simply build nor repair themselves, and without these robots the need for massive infrastructure spending will continue without end.

Public Transit investment makes little sense except in only the largest urban settings as driverless cars will make point-to-point transit dramatically less expensive than today's inconvenient and expensive buses and drivers.

A robotic road builder, home builder, point-to-point driverless transit etc. will take one to two years to design and build a first v1.0 Pilot.

We would use these solutions ourselves and then we could resell it internationally as well.

Russia failed to sell its cars and watches where China and German succeeded; the difference between monetizing and not monetizing is in the attention to features and finish quality – so incent workers to build great robots. China has been 3D-Printing six-story buildings since 2013 and its cars have begun to rival German cars in just ten short years.

Citizens want their country to be a World Leader.

A country cannot usually do it all, so focus becomes key to success.

Canada can be a World Leader and make a positive impact very quickly, by supporting and promoting #WPProjects as a Canadian Plan – and so can your country. China has one-billion people and is rich from great planning too. One or two countries in the world can go head-to-head for technology leadership against China in everything at this time.

To become a World Leader, a country has to focus based on a long-term plan. South Korea focused on electronics; Japan on electronics, scientific equipment and cars; Hong Kong – cars; Germany – transportation and manufacturing equipment, and so on.

The #WPProjects' global approach assigns 250 automation projects to 200 countries so that everything that every country can be a leader at the same time that all of society's automation needs can be built in a quick and coordinated way. WP Projects assigned the following sustainable renewable automations to Canada for example:

In Tier 1 - Food, mining, farming, lumber, raw resources: Satellite Water Divining, Collection, and Packaging & Distribution

Tier 2 - Manufacturing, Baking, Food Prep, etc.: Drone Jets & Air Transport / Logistics

Tertiary Supporting industries - Energy: Clean Energy - Cold Fusion

Build an Engineering Safety Net

Income supports and funded education for individuals and small startup companies that want to build Sustainable Renewable Automation and Local IP (Intellectual Property) are essential.

Traditional Businesses, and especially startups, have to afford expensive finance and tax avoidance people to make their way. 50% of Waterloo Engineering grads leave the country immediately after graduation because engineering careers are not supported locally.

Governments can create "safe zones" for uninterrupted development – and they absolutely need to do this as well.

Engineers just want to build - and that is not always possible in many job settings.

Even large world-class engineering organizations have realized this problem and had to make this shift. NASA is a good. We have thousands of retired and out of work engineers in every country right now - let's put them to work.

Being a success just takes support. Salesforce is a mult-billion-dollar company that was started by Larry Ellison of Oracle when he signed a cheque for $30 million to one of his in-house VPs over in the lobby of their Mississauga Matheson offices. Multi-billion-dollar companies take support and engineering leadership to build. The VP assigned to CEO Salesforce was a weak engineering lead so it took the company many years to prosper, but support was consistent and so are the results.

Canada has not focused on its support of startups, they offer very small accelerator and $10k, $100k contest gifts but investment capital is scarce and decision-makers are uninvested finance leads - and as a result they have no skypes, no Airbnbs, no Microsofts; MARs and Innovatech are local Hi-tech Incubators that have really been wasted investments for the Governments of Canada as a result.

I brought an AirBnb ($25 billion market-cap in 2015) "Killer" company called TekRealtor/TheHomeDeal to Innovatech and MARs in 2009. I sat in large halls full of other startup companies, and comment after comment from the group was that none could find the sales funding that they needed.

Engineers must Lead

I heard this message loudly and clearly at a recent CEO Workshop that I attended with the Canadian Federal Innovation, Sciences and Economic Development Ministry. Progress is too often held back by finance and administrator generalists who are either not invested in moving society forward or simply do not know how. I talked about this historically confirmable phenomenon in my last book as well.

#2 Technology Leadership
Engineers were Marginalized and Business Ethics Grads took to the Boardrooms

Copywrite 2015 World Peace – The Transition at CSQ1.org

Engineers are not necessarily just tin ring holders, by using the term "engineers" I am also referring to career big-project builders and startup leads. People who understand a bit of everything from programing, to business cases, to leading 200 project staff and who have a mastery of SUSTAIN Project Management Method as well.

I am a career hi-tech lead and engineer; I can assure that Canada like every country, have tremendous, bright engineering minds. The weak link for many countries is in failing to find this engineering and entrepreneurial mindset in Government administrators and elected officials.

When thought-leadership is not revered; when it is not supported, the country will have suffered in the same way that academia has suffered from its ultraconservative and inward-looking peer-review processes - and the end product observation of its very poor result. Canada - as evidenced in its place among collapsing economies; and academia in it's supplying the economists, lawyers and business grads that have created a world economy with a 72% collapsing rate.

Life's messy, Clean it up

Business Accountability laws, tax evasion corrections, housing and anti-eviction controls, foreign ownership limits, engineering safety-nets and protections from offshoring, legal system acknowledgement of social obligation and freedoms, to name just a few policies that governments need on top of. Here is a hint: The Netherlands did it and so should you.

Chapter 13

-

Democratic Reform

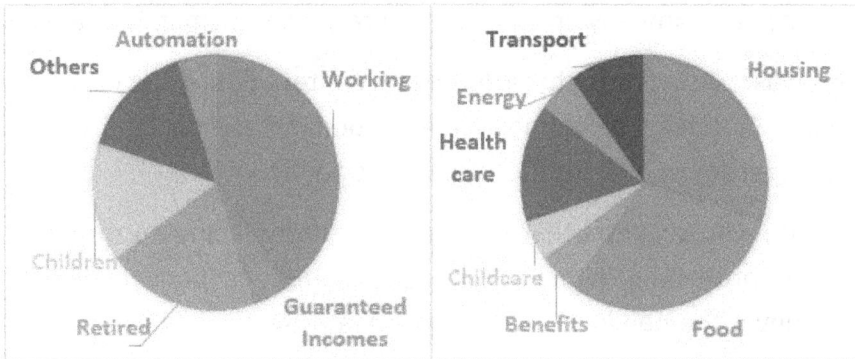

The improvement of democracy is a ongoing necessity that we must recognize and all stand in support of over time. An important part of part of democracy's success will be the ability to make changes based on expert direction too. With time, any system – regardless of its merits - can be corrupted. Corrupted, and systems turned counter to the tenants of democracy and the definitions of the first written Constitution – the Mayflower Compact, which succinctly stated:

*"**We** ... covenant and **combine ourselves together into a civil body** politic; **for our better** ordering, and preservation and **furtherance of** the ends aforesaid; and by virtue hereof to enact, constitute, and frame, such **just and equal laws**, ordinances, acts, constitutions, and offices, from time to time, **as shall be thought most meet and convenient for the general good of the colony**; unto which we promise all due submission and obedience."*

Abridged   November 11th, 1620

You might as well have laughed as cried over having to vote for the best-of-the-worst in North America this year, and most other G20 nations have similarly upset citizenry grasping to demand "Change".

This was the setting in the last K-Wave Winter - during the very early 1930s. European electorate chose Hitler, Mussolini; and elected fringe parties to high positions similar to today.

Anyone who suggests that Democratic Reform is undemocratic - is clearly protecting either a special interest or poor judgment. Whenever the needs of the democracy are overlooked to the point of a protest vote such as these, Democratic Reform is in fact, an imperative.

Those who make peaceful revolution impossible, make violent revolution inevitable.

John F. Kennedy

The coming years will really have to be spent reforming democracy in order to give voters the technology and training to let them vote for policy directly. The election of an individual to speak for voters was a limitation forced on us by practical considerations that don't exist any longer.

Benjamin Franklin said that "When the people find that they can vote themselves money, that will herald the end of the Republic", he was right of course, and the wealthiest 1% certainly have that now as well.

Whenever money can influence both elected officials and policy creation, you have the essentials of corruption and the mandate to design corrections that mitigate the problem.

In the U.S., a golden opportunity was missed with Bernie Sanders who would have also soundly defeated Donald Trump. The U.S. loses $500 billion annually to Inequity; the cost of leaving 160 million fellow citizens with nothing - without the ability to start businesses that generate GDP Export Wealth and prosperity for the country.

Superficial or unfounded messages of transparency, gender equality and accountability are tossed around with no intention of tracking progress, following up on, nor improving routinely today. It seems like wherever it is possible to appear inclusive but not to not be inclusive at the same time, that is the direction most politicians and their party leads prefer take.

Managing thousands of voices is impossible without terrific processes and most countries are in a varying state of maturity.

The role of Government in Economic Policy is straightforward – keep the economy's wealth distributed and growing. Unfortunately, this responsibility of governments both left and right, is not well understood by democratically elected politicians, nor voters, who need to make correct course corrections at specific turning points in a Capitalist K-Wave cycle.

Capitalism troughs every 60 years due to compounding Interest, the year-over-year expectation of higher profits; the rich begin earning day and night; after enough time passes there are only rich and poor – just like any game of Monopoly that you will ever play. These cycles have repeated within our capitalist civilizations for at least 4000 years - as mentioned, and so we can only hope to change this inherent instability of Capitalism when we manage wealth distribution proactively.

The start of a new economic cycle, the one right after World War II for one example, is a time in which the distribution of wealth within a society is relatively even. Everyone has what they need, a single family income provides all the basics, and a good life is available to everyone in society. This beginning is referred to by economists as the Spring of a Capitalist K-Wave Cycle.

Spring carries on like a monopoly game would - players buy houses easily, begin to collect preferred, high earning property and businesses and then start generating revenue by renting them out and earning income from these investments. Incomes were distributed across society somewhat evenly – similar to this pie-chart below where there are rich people, but that those top 20% of high-income earners control 35% of the wealth; the next 20% had about 25%, and the Lowest had 11 % of the wealth.

Michael I. Norton and Dan Ariely suggested the following arbitrary targets in their report "Building a better America – One Wealth Quintile at a time" (Norton & Ariely, 2011). The actual values assigned to each quintile are less important; the important task here is to create targets and manage wealth distribution to those targets.

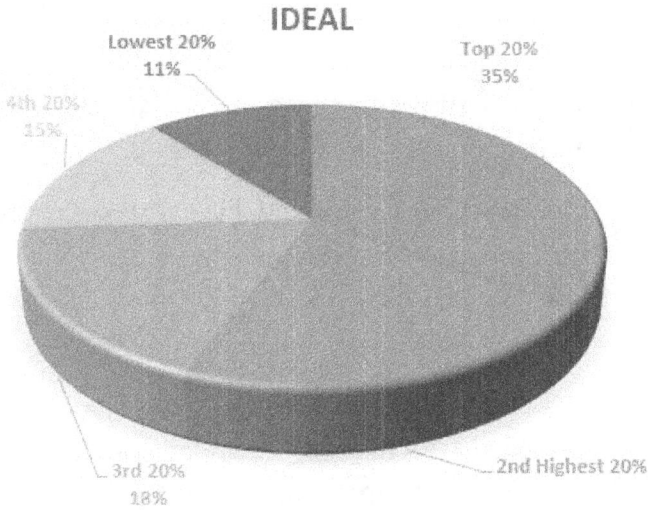

IDEAL

Lowest 20%
11%

Top 20%
35%

4th 20%
15%

3rd 20%
18%

2nd Highest 20%

In K-Wave Summer, some business owners start to make investment money available – initially at a higher interest rate. There are relatively few takers but still a few members of society start amassing wealth. Speculating and rental investment continues until all houses are gone and competition for homes drives up prices quickly. In the Toronto suburbs in 1982, a home could be bought for $30,000 at 22% interest annually. By 1986, four years later, the same house cost $90,000, and rates were 10%. By 2012, the house could be worth $500,000 with an interest rate at 3%. The notion of reality left real estate prices somewhere within this window of time.

As K-Wave summer ends, the Good Life too is ending now for many, and will be available for fewer and fewer families going forward now - until young adults do not have the same easy start in life that their parents did. Many families feel they need two salaries to afford a living at this time.

The end of a summer K-Wave is the time, in economic terms, to begin reducing tax to low-income individuals and increase the tax to successful businesses and high-income earners.

In K-Wave Autumn, interest rates can be expected to fall and fall, houses should soar in cost, and bankruptcies should rise in response to higher mortgage needs. Higher rates of mortgages will default as people lose jobs or cannot keep up with their bills.

The correct economic controls would have taxed the rich more heavily, and the poor to a lesser degree – but in the following chart "Historical Marginal Tax Rate for Highest and Lowest Income Earners", the opposite happened throughout the 1980s.

Tax rates of 91% and more were levied on High-income earners in the 1940s through 1960s. By 1985, high-income tax rates were reduced to 28% and 35%. In 2012, the highest tax rate was lifted to 40%.

Taxes on the lowest income level hovered around 15% throughout the boom years of the spring and summer K-Wave, until the tax rate was reduced to zero for the poor in 1977. In the late 1980s, the tax rate for the lowest income earners returned to 15% and then has remained at 10% since 2003. (Blodget, 2011)

You have seen the Federal Reserve Pie Chart in Chapter 2 that describes 2010's income distributions – where today the bottom 40% of American's share 0.3% of the wealth, and the top 20%, share more wealth than all of the GDP of the G20 combined.

The point here is, that we all should have been able to see inequity of this magnitude coming - and then our government and voters should have prevented it from becoming as extreme as this was obviously going to become as well.

Historical Mariginal Tax Rate for Highest and Lowest Income Earners

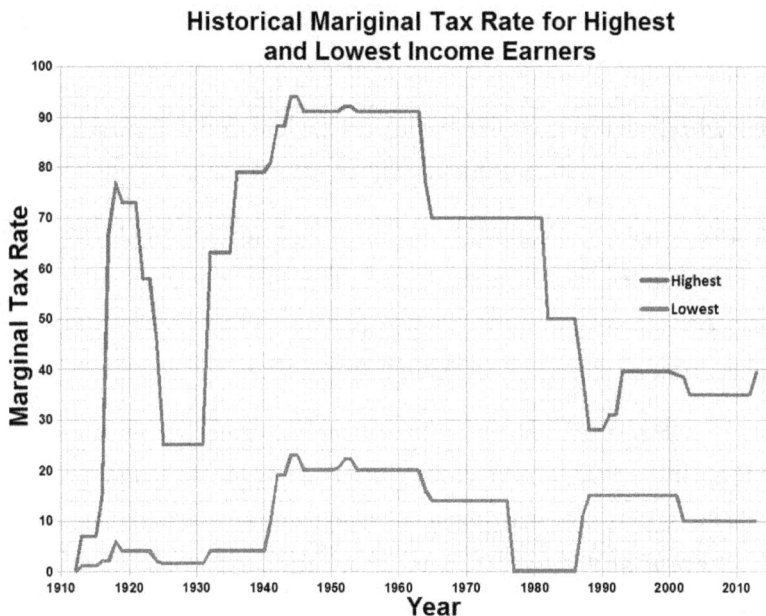

Today our income distributions are extreme for two groups; the rich, who should have stood up to insist on doing the right thing by society; and second, to every other one of us who voted for low taxes in every election since the 1970s.

The Pitfalls of Managing Proactively

What if our country had a President, Prime Minister, or Monarch who knew enough about Capitalist Economies and K-Waves to realize that a sixty-year cycle of wealth inequity was headed our way? As a good and responsible leader, he or she would have decided to prevent a calamitous outcome by implementing appropriate economic controls when wealth was still quite distributed in the Spring or early Summer - back in the 1950s through 1970s.

Finding a leader with a good grasp of K-Wave Economic Controls would have been a tall order. Although documented in 1925 - and in many economic thesis since, my five High School and University economics courses made no mention of it.

John F Kennedy acknowledged the need to manage society's revolutions proactively in 1962 with his famous quote:

"Those who make peaceful revolution impossible will make violent revolution inevitable."

Without fail, every politician that ran for election in the United States with a message of the importance of economic controls that tax the rich and proactively ensure wealth distribution – was voted down and never had a chance of making it into office.

At this crucial time, Americans voted instead for a wonderful, charming, untrained leader with a heart of gold - in Ronald Reagan. Reaganomics was an economic policy that embraced the Trickle-Down Theory and next it was also adopted into the U.K. as Thatchernomics.

Trickle-down said that "What was good for the rich and good for business, was good for society." Reaganomics gave money to the rich, and the rich would administer its trickling down into society with virtually no monitoring of the policy's success or failure by the government after that.

The campaign message of "Low Taxes" got Reagan nominated; "Low Taxes" got him voted President in 1981, and it reelected him again in 1985 – echoing a too long period of previous campaigns promising "low taxes" at a time when roads and highways were crumbling. Citizens began to abandon Major city centers due to neglect and security concerns. I can remember that administrators decided to close sidewalks in Buffalo rather than to repair collapsing buildings in their city center.

To not campaign based on "Low Taxes" was not to get elected in the United States and soon "Low Taxes" encouraged irresponsible administration too.

Outside the G8, Norway enacted strong economic controls proactively 25 years ago. Today they have very low unemployment (3%), universal healthcare, a $20 minimum wage, the seventh best income equity in the world, and the highest GDP exports per capita (wealth generation) annually for the past 20 years. Anyone looking for clues as to where the "American Dream" went, can look to Norway to find it protected and thriving here.

Norway's economy looks like a very smart Government Management Team's Performance Report. I suspect that it is no mere coincidence that the Nobel Peace Prize, and the Nobel Prize for Economics in neighboring Sweden, were founded here within Norway's very sustainable society.

Economic Controls - Right and Left

When wealth distributions can become this extreme, with all the negative social problems and embarrassment associated, neither Right nor Left parties are enforcing responsible economic controls.

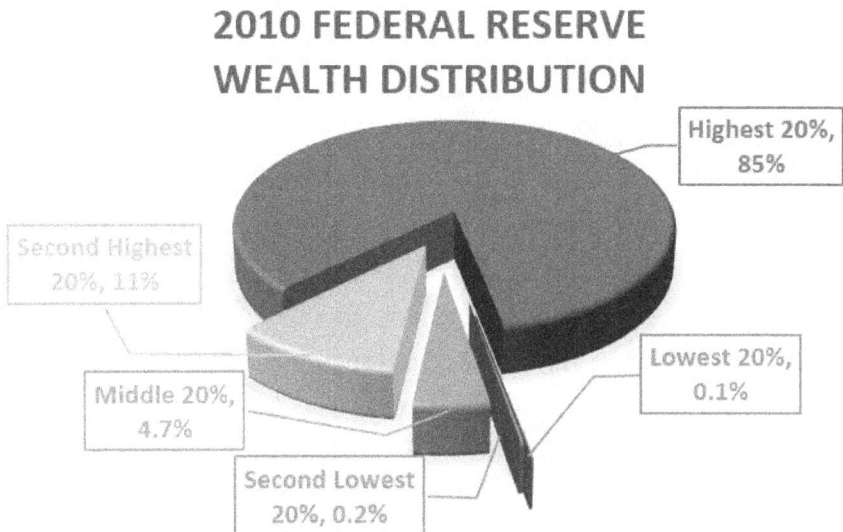

2010 FEDERAL RESERVE WEALTH DISTRIBUTION

Highest 20%, 85%

Second Highest 20%, 11%

Middle 20%, 4.7%

Second Lowest 20%, 0.2%

Lowest 20%, 0.1%

Essential services like hospitals must remain open, the ambulance must come when called, school children have to take a good education within secure communities – and we must avoid trough wars that gain support from destitute citizens in every economic depression.

For the first time, our technology is within just twenty years of ending our reliance on money altogether as well. Now is finally the time to stop voting for "Low Taxes" and look at our Wealth Distribution challenge as one that just needs resolving now.

The government's "Right" tend to be the more conservative managers between the two sides. The Left will support more social and communal services at higher cost and risk to the government – but both sides have the mandate to present an affordable suite of policy offerings to put to the decision-making hands of their voters.

For either Right or Left parties to ignore its responsibility to Economic Control is not Left nor Right behavior specifically – rather it is poor management, as permitted by poor voter education.

In 1980 America, and in other G7 countries, voters followed poor policy as political campaigns exploited the public's low education level to win election and further personal business interests.

Rather than to educate the public in how to judge what responsible financial controls for society are, political campaigning appealed to our emotions – and not to logic, because they could. Voters were told that if they didn't support "Low Tax", they were "a socialist" or "Un-American" - basically. The American Dream ended for most of the poor minority whose voting strength was smaller than the richer majority during these years. The cost? The U.S. loses $500 billion annually due to 160 million citizens (40%) who have nothing and have no vote either because they are not 51%.

Democracy is an important building block of a Good Life, so sound Financial Controls are important to a Good Life as well. Every democratic voter must be educated well enough to stand on guard against this, or Democracy itself becomes unsustainable over time.

The responsibility of the right and left should always extend to the "greater good" as a minimum precept, general rule, and guiding principle. If there are not enough resources to move everyone forward, then work on revenue growth until there is enough wealth – but once there is enough wealth, as is the case for the G20, keep it distributed by graduating tax.

Policy Creation and Policy Committee Reform

Political Party Policies are selected based on a variety of approaches. The constitutions of many political parties, offer a documented process to forward policy by democratic election – and this is a concern.

Policy Committees are not necessarily Subject Matter Experts - SMEs, and they are not screened for conflicts of interest in many cases. All policy reviewers should fully disclose conflicts that can include employment incomes from other members of committee - first. Second, you should be elected a Subject Matter Expert before being invited to vote on policy as well.

Ideally, SMEs come to agree based on expertise earned through a career and higher education in the subject area discussed. A 25-year career is considered PhD equivalent in that area of employment and experts both academic and practical only should be participating in policy creation.

When a career Engineer, Doctor, Lawyer, or Economist votes on Policy in which they are an SME, that vote cannot be weighed equally against a sprinkler repair technician who is voting as he feels his father might have voted when he was alive (or some other emotion-based voting).

Even within professional fields, there are experts and generalists; a cancer specialist needs to weigh in more heavily on Policy specific to Cancer, than would a GP General Practitioner - for example. As you drill down within a community of Cancer physicians, opinions are often divided here as well.

When SMEs are not valued above other voices, genius and best-and-brightest get tucked into a corner and democracy languishes. If you don't do this - Einstein, for just one example, was made to "sit out" by academic rivals for two decades so they could figure out his thinking; Alan Turing was abandoned by peers and dead at 41, Pons and Fleishman were disgraced for 25 years for discovering Cold Fusion – we are just finding that their discovery was valid finally this year.

A long time association and volunteering record with your party is terrific, but it does not however, justify your cancelling out the vote of an expert in a policy field. Invariably, there are far fewer experts in this world than not – so do not be offended if you are declined the vote in one subject area.

If, however, you believe you are an expert and have been denied your right to participate as an SME, an appeal process should be available to you.

Each policy typically makes its way from city riding offices throughout the country to a regional review. When policies are ratified at a regional level, the policy next moves forward to a vote at a national convention.

Poland is the world's longest running democracy; it was a Super-Power in 1600 and six-times the size that it was at the start of WWII. World War II almost killed 20% of its population in large part due to 400 years of democratically elected compromise and weakening. Point is, in a democratic system, once we create well-vetted policy, we have to protect it, we have to control or permit revision by brilliant authors carefully, and then we have to communicate it well too.

Democracy is very important - and history teaches us that Democracies dumb-down and weakens itself if we don't stand on guard in this way.

Left & Right Must Support Important Policy

If a marketing survey shows low voter support for an Important Policy or Economic Control, that policy's Business Case must be communicated and then implemented by parties both left and right to voters trained to expect a professional Business Case and argument for acceptance.

In our current system, the election marketing teams on both Left and Right, feel they must discard important policy in order to win elections - and will bring forward a platform of policies that they believe will win power in an election. In this way, Society's sustainability is discarded by political teams that simply want to win elections.

Voters must be able to vote their values. When a political party supports middle-class-only policy, they do so forsaking important low-income productivity that is proven to turn economies around. An educated voter will vote for these low-income supports, but others may vote selfishly - not realizing nor caring that their society will pay a steep opportunity cost that may even lead to social collapse.

Reagan's Policies of Low Tax and Trickle-Down, with no monitoring by small government, were popular policies because voters were never made aware that their kids would suffer Economic Recession and Depression as a direct result today.

Reagan won because no credible objection was raised within his party; today however, Reagan is regarded as the Salesman of today's Economic Collapses and is a shining example of what not to do.

INCOMES DISTRIBUTE	Transition Economics Mature Policy 5% to 10% in Collapse	Collapse Policy 72% of All Countries are in Collapse
Working Families & Individuals	Graduated Tax, Big-Business Tax Avoidance Crackdown, Inequity targets, Local Business Ownership, Local Govmt Business Ownership	Low Tax, Trickle-down, Middle-Class Focus, Diversity, Cheap Imports, Immigration, Small Business w/o support
Unemployed	Guaranteed Cost of Living Incomes, Business Automation Revenue Sharing	No benefits for underemployed nor all unemployed
Retirement	Employee & Pension Fund Protections, Cost of Living minimums, CSR & Business Accountability	Offshoring, Misuse of female diversity rules, ignoring pensions
Children	Free Mastery-based Education & Transition Economics Voter Education	Failure to support 20-year-olds starting families, High Divorce Rates
Others	Cost of Living Benefits for Disabled	Insufficient Support, High Debt Servicing Costs
Automation	Engineering Safety Nets, #WPProjects & Renewable Automation Support, Multi-Party Long Term Strategic Planning	Innovation programs that fail to support Renewable Automations and Trade & Selling Needs

SPENDING POWER RETURNS	Transition Economics Mature Policy 5% to 10% in Collapse	Collapse Policy 72% of All Countries are in Collapse
Healthcare & Benefits	Universal Healthcare, Employee Benefit Plans to Revenue Neutral Business Case targets	Private Plans, Patents that externalize Government R&D
Childcare	Universal Daycare & Free Education incl. University	Unaffordable Childcare
Housing	Public Housing (30%) Controlled to Inflation, Land Grants, Anti-Eviction, and Foreign Ownership Taxes	Energy Poverty, Housing Bubbles created by lax controls
Food & Goods	License Renewable Automation, Local Harvesting, Driverless Transport & Distribution, Local Self-Sufficiency & Abundance	Insufficient Farm Compensations, Failure to develop automation, Dollar & 99p Stores, Cheap Imports, Austerity Measures
Energy	Abundant Geo-Thermal, Hydro, Cold-Fusion, Thorium Nuclear, Zero-Pollution Fuels	Part-time Wind & Solar, Fossil Fuel Oil Pipelines, Energy Poverty
Transport	Driverless-cars & Automated Goods Delivery, Auto Road & Rail Construction	Infrastructure w/o Automation & Trickle-down Protection, Transit

Believing in a Party Policy Process that is failed by design – amounts to not understanding that the results of that process can never work for any country. Now that you understanding and acknowledge the problem - is the first step to resolving it. Ensure that you work to resolve this problem within your party with priority.

This list is a summary list of all of the TE-Mature Policies discussed throughout this book.

Chapter 14

-

Cost of Divorce in Society

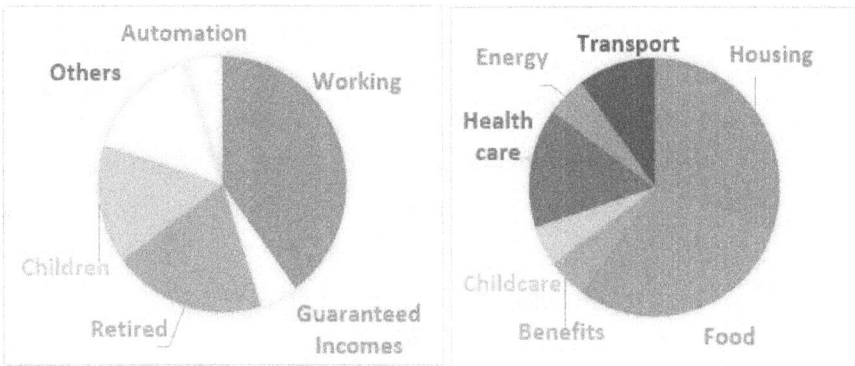

When marriages end, the finances of the couple split and the need for two homes replace a single shared home; separate retirement incomes and savings are now needed as well. The impacts of Divorce, to every facet of society, are not obvious until we begin to add up the cumulative costs.

Separations will mean that one or both of the spouses must spend more years in the work force. Because children are also born later in life today, many 50-year old parents are supporting University costs on top of alimony payments and retirement plans.

These changes often force people to need to work; to draw a workforce income, well into their late sixties; well beyond the point where retirement income structures would otherwise be providing for their needs.

With fewer jobs available, and more graduates needing jobs year over year as well, the chance that these 50 years olds will be able to stay in productive employment reduces and the need for support of these people by the state increases.

Effectively, the combination of high marriage failure, combined with economic downturn, much higher housing costs, automation-driven job losses, and later starting families, may make divorce a choice, and "Right", that our economy simply cannot afford.

The socio-economic impacts and cost of a 50% to 70% divorce rate when combined with a high male unemployment rate may not appear high at first glance. On closer examination, the costs when multiplied by 50%-70% of the population base, are staggering. According to the latest official statistics, Divorce to Marriage Ratios were 48% in 2011 on average in the United States (see en.wikipedia.org/wiki/Divorce_demography).

- Cost of sale of primary residence - $25,000+ commissions
- Purchase and move to other residences $36,000 in land transfer and fees
- Twice the Utilities, House Taxes, etc.
- Rental accommodations delay retirement savings - $100,000-$1,000,000 per pensioner
- $6,000 to $25,000++ divorce legal costs
- $2000 additional tax & accounting costs
- Purchase, maintenance and insurance for two cars - $6500 annually
- Additional Cell phones - $2000 to $6000 annually
- Jobs & support needed in society for two full-time workers - $100,000

- Retirements will be delayed to at least 65 or later.

- Double the clothes, computers, sundries for kids - $6,000

- School councilor costs increase as 50% of kids are now high-stress - $50,000 per school

- Help Line volumes increase as kids struggle with all aspects of change in family - $1 million annually per 100,000 population.

- If incomes are not steady, and jobs are scarce, all costs hit the social welfare and housing system - $40,000+ annually.

Actual numbers are very hard to guess because two divorces are never the same, divorces within housing bubbles are much more expensive than non-bubble divorces, and so on. Although I took two very different tacts to get to these estimates, the $12 trillion dollar cost came out just the same with these input costs. $12 trillion is 2/3rds of the U.S.'s total GDP and so I realize that these numbers have to be too high. The important thing to take away from this discussion is that social problems – from divorce, incarceration rates, and military spending and similar – probably accounts for very near half of the total GDP of the United States. If I add this cost to the opportunity costs lost by not supporting guaranteed income programs, universal healthcare, and similar, the United States is paying a very high cost to protect its inequity indeed.

Total Estimated additional cost of divorce per 100,000 population is between $6 and $7 billion first year, and half of that - $3 to $4.5 billion is needed annually thereafter, if you do not count an additional new salary requirement as a social burden. If I don't count additional income needs nor welfare costs, the cost of divorce for the population of Canada's 30 million people is $1.6 trillion best case; and trillions upon trillions for the U.S. See the detail chart for the worksheet that supports these cost estimates.

Cigarette Smoking kills 480,000 Americans annually; Smoking related illnesses cost more than $289 billion in a 45/55% split of medical costs and lost productivity. In 2012, 18.1% of the US's 350 million citizens were smokers.

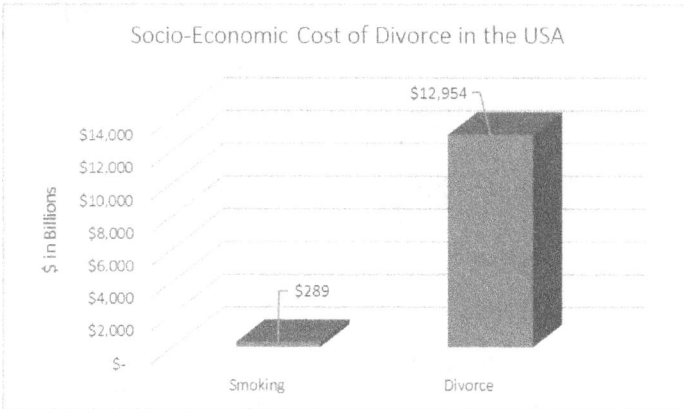

Socio-Economic Cost of Divorce in the USA

A comparison of costs shows that divorce dwarfs the cost of smoking in our society.

In the same way that we ban smoking because of its staggering health-care cost, we may find that our society has to control divorce rates in an effort to curb runaway social pensions as our citizens are unable to pay for their own retirements.

Socio-Economic Cost of Divorce (per Capita)

Costs Per Family	People Affected	Monthly Cost per	One Time	Annual per Family	Total One-time
Residence Sale	1		35000		35000
Purchase of New Homes	2		$18,000		36000
Rental or Utilities @ taxes & insurance	2	2300		55200	
Divorce Legal	2		3000		6000
Accounting	1			2000	
Extra Car	1			6500	
Insurance	1			1500	
Cell phones	3	110		3960	
Extra Full-time salary $60,000	1	5000			
Public Pensions	1			5000	
Extra Clothes	2			3000	
School Councellors	2			50	
Help Line	4	40000		1.6	
Social Housing	1	40000			
				$ 77,211.60	77,000.00

Column1	Column2	Column3	Annual	One Time	Year One
People	30 Million	30,000,000	$ 2,316,348,000,000	$ 2,310,000,000,000	4,626,348,000,000
Divorce Rate	x 70%	0.7	$ 1,621,443,600,000	$ 1,617,000,000,000	3,238,443,600,000

* Assume either social housing or Rental Cost - but not both
* Rental Costs is assumed equivalent to carrying cost for a home
* Variables include Divorce Rate, Population
* Housing Costs assume $400k and 5% Mortgage

Chapter 15

-

Responsible Transition

Transition Economics is the first Theory in Economics to require a profound understanding of a very specific definition of sustainable Change and Project Management methodology.

The adoption of mature, well-proven, and scalable processes for change are fundamental to the success of any change large or small. For this reason, Transition Economics mandates a specific process to communicate, monitor and manage change well across a broad group of Government Policy changes for Business, Legal, Engineering, faculties, organizations, countries, and all other change.

Transition Projects are often large change programs containing dozens, and even hundreds, of social and engineering sub-projects. Having these all run under a common program reporting process ensures that all know next-steps at any point in a change.

Only SUSTAIN Project Management Method is suggested to manage these changes as only this methodology ensures that each project meets sustainability targets at appropriate points.

SUSTAIN PMM is the only certified Project Method certified as "Transition Economics Compliant" at this time - and is introduced in Chapters 27 & 28.

Training in Project Process is the first place to start to ensure successfully making a change across many faculties and organizations with varying levels of expertise, experience, and even education, reliably.

Using SUSTAIN Project Management Method, all current and soon-to-be-affected organizations become empowered Project Owners and their Engineering Teams, Policy Management Teams, Legal, 3rd Party Consultants, Auditors, and Governance Team members become Steering Committee Stakeholders who are responsible to assign members of Working Teams. Programs are led by a Program Manager with one Project Manager assigned to at least one of each Project or Sub-Project.

All current processes: those of legal departments, governments, corporations and engineering teams are listed as "Inventory" and all are documented in the Requirements Document of an appropriate individual project or projects.

Program Charter Documents contain a list Stakeholders, Owners, Steering Team members, Projects, and other specific Program

I've worked in environments where 500 of these individual projects were running in a dozen large programs managing billions of dollars, so this process scales and executes reliably regardless of the number of stakeholders and complexity.

Individual Projects take on-average, six months to communicate and deliver with high quality, proper training and status reporting. Never advance a project past a sign-off milestone until all stakeholders sign to advance the project; you add risk to your successful outcome every time you do – and responsibility for delays becomes that of stakeholders alone.

It is always true to say that a **Great Process Never Takes Longer**.

TE Throttles and Throttle Rates

In Transition Economics, throttles are algorithms or ratios that suggest a safe rate of automation change. The rate that change can take place responsibly is referred to as the adjustable TE Throttle Rate.

For example, if automation can replace 50% of the world's five billion jobs (this assumes that approx. 70% of the world's population take incomes via a job; in the U.S. 63% have jobs) over the next 20 to 30 years, throttles must predict how to absorb 7 million lost working incomes per month globally over that time. 7 mil x $1,500 per month Cost of Living (CoL) means automation must offset $10.5 billion monthly or $126 billion annually.

That's a calculated cost of $17.5 million annually per every one million population; and it is also a cost that could easily be recovered through simply cleaning-up half of the tax avoidance estimated by major companies and financial institutions.

Calculation	Value
Global Population	7.2 Billion
% in Jobs	70%
Working	5.04 Billion
Targetted Job Automation	50%
Years to Automate Target	30
Months per Year	12
Jobs Automated per Month	7,000,000
Cost of Living Guarantee Income	$ 1,500
Monthly Cost of Automation	$10,500,000,000
Annual Cost of Automation	$126,000,000,000
Cost per 1,000,000 Population Annually	$17,500,000
Monthly Jobs Automated / 1 mill	972

Note Minimum guaranteed incomes differ based on Cost of Living

(CoL) per country and also per municipality. For example min CoL for Toronto is $3000 CAD, London, New York, Chicago, Rome, etc. are all different.

With budgets in place and offset by tax or automation incomes, the acceptable Throttle for Jobs to switch to Guarantee Incomes - in Canada with its population of 36 million, would therefore be 972 monthly job automations multiplied by 36 (million) which is 35,000 jobs will be automated in Canada monthly. **If budgets cannot accept** these rates, throttle rates must calculate affordable compromises – both in spending and incomes.

The Goal of Transition Economics and adjustments in Throttle Rates is intended protect citizens in change while ensuring that every possible opportunity to avoid collapse with the economy has also been employed.

The goal is not - to compensate citizens undertaking a change automation change with the lowest standard of living possible over long stretches in time. For example, a $3,000 income in Toronto will not build a Good Life if all other costs remain unchanged or continue to increase. Whether Salaries increase or Cost of Living decreases, the better measure of any successful community is by the definition of a Good Life; one that can afford all of the things that we need.

Chapter 16

—

Terror, Race, Gender, Religion or Empathy

The Business Case for Empathy

The Business Case for Empathy is compelling. So much so in fact, that if you are arguing against Empathy, no matter the context, you are arguing on the wrong side. Let's discuss why this is true next.

After writing three books in Economics, and in years of research and fact finding, I have never been more convinced that Reliable Incomes and renewed spending power, permit abundance of our basic needs of food, water, shelter, energy, education, healthcare, and security in family friendly communities. This Good Life was the basis of the American Dream of the 1950s and 60s throughout the G8 in the 1950s and 1960s.

Citizens that lived within that society had time to volunteer, to raise families, to invent, and they had the freedom to make decisions based on moral grounds without concern that they might do without something and feel forced to make socially irresponsible decisions. Citizens built the stable neighborhoods, schools, and the infrastructure needed to sustain commerce and a Good Life that would become the highest standard in the world.

There were concerns for race, gender equality, and religious persecution as in any society back then, but this period was the one that broke America out of racial segregation on buses and in schools too. It was not until wealth distribution began to become very unequal again in the 2000s that Race, Gender and Religion tempers began to flare once again.

Scarcity drives even the most passive creatures to both offensive and defensive violence. The Venus Project documented a terrific example of this in their video "Paradise or Oblivion" (available to view on YouTube): Picture two cows grazing in a late-spring pasture. With as much grass as they might want, the entire lifetimes of these two cows might be spent without a care nor conflict - and as much grazing as they might ever need sustainably. However, if you introduce a scarcity; if you offer one portion of carrot or honey to one of the two, they will kick, bite and violently fight the other for access to the new scarce resource.

I noticed that a number of popular Google+ forums had also become swamped, along with our news reports — with stories of Religion, Gender Issues, and Racial intolerance.

I found myself defending Socialistic Policy during a recent friendly lunch discussion — and that discussion sent me back to one of my articles and books, to assure the group that Socialistic Policies are very, very good for business at the same time that they are good for people too — as supported by the statistics shown below.

Are these two topics related? The widely published GDP statistics of every country did support that countries whose citizens have a Good Life; a life with strong Wealth Distribution and Wealth Equity (GINI), did also create more Wealth for their country and their social problems were lower as well.

Are concerns about Religion, Race and Gender problems, just symptoms of Wealth Distribution Inequities?

To answer the question, I will offer my conclusions below — but rather than convince the reader with my summary, I will give you the raw data to support your own analysis as well. I have assembled the statistics for countries that generate the most wealth per citizen (Export GDP per Capita) and compared these numbers for just a few example countries. You saw these stats in Chapter 11 as well.

Country	GDP Export per Capita	Multiplier to Dutch Export/Cap	GINI Wealth Equality	HDI	Leaning	American Dream?	Population (In Millions)	Export Quality
Netherlands	$33,652	100%	31	0.915	Socialistic	Yes	17	High
Norway	$28,807	117%	25	0.944	Socialistic	Yes	5	High
United States	$5,057	665%	45	0.914	Capitalistic	No	324	Very High
Sweden	$18,688	180%	23	0.911	Socialistic	Yes	10	Mid
Germany	$18,316	184%	27	0.911	Socialistic	Almost	80	Very High
Canada	$13,286	253%	32	0.902	Capitalistic	No	36	Low
United Kingdom	$7,378	456%	32	0.907	Capitalistic	No	65	Mid
Australia	$10,446	322%	30	0.935	Capitalistic	No	24	Low

GINI — is a statistic that measures country-wide wealth distribution pretty efficiently.

HDI – is the UN's less-than-perfect Human Development Index; I say less-than-perfect because 45% of Hong Kong's residents live in 8×8 apartments without a window – and still the country gets a quite-high HDI. Wealth Distribution is considered little in this calculation.

GDP Export Quality – is an assessment of export quality, and not necessarily quantity. The diversity of exports and the per-unit profitability of exports are important measures as well. For example, selling your mining resources at pennies a ton are low quality exports that put your country at much risk of commodity market fluctuation; far better to sell and ship manufactured pharmaceuticals, or engineered tunneling and automation equipment, at $1000 per box.

Compare the Exports and per Capita Exports of your Country to understand how much revenue that your country is failing to earn every year by not engaging every citizen in commerce. I have called this number "Opportunity Cost" in the chart below.

Country	GDP Export per Capita	Multiplier to Dutch Export/Cap	Export 2015 (in billions)	Opportunity Cost New Export (in billions)	Collapse or Advance Trending?
Netherlands	$33,652	100%	$477	$0	Advance
Norway	$28,807	117%	$103	$17	Advance
United States	$5,057	665%	$1,510	$8,538	Collapse
Sweden	$18,688	180%	$151	$121	Advance
Germany	$18,316	184%	$1,309	$1,096	Advance
Canada	$13,286	253%	$411	$630	Collapse
United Kingdom	$7,378	456%	$436	$1,553	Collapse
Australia	$10,446	322%	$188	$418	Collapse

Enabling the success of The Netherlands' citizens, are some of the strongest policies and economic controls in the world. Dutch Government controls protect spending power, employment, housing, and foreign investment and business ownership. Education at all levels is free, daycare, healthcare, guaranteed incomes and even retirements are all paid for through a graduated tax structure that permits all citizens to participate in businesses and other commercial work.

Taxes are higher here in Holland than in G7 countries presently, but these differences can be considered tax and revenue-neutral in that they cover healthcare, retirements, and other living costs that other countries do not call "taxes".

Conclusions

The Export per Capita statistics of Holland prove conclusively that citizens do take advantage of social benefits to improve both their productivity and the standard of living for their communities as well.

The last G8 country to support "The American Dream" was Russia when Perestroika ended support for a Good Life for all citizens in 1986. Once that universally sustained Good Life was lost, social problems began.

Incarceration Rates and divorce increased; longevity and birth rates decreased, and other stats confirmed too that social problems appear to simply be symptoms of economic inequity that are leading to social collapse.

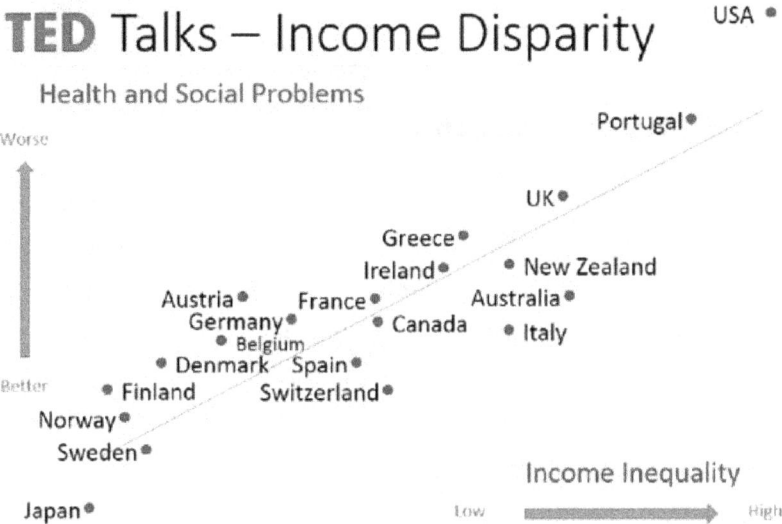

TED Talks – Income Disparity

Health and Social Problems

USA •

Portugal •

Worse

UK •

Greece •
Ireland •
Austria •   France •   • New Zealand
Germany •   • Canada   Australia •
• Belgium   • Italy
• Denmark   Spain •
Better   • Finland   Switzerland •
Norway •
Sweden •

Japan •

Income Inequality

Low ➡ High

Country	Incarceration Rate per 100,000		Longevity	Government System
United States	707	75		Pure Democracy Presidential Elections
UK	148	79		Parliamentary Monarchy Public Healthcare Democratic Elections Prime Minister by MP vote
Canada	118	81		Parliamentary Monarchy Public Healthcare Democratic Elections Prime Minister by MP vote
France	103	81		Socialist Parliamentary Republic Public Healthcare Presidential Elections
Italy	100	81		Parliamentary Monarchy Public Healthcare Democratic Elections Prime Minister by MP vote
Germany	78	80		Socialist Parliamentary Republic Public Healthcare Presidential Elections
Japan	49	82		Constitutional Monarchy

Lack of Empathy in History

The Nuremburg Diaries summarized Evil as the Absence of Empathy in 1946. This was a summary meant to highlight not only death camp atrocities to twelve-million Polish, Ukrainians, Russians, and European Jews in World War II, but it was also a commentary on the starvation-wage treatment of labor by business interests and governments putting World War I's Versailles Treaty compensations upon German's until it drove them to prefer a second war to untenable living conditions.

The Golden Rule is a Philosophy Lesson and Sustainability Model that is repeated in every religion; even the ones in antiquity that we know about and are no longer practiced. Ensure that your neighbor has what he needs; just as you have what you need. Remember, Philosophy – is not poetry nor verse, philosophy is the basis of all of our systems of education, school curriculums, and scientific method globally today.

Our secular education and government systems threw the baby out with the bathwater when we failed to recognize that flawed religious organizations should be separated from the infallible social sustainability lessons that fallible organizations, and even religious teachers, were originally charged to protect.

Chapter 17

-

Values and Sustainability

World Peace – The Transition is a book that invested two hundred pages of research to explain the important economic benefits for philosophy that asks us to build sustainable solutions in society. That work & effort seemed appropriate for a book titled "World Peace".

In Transition Economics, we want to understand that there is also a compelling business case for maintaining strong social values and building Right Plans.

Values and Philosophy that build sustainable economies that resist collapse – and sustain a higher level of Human Rights in a society of abundance - include:

The Golden Rule

The ultimate sustainability lesson as taught by every religion, philosopher, and playwright of note in history. Even religions of antiquity that are no longer practiced recognized that to respect and treat your neighbor as you would treat yourself and your family, was important to your own success as an individual and as a society.

The Golden Rule mandates win-win solutions in every business and personal transaction.

This chart of the Ten Things Great Leaders say to Highly Engaged Teams came to mind as I wrote this and thought to share it here.

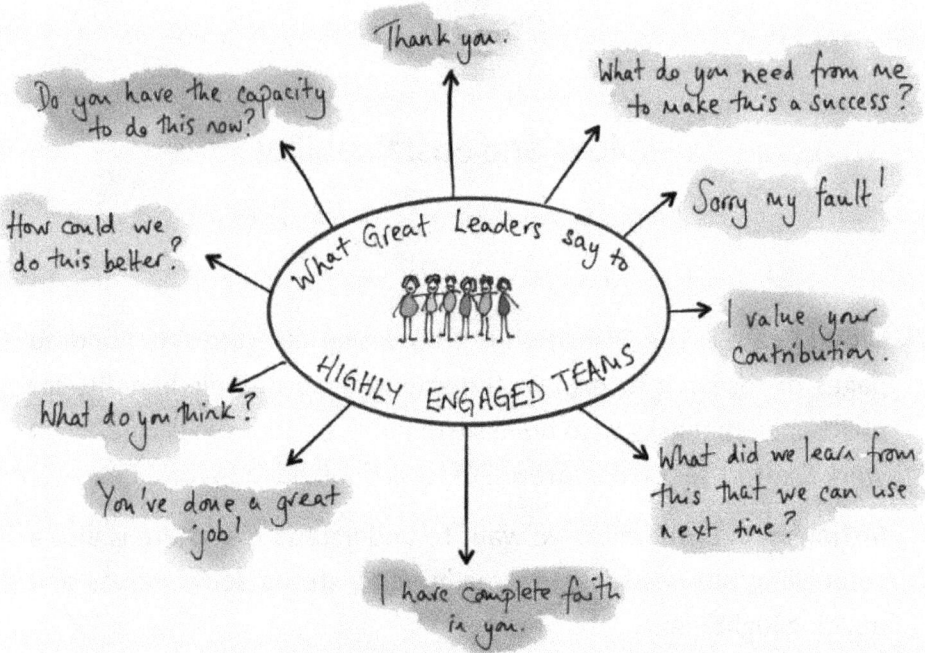

Great Leaders say: Thank you! What do you need from me to make this a success? Do you have the capacity to do this now? How could we do this better? Sorry, my fault! I value your contribution! What do you think? You've done a great job! What did we learn from this that we can use next time? I have complete faith in you!

The Definition of Evil

Dr. Gustav M. Gilbert summarized the atrocities reported during the trials of 1945 in Nuremburg, Germany after World War II. Dr. Gilbert was the U.S. Army Psychologist assigned to study the thoughts and motivations of the Nazi Generals put on trial after the war. In his book

"Nuremberg Diary", published in 1946, Dr. Gilbert summarized "Evil as the endemic failing of finding empathy for the situations and suffering of others"; "Evil, I think, is the absence of empathy".

This statement meant to summarize the Nazi Government's atrocities in death camps to Jews, Russians, Poles, Ukrainians, of course, but it also spoke to the "It's just business" attitudes of uncaring wealthy Jewish, and other, business owners who employed slave-wage tactics widely in Germany at the start of the 1929 Great Depression.

CSR – Corporate Social Responsibility

BSR - Business Social Responsibility and CSR – Corporate Social Responsibility, go a long way toward assisting the efforts of Business and Governments to bolster a Good Life worldwide.

By not permitting investment nor lending to projects that would harm society and the earth as well, we prevent situations like Montana – where 100 year old tailing ponds from mining operations long retired, are bursting through decaying reservoir dams.

By directing investment toward sustainable automation, we spend once and realize benefit many times. In the example of tailing ponds, robotic dredgers could process contaminated soil with eco-friendly solvents separating component arsenic and other mining acids from soil. Unrecyclable chemicals can be converted to energy through a plasma-based waste elimination process and reusable chemicals can be transported to working mining installations. Once cleaned, the land can now be made-over to parkland by Spain's automated Park builder.

By monetizing while protecting the environment and society, we build strong, sustainable communities.

Sustainability Planning

When solving global social projects, consider the following definition of Sustainability:

1. Feed a man a fish - and he can eat for a day. It works, but benefits are often unsustainable over time.
2. Teach a man to fish, and he will eat for a lifetime. This is a Bottom-Up plan that ensures self-sufficiency and food for a family for a lifetime.
3. Build automated tools that deliver fish automatically to everyone. This plan is a Sustainable Bottom-Up plan because he will have food and he will not be a "have" among neighbors who are "have-nots".

Inequity versus Diversity

Inequity is by far the most expensive social problem of the Winter Phase of any economic cycle. Although well-to-do individuals and organizations can often work diligently to divert attention from this reality, there is little business case for Diversity and only compelling business cases against Inequity.

I mention these two topics together here simply because a number of very large and important organizations are deflecting inequity discussions with diversity campaigns recently.

Diversity and Gender Equality Campaign examples include those sponsored by Harvard University, and the recent Canadian Government drive for equal numbers of each gender in Parliament.

Diversity campaigns sound like well-intended programs in support of resolving social problem effects/symptoms between genders and minorities, but these can never be used to divert attention from the cause/disease of far more important problem of inequity; Rich and

Poor.

Merit & Reward

"Merit" is the useful product that our work results in; "Rewards" are our compensation for the work that we perform as well. Our work might feed others, we might build schools, teach university students to build the future; we might run businesses that provide good jobs, provide healthcare, build airplanes or build driverless automobiles, and so on. Ideally, our work's reward will increase while our merit to society but this is a difficult discussion in Capitalistic societies where Merit and Reward can even often have an upside-down relationship.

Revere Thought Leadership

The surest way to disincent someone who does ground-breaking, thought-leadership work with fantastic performance, is to not acknowledge, recognize their value, nor permit their contribution.

Alan Turing, founder of the Computer Science and one day perhaps even World Peace itself, was ostracized and chemically castrated with the result that he committed suicide at the age of forty-one. Over four years, from 1940 to 1943, he built and made work from concept, an electro-mechanical computer capable of deciphering Enigma - the most sophisticated mechanical encrypting computer ever built. Enigma was used to protect messages to German assault forces throughout World War II.

Alan's "Turing Machine" was an initial trial and pilot of the binary computer that all digital computers are based on today.

Mr. Turing's genius and contribution are estimated to have saved the lives of twelve million people and reduced World War II by two years. I recommend that everyone and young people especially, take some time out to watch the 2014 movie "The Imitation Game".

Albert Einstein (founder of the Theory of Relativity and Atomic Energy) was relegated to a patent clerk and ignored by academia for two decades; in 1989, Stanley Pons and Martin Fleischmann discovered Cold Fusion but academic peers condemned them to disgrace and took twenty-five years to rediscover formulations of nickel and palladium nano-powders that created cold fusion reactions.

Years lost; promise squandered; contributions ignored, and a future of clean energy delayed.

Everyday examples include resume pre-qualifiers that modern Human Resource interviewers and heuristics software use today. These tools and individuals are not SMEs (Subject Matter Experts) - and neither are MBA leads either, and this means that twenty plus year hi-tech leads with many hands-on roles and major project successes are considered poor candidates and, therefore, unhirable in a competitive job market.

Stereotypes of inflexibility, high cost, pension risk, non-relevant skills, distance of past training, ageism, racism, sexism, academic and other biases, and the dismissal of volunteerism, community leadership, and other life experience and measures - all work to increase a growing sense of arrogance in a greatly dumbed-down workplace.

The reality that experience and value are not always well considered is highly detrimental to a society because many of our best and most experienced engineers, sit at home without productive lives while business leaders call for the immigration of offshore experts and immigration. Both of these are among the most short-sighted policies that a government can endorse.

These are all problems that can be solved with an update to Business Ethics courses and governments must control this when required.

Freedom

Worth repeating from previous Chapters, Freedom - is a 20-year-old who can choose to start a family; one who can choose an education or work as he or she wishes; one whose children and children's children will live in family-friendly communities that promise lifetimes of interesting worthwhile projects, learning and exploration.

This Freedom is within our ability to build and an imperative of responsible citizens worldwide to ensure.

Values

Why did some Nordic State countries reject the capitalist notions of "Greed is Good" and "Everyman for himself" that became synonymous in the movies with being American? There were a number of very good reasons.

First, the basic communal values of these countries taught them that helping neighbors ensured that their families could find help if ever needed too; often these families lived in a harsh climate with regular occurrences of severe scarcity. An unlucky fire or water damaged food store, could leave whole communities without provisions for winter – and so fathers taught sons to help others first and foremost as needed because, of course, the next natural disaster could as easily befall his own family.

Second, these countries were much smaller – smaller in size, resources and population - so when foreign businesses swooped in and ran off with profits, or polluted the land, or offshored engineering work, the economy felt the job losses of its educated citizens and lost incomes very quickly.

Third, these decisions were morally defendable and the Dutch, albeit progressive and not prudish, were ever-productive and pragmatic. From these values, a pervasively big-picture ethical society evolved dating back from well before the time of the 16th century Puritans.

It's ironic that Amsterdam, Holland's capital city, is also famous for legalized drug use and prostitution. Tourists are quite curious about Amsterdam's Red Light District and yet the overwhelming majority of Dutch population makes more-worthwhile use of their time and personal lives.

What is the reason for the pervasive success of prostitution in a Puritan stronghold? Amsterdam is a major port city since the 1500s and the steady influx of hard-drinking men on shore-leaves resulted in rapes within the local population. It became obvious that prostitution, albeit "lowly", was also indispensable. By legalizing prostitution and centralizing it first outside city walls - and later into one area of the city, authorities actively protect minors, eliminate forced prostitution and combat the new phenomena of human trafficking. ("Prostitution in the Netherlands," n.d.)

In the Netherlands, guaranteed incomes ensure that its young women do not have to choose between sex work and destitution - as many young women now do in the U.S. where sex-workers are unregulated and growing rapidly. Approximately half of the 3000 Amsterdam women who choose a sex-worker role are battling drug or alcohol addiction. 80% of sex workers are foreign; those people who *are* running from destitution, are protected by this legalization. Sex workers in the U.S. are often students and low-wage workers battling against a $7 minimum wage and high education costs – conditions that do not permit them to make ends meet; this is the definition of destitution. The Dutch are pragmatic and responsible - and the U.S. is, arguably, enacting social governances in a much less responsible way.

Why am I choosing to compare the United States and Holland? I am comparing the two, because at a point their values were absolutely one and the same.

The Mayflower, the ship chartered by America's Puritan founding fathers, was a Dutch ship and America's British forefathers were cut from this Puritan cloth as well. No mere farmers, Puritans were Britain's scholars, lawmakers, great writers, and merchant-class who served as social architects to the British and European Royals.

When some of the Mayflower's passengers expressed their wish to settle with no order of law - and to live under "their owne Liberte", community leaders insisted that each of the ship's 41 settlers were required to sign an accord before off-boarding. That letter became the world's first written Democratic Constitution – the Mayflower Compact. (Foner & Garraty, n.d.)

The American Constitution was influenced by a collection of 150-year-wealthy landowners with influences from the French, Dutch, and Spanish Monarchies, and from private investors who made the eight-year war for American Independence possible.

England became America's largest trade and debt partners immediately after the revolution, and the $1.3 billion Livres that France committed to this war bankrupt the country and set off the French Revolution. Spain invested $600 million Reales and both France and Spain assumed huge land grants in America for their support in armaments and military consulting.

Modern American governments highlight the Constitution of 1776 as being the guiding values and viewpoints of their first forefathers, but that is certainly not a claim supported in fact by history. (Smith, 2015)

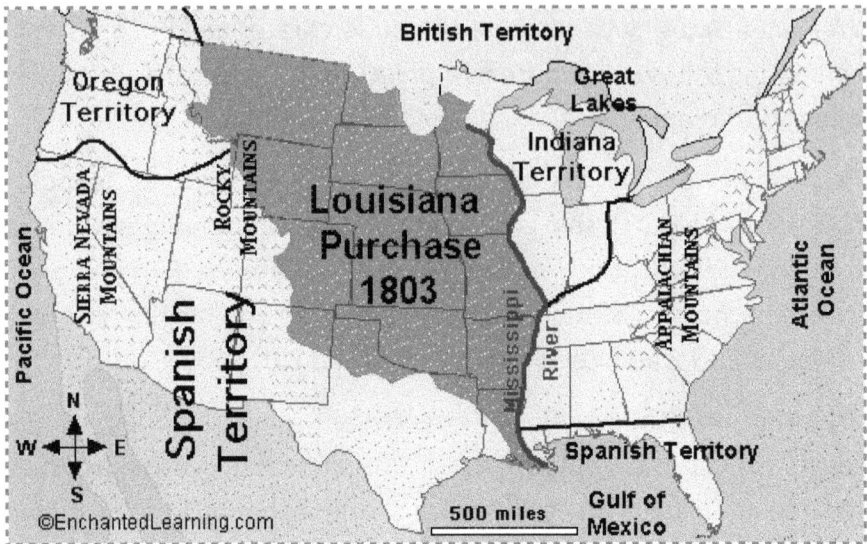

Map showing the Louisiana Purchase 1803, with labels: British Territory, Oregon Territory, Great Lakes, Indiana Territory, Sierra Nevada Mountains, Rocky Mountains, Spanish Territory, Pacific Ocean, Appalachian Mountains, Atlantic Ocean, Mississippi River, Gulf of Mexico, Spanish Territory, 500 miles. ©EnchantedLearning.com

Values are an important sustainability measure for any society, as was seen clearly in Populist election results in Canada, the U.S. and Great Britain in 2015 and 2016.

Human Rights

The way that we set our "low-bar" for acceptable Human Rights as a society often dictates the future for our society as well.

Rape cultures, gender inequality, slave trades and indentured servitude, corporate greed, endemic bullying are examples of injustices in communities who systematically engage in behaviors that disregard the human rights of others.

Human Rights exist to explain our minimum expectations for respect for life, for equality, women and children's rights, respect for family, respect for elders, neighbors, free speech, and healthcare.

#WPProjects discusses that building infrastructure beyond even the goals reached for in the U.N.'s Global Goals, can also ensure the right to a Good Life.

A "Good Life" – was first defined by Aristotle in 325 BCE. Contemporizing his writings in "Politic", a Good Life is the freedom to start a family as a young adult - if you wish, in a family-friendly community, with shelter, food, higher education, transportation, healthcare and the ability to pursue worthwhile projects for a lifetime.

Chapter 18

-

Summary

Capitalism does work and it is sustainable, but not by itself. Without economic controls, managed targets for wealth distribution, or a proactive reset like "Jubilee", predictable 60-year Great Depressions have repeated consistently throughout our history. Great Depressions, therefore, are perfectly normal and will go on for longer or shorter lengths of time depending on how long it takes for us to reset these Economic Cycle and get incomes with spending power back into the hands of citizens.

Responsible economic controls look like those put in place by the Netherlands and Scandinavian countries twenty-five years ago. Citizens there continue to ensure that wealth stays somewhat distributed and that all citizens can benefit from universal healthcare, childcare, incomes, pensions, drug benefits, and so on.

Because Dutch citizens have the economic and personal freedom to engage in commerce, the average citizen here produces three times as much wealth (GDP Export) than a Canadian citizen – and 50% more than an American. That's another half-trillion dollars of new wealth lost to the U.S. economy annually; and $60 billion to Canada, the U.K. and Australia. That's is an incredibly large opportunity cost to lose in defense of inequity.

Recall that the social systems of capitalist G7 nations like America, Canada, Germany, France, etc. for systems like housing, debt, employment, insurance, pensions, bonus and reward, were all built on the notion that one-job-per-family would afford the family's retirement, education, and all other needs. When the one-job-per-lifetime job model stopped working over these past twenty years, these systems no longer sustain families who now have to resort to dual-incomes, poverty, homelessness, high divorce rates and other well-documented social problems.

At the end of any Capitalist Cycle that has failed to manage inequity, we need to ensure incomes now and we have to reverse years of market bubbles and inflation so as to give families spending powers again. One income per family must affords our basic needs again.

Renewable Automation eases the impact of future inequity and reduces the importance of money in society. This also promises a return to a value-based rewards system for socially beneficial moral decisions and actions once again.

Building communities that support families and Good Lives needs a supporting infrastructure. People need guarantees of income, food, healthcare, education, in family friendly communities, in order to be able to think seriously about helping others. Resetting an economy according to a Plan means that all policies must be driven by a compelling Business Case as well.

A summary of the decisions that we took to restart a cycle and maintain equality are summarized in this v1.0 assessment as follows:

INCOMES DISTRIBUTE	Transition Economics Mature Policy 5% to 10% in Collapse	Collapse Policy 72% of All Countries are in Collapse
Working Families & Individuals	Graduated Tax, Big-Business Tax Avoidance Crackdown, Inequity targets, Local Business Ownership, Local Govmt Business Ownership	Low Tax, Trickle-down, Middle-Class Focus, Diversity, Cheap Imports, Immigration, Small Business w/o support
Unemployed	Guaranteed Cost of Living Incomes, Business Automation Revenue Sharing	No benefits for underemployed nor all unemployed
Retirement	Employee & Pension Fund Protections, Cost of Living minimums, CSR & Business Accountability	Offshoring, Misuse of female diversity rules, ignoring pensions
Children	Free Mastery-based Education & Transition Economics Voter Education	Failure to support 20-year-olds starting families, High Divorce Rates
Others	Cost of Living Benefits for Disabled	Insufficient Support, High Debt Servicing Costs
Automation	Engineering Safety Nets, #WPProjects & Renewable Automation Support, Multi-Party Long Term Strategic Planning	Innovation programs that fail to support Renewable Automations and Trade & Selling Needs

	Transition Economics Mature Policy 5% to 10% in Collapse	Collapse Policy 72% of All Countries are in Collapse
Healthcare & Benefits	Universal Healthcare, Employee Benefit Plans to Revenue Neutral Business Case targets	Private Plans, Patents that externalize Government R&D
Childcare	Universal Daycare & Free Education incl. University	Unaffordable Childcare
Housing	Public Housing (30%) Controlled to Inflation, Land Grants, Anti-Eviction, and Foreign Ownership Taxes	Energy Poverty, Housing Bubbles created by lax controls
Food & Goods	License Renewable Automation, Local Harvesting, Driverless Transport & Distribution, Local Self-Sufficiency & Abundance	Insufficient Farm Compensations, Failure to develop automation, Dollar & 99p Stores, Cheap Imports, Austerity Measures
Energy	Abundant Geo-Thermal, Hydro, Cold-Fusion, Thorium Nuclear, Zero-Pollution Fuels	Part-time Wind & Solar, Fossil Fuel Oil Pipelines, Energy Poverty
Transport	Driverless-cars & Automated Goods Delivery, Auto Road & Rail Construction	Infrastructure w/o Automation & Trickle-down Protection, Transit

A Leadership TODO list is:

1. Call every CEO to start hiring - free stimulus
2. Anti-eviction protections – put an end to homelessness.
3. Restore spending power - Day Care Affordability, Rental & Housing controls,

4. Look at foreign support spending - push for real sustainability and not an endless, increasing stream of outgoing cash.
5. Remove Tax Evasion's Legal protections
6. Restore Pensions
7. Target Wealth Distribution by introducing economic stimulus from new sources like the unemployed and retired through income programs.
8. Donald Trump is right - let's get our engineers working here again by putting an end to offshoring - like the Netherlands did 20 years ago; their hi-tech industry is thriving and engineers are in demand.
9. Automate of our basic needs - food, basic goods, roads, rail, housing, transport, energy. Invest in Livingry instead of Weaponry and endless infrastructure spending.

The social projects needed to reset the Economic Cycle have already started in Transition Economics "Mature" Countries and the renewable automation projects are just beginning.

Funding Local Renewable Automation Hi-Tech Companies will pay dividends to both countries and private investors the same. Governments who have lagged in the support of Renewable Automations should be focusing on these technologies directly for the far more promising future and for investment returns.

The Transition

Assuming governments adopt Transition Economics Cycle Management strategies, the work to automate our production economies will continue uninterrupted as jobs transition to new income safety-nets at a rate governed by GDP Export Targets, unemployment quotas, and retraining program budgets as described in TE Throttles above.

Without these safety nets, our society risks having our most senior engineers unemployed due to their pension risk and then turned into underemployed or unproductive assets. With safety nets, our best and brightest engineers build a technology safety net that makes money irrelevant and a Good Life sustainable.

None of these automation projects are beyond our reach over just the next few years. We can ignore this disruptive automation - and it will happen painfully anyway, or we can plan for the change and implement it professionally and intelligently.

Rollout Worldwide

As countries around the world are fine tuning their TE-Mature Right Plans and new policies, Automation Projects continue to mature. New engineering teams come online to help the automation efforts, sustained by Transition Economics throttling algorithms that ensured resources were available after solutions were built locally.

Standardized status reports manage country budgets and other SUSTAIN Method Project KPIs. Administers coordinate status reports and World Wide Coordination rolls up to a #WPProjects countdown clock.

With-in a surprisingly short time, our automated economy will begin to take on the heavy lifting and make a Good Life sustainable for us all.

For me, it is never enough to stop at explaining "What" the future holds, it is important to explain "How" to achieve great things too. By explaining the how step-by-step, I think you will find it different from any other book in Economics that you have ever read.

Building sustainable is very little different from building futuristic robots in the way that we build plans for these projects in just the same way. TE-Mature Policy builds excellent lives all by itself – as mentioned. Renewable Automations make our societies easily sustainable. Both programs require smart planning, good project process, brilliant engineers, hard work, strong leadership, and then with your support - anything is buildable.

We've tackled a trip to the moon, we already have robotically-built self-driving cars; ask yourself - What's Next? When will we have a robotically build home, a two day work week, a Great Life in a robotically built family-friendly community?

So many books in Economics set out to discuss problems in economics and stop there. I hope that Transition Economics sorted out a lot of questions in real-world events for you; as it did for me.

The exercise of researching and writing this book, and then summarizing all of my researches into easy to understand, buildable lists, allowed me to feel very confident that your country and our world have some very exciting times ahead.

Vote in support of – and become a project lead or team member for - a successful Transition Economics Policy and Project in your country. When you do – you can feel very confident that this effort can make your life's work meaningful and worthwhile too.

A successful economy and an automated society is our generation's Moon Launch-like mega-project – so let's get this Business Case approved and funded.

ABOUT THE AUTHOR

The process to transition to sustainable new economic cycles and automation heralds from learnings in economics, history, leadership, government, technology, engineering, business, physics and the social sciences. I hope that readers leverage my example and are inspired to keep their studies wide and goals important.

To give you some idea where these books come from; I have raised five terrific kids, built six high-tech startup companies, I learned something new every day of a 25 year high-tech engineering career after four years of post-secondary study.

I am a Lecturer, CEO; CIO, CTO and I have led 300+ complex projects in dozens of major programs with budgets up to $100+ million, 100,000 staff, and 200+ project team members in organizations that ran more than 500+ projects year after year. I have terrific coping skills that I exercise and practice often; I have worked with terrible bosses and terrific bosses.

Joseph Schumpeter had a famous line in the 1940s that I like - I know how to make a dance partner shine. I ran a full marathon a couple of years ago, I love mountain biking and hold my own sparing with a couple of different Marshall Arts belts; I read widely, travel, study languages, cultures, Religions, Academia, Business, Technology, Geography, and History.

I can say easily that I am a capable big-picture, process-minded and strategic thinker with a well-balanced resume for someone who thinks they know enough about building a Good Life - to be able to write an authoritative book that figures it all out too.

Family and society are important to me. My forefathers were Puritans and Founding Fathers, and so my history connects me to the importance of leveraging lessons from the past.

In community life, I founded one of the largest local Minor Football organization in Toronto, and that volunteer work gave me the chance to hire eight management teams annually and to get to know 800 young people and their parents every year as well. Volunteerism connected me to the next generation and to their hopes for a bright future.

Transition Economics is an important subject and book and I hope that I've provided a valuable foundation to begin from here. Writing it has changed the way that I look at politics and policies.

I choose to write books that are prodigious and to build projects that are worthwhile and can change the world for the better. I hope that your life is filled with successful worthwhile projects too.

Everything is Buildable - just keep working the problem.

Wishing you All the Best.

Edward Tilley

PS.

Look for my new books Teaching Doers and Modern Love in 2017.

Bibliography

4 commit suicide in Spain over evictions as EU struggles with unemployment — RT News. (2013). Retrieved from https://www.rt.com/news/spain-eviction-suicide-homeless-184/

Acland, F. (2016). New Scientist: Cold Fusion is Back |. Retrieved from http://www.e-catworld.com/2016/09/16/new-scientist-cold-fusion-is-back/

American Press. (1995). A 120-Year Lease on Life Outlasts Apartment Heir - NYTimes.com. Retrieved November 23, 2015, from http://www.nytimes.com/1995/12/29/world/a-120-year-lease-on-life-outlasts-apartment-heir.html

Amnesty launches Spain anti-eviction campaign - The Local. (2015). Retrieved from https://www.thelocal.es/20150624/amnesty-launches-first-campaign-against-spanish-evictions

Babcock, J. (2015). Spain's Ruling Party punished in local elections. *The Telegraph*. Retrieved from http://www.telegraph.co.uk/news/worldnews/europe/spain/11627935/Spains-ruling-party-punished-in-local-elections.html

Beck, R. (2010). Immigration, World Poverty and Gumballs - NumbersUSA.com - YouTube. Retrieved from https://www.youtube.com/watch?v=LPjzfGChGlE

Blodget, H. (2011). TRUTH ABOUT TAXES: Are Today's Rates High? Retrieved November 8, 2015, from http://www.businessinsider.com/history-of-tax-rates

Bourbeau, J. (2016). Rural Ontarians left in the dark as electricity bills skyrocket | Globalnews.ca. Retrieved from http://globalnews.ca/news/2796958/rural-ontarians-left-in-the-dark-as-electricity-bills-skyrocket/

Brooks, M. (2016). Cold fusion: Science's most controversial technology is back | New Scientist. Retrieved from https://www.newscientist.com/article/mg23130910-300-cold-fusion-sciences-most-controversial-technology-is-back/

Calkins, D. (n.d.). How to make CO2 (Carbon Dioxide). Retrieved November 8, 2015, from https://www.youtube.com/watch?v=b_qdkKnftt8

Clemente, J. (2014). Americans Can't Afford Higher Electricity Prices. Retrieved from http://www.forbes.com/sites/judeclemente/2014/11/24/americans-cant-afford-higher-electricity-prices/#3066b5ec7261

Combustion Efficiency and Excess Air. (n.d.). Retrieved from http://www.engineeringtoolbox.com/boiler-combustion-efficiency-d_271.html

Davis, J. (2015). Diesel From Water And Carbon Dioxide | IFLScience. Retrieved November 8, 2015, from http://www.iflscience.com/chemistry/audi-make-diesel-water-and-carbon-dioxide

Diggs, C. (2015). Russian Floating Nuclear Power Plant. Retrieved November 8, 2015, from http://bellona.org/news/nuclear-issues/2015-05-new-documents-show-cost-russian-nuclear-power-plant-skyrockets

Edward Tilley. (2015). World Peace 1.8.pptx - Google Slides. Retrieved from https://docs.google.com/presentation/d/1c-7y2VknAT62acnBr42RF_FOAz_7SCYy2HmalbaeDU8/edit#slide=id.p4

Elia, J. A., Baliban, R. C., & Floudas, C. A. (2012). Nationwide energy supply chain analysis for hybrid feedstock processes with significant CO2 emissions reduction. *AIChE Journal*, *58*(7), 2142–2154. http://doi.org/10.1002/aic.13842

EPA. (2001). AMENDMENTS TO THE CALIFORNIA ZERO EMISSION VEHICLE PROGRAM REGULATIONS: December 2001. Retrieved November 8, 2015, from http://www.arb.ca.gov/regact/zev2001/fsor.pdf

Erin Davis. (2015). Notable.ca | The Minimum Amount of Money Needed to Live in Toronto. Retrieved from http://notable.ca/breakdown-this-is-the-minimum-amount-of-money-a-young-professional-needs-to-live-in-toronto/

Foner, E., & Garraty, J. A. (n.d.). Mayflower Compact - Facts & Summary - HISTORY.com. Retrieved from http://www.history.com/topics/mayflower-compact

Garrett, R. (2015). Inside An Eviction Party—For Two Anti-Eviction Groups

| Hoodline. Retrieved from http://hoodline.com/2015/12/inside-an-eviction-party-for-anti-eviction-groups

Gas Turbines. (n.d.). Retrieved from https://en.wikipedia.org/wiki/Gas_turbine

Govan, F. (2016). Spain's suicide rate jumps to record high in economic crisis - The Local. Retrieved from http://www.thelocal.es/20160331/suicide-rate-in-spain-reaches-new-record

Gray, R. (2015). Audi creates DIESEL from air and water and its already powering a car | Daily Mail Online. Retrieved November 8, 2015, from http://www.dailymail.co.uk/sciencetech/article-3059025/Audi-creates-DIESEL-air-water-fuel-future-powering-car-driven-German-minister.html

Hamilton, K. (n.d.). What's At The Bottom Of The Deepest Hole On Earth? | IFLScience. Retrieved from http://www.iflscience.com/environment/deepest-hole-world/

Hargraves, R. (2016). Thorium Energy Alliance. *Thorium Energy Alliance.*

Homeless in Russia: A visit with Valery Sokolov, by Jan Spence, Share International Archives. (1997). Retrieved from http://www.share-international.org/archives/homelessness/hl-jsrussia.htm

Hussain, Y. (2015). Oil-by-rail economics suffers amid narrowing spreads | Financial Post. Retrieved from http://business.financialpost.com/news/energy/oil-by-rail-economics-suffers-amid-narrowing-spreads?__lsa=240d-a4ea

HUTZLER, M. (2014). U.S. SECURITY IMPLICATIONS OF INTERNATIONAL ENERGY AND CLIMATE POLICIES AND ISSUES. *THE INSTITUTE FOR ENERGY RESEARCH.* Retrieved from http://www.foreign.senate.gov/imo/media/doc/Hutzler_Testimony.pdf

IANS. (2016). India doesn't lag in developing thorium-fuelled nuclear-reactor: MR Srinivasan, former AEC chairman - The Economic Times. Retrieved from http://economictimes.indiatimes.com/news/science/india-doesnt-lag-in-developing-thorium-fuelled-nuclear-reactor-mr-srinivasan-former-aec-chairman/articleshow/52489649.cms

Kerr, F. (2016). Kerr: Nenshi is right — NDP power lawsuit is "outrageous" | Calgary Herald. Retrieved from http://calgaryherald.com/opinion/columnists/kerr-nenshi-is-right-ndp-power-lawsuit-is-outrageous

Klein, J. (2014). Can Thermoelectric Generators Compete Against Solar Photovoltaics? Retrieved October 26, 2016, from http://insights.globalspec.com/article/98/can-thermoelectric-generators-compete-against-solar-photovoltaics

Knapton, S. (2015). "Impossible" rocket drive works and could get to Moon in four hours - Telegraph. Retrieved from http://www.telegraph.co.uk/news/science/space/11769030/Impossible-rocket-drive-works-and-could-get-to-Moon-in-four-hours.html

Lopoukhine, R. (2014). Top 5 Reasons Why Geothermal Power is Nowhere in Canada | DeSmog Canada. Retrieved from http://www.desmog.ca/2014/02/26/top-5-reasons-why-geothermal-power-nowhere-canada

Messerly, J. G. (2013). Aristotle on the Good Life | The Meaning of Life. Retrieved November 9, 2015, from http://reasonandmeaning.com/2013/12/19/aristotle-on-the-good-and-meaningful-life/

Ministry of Economic Development. (n.d.). Price - New Zealand Geothermal Association. Retrieved from http://www.nzgeothermal.org.nz/price.html

Mirza, J. (2015). The great Canadian tax dodge | Junaid Mirza | Pulse | LinkedIn. Retrieved from https://www.linkedin.com/pulse/great-canadian-tax-dodge-junaid-mirza

Moir, R. W., & Teller, E. (2004). THORIUM-FUELED UNDERGROUND POWER PLANT BASED ON MOLTEN SALT TECHNOLOGY. *Laurence Livermore National Laboratory*, *1*, 7. Retrieved from http://web.archive.org/web/20101005073843/http://www.geocities.com/rmoir2003/moir_teller.pdf

Moon, H., & Zarrouk, S. J. (2012). EFFICIENCY OF GEOTHERMAL POWER PLANTS: A WORLDWIDE REVIEW. *New Zealand Geothermal Workshop, 19*.

Moore, P. (2016). The TRUTH about carbon dioxide (C02): Patrick Moore,

Sensible Environmentalist - YouTube. Retrieved from https://www.youtube.com/watch?v=5Smhn1gL6Xg&feature=youtu. be

Neate, R. (2014). Scandal of Europe's 11m empty homes | Society | The Guardian. Retrieved from https://www.theguardian.com/society/2014/feb/23/europe-11m-empty-properties-enough-house-homeless-continent-twice

Noor, J. (2013). Detroit Anti-Eviction Campaign Keeping Families in Their Homes. Retrieved from http://therealnews.com/t2/index.php?option=com_content&task=view&id=31&Itemid=74&jumival=9738#newsletter1

Norton, M. I., & Ariely, D. (2011). Building a Better America--One Wealth Quintile at a Time. *Perspectives on Psychological Science*, *6*(1), 9–12. http://doi.org/10.1177/1745691610393524

OKBM. (n.d.). Reactor Plants. Retrieved November 9, 2015, from http://www.okbm.nnov.ru/english/npp

Parussini, G. (2013). U.S. CEO Blasts French Work Culture - WSJ. Retrieved from http://www.wsj.com/articles/SB10001424127887323549204578316 101127838118

PragerU. (2016). Are Electric Cars Really Green? - YouTube. Retrieved from https://www.youtube.com/watch?v=17xh_VRrnMU

Prostitution in the Netherlands. (n.d.). Retrieved from https://en.wikipedia.org/wiki/Prostitution_in_the_Netherlands#History

Refugees of the Syrian Civil War. (n.d.). Retrieved from https://en.wikipedia.org/wiki/Refugees_of_the_Syrian_Civil_War

Safety of Nuclear Reactors - World Nuclear Association. (2016). Retrieved from http://www.world-nuclear.org/information-library/safety-and-security/safety-of-plants/safety-of-nuclear-power-reactors.aspx

Smith, J. L. (2015). How was the Revolutionary War paid for? - Journal of the American Revolution. Retrieved from https://allthingsliberty.com/2015/02/how-was-the-revolutionary-war-paid-for/

Snyder, M. (2014). If Economic Cycle Theorists Are Correct, 2015 To 2020 Will Be Pure Hell For The United States. Retrieved from http://theeconomiccollapseblog.com/archives/if-economic-cycle-theorists-are-correct-2015-to-2020-will-be-pure-hell-for-the-united-states

Solar Thermal Tower. (n.d.). *Wikipedia.* Retrieved from https://en.wikipedia.org/wiki/Solar_power_tower

TaxPayer.com. (2016). Canada's National Debt Clock : The Canadian Taxpayers Federation. Retrieved from http://www.debtclock.ca/

Thorium Energy Generation. (n.d.). Retrieved from http://www.thoriumenergyalliance.com/downloads/thorium_Energy_Generation.ppt

US Census Bureau, D. I. D. (2015). Income - US Census. *US Government.* Retrieved from http://www.census.gov/hhes/www/income/data/historical/household/

Weston, J. (2016). Car gets 400+ MPG – Fuel-Efficient-Vehicles.org. Retrieved from http://fuel-efficient-vehicles.org/energy-news/?page_id=968

Wiki. (2016). Geo-Thermal Energy. Retrieved from https://en.wikipedia.org/wiki/Geothermal_power

Wikipedia. (2016). Bashar al-Assad. Retrieved from https://en.wikipedia.org/wiki/Bashar_al-Assad

William Thompson | Department of Political Science | Indiana University Bloomington. (2016). Retrieved from http://polisci.indiana.edu/faculty/profiles/wthompso.shtml

Wolf, E. N. (2015). Wealth Inequity in the United States. Retrieved from https://en.wikipedia.org/wiki/Wealth_inequality_in_the_United_States#cite_note-levyinstitute.org-12

Index